Heritage Signature® Auction #5312

Fall Fine Jewelry Auction

September 25, 2017 | Beverly Hills

Signature® Floor Session 1
(Floor, Telephone, HERITAGELive!®, Internet, Fax, and Mail)

Heritage Auctions, Beverly Hills
9478 W. Olympic Blvd. • Beverly Hills, CA 90212

Monday, September 25 • 10:00 AM PT • Lots 55001–55393

Signature® Internet Session 2
(HERITAGELive!®, Internet, Fax, & Mail only Session)

Monday, September 25 • 3:00 PM CT • Lots 55394–56328

LOT SETTLEMENT AND PICK-UP
Lots will be available for pick-up immediately following the floor session and Tuesday, September 26, 10:00 AM – 1:00 PM PT at the Beverly Hills location. If you wish for your purchases to remain in Beverly Hills for pick-up after this time, please notify FloorManagers@HA.com no later than 1:00 PM PT on Tuesday, September 26. After this time, all property will be transported to Dallas where it will be available for pick-up on or after Friday, September 29, weekdays, 9:00 AM – 5:00 PM CT by appointment only.

Lots are sold at an approximate rate of 80 lots per hour, but it is not uncommon to sell 60 lots or 100 lots in any given hour.

Buyer's Premium Per Lot:
This auction is subject to a Buyer's Premium of 25% on the first $250,000 (minimum $19), plus 20% of any amount between $250,000 and $2,500,000, plus 12% of any amount over $2,500,000 per lot.

CA Auctioneer Bonds: Heritage Auctioneers & Galleries LSM0889114; Heritage Collectibles, Inc. LSM0889990; Heritage Numismatic Auctions, Inc. LSM0818768; Hayley Minshull Brigham LSM0606157; Paul Minshull LSM0605473; Carolyn Mani LSM0889980; Jennifer Jayne Marsh LSM0592983; Alissa Ford LSM0639742; Fiona Elias LSM1022035; Teia Baber LSM0606714; Ed Beardsley LSM0626564; Samuel Foose LSM0746370; Kathleen Guzman LSM0594811; Marina Medina LSM0744324; Bob Merrill LSM0868760; Brian Nalley LSM0746365; Scott Peterson LSM0594796; Michael Sadler LSM0737853; Barry Sandoval LSM0857626; Andrea Voss LSM0602700; Brent Lewis LSM1021608.

PRELIMINARY LOT VIEWING
Heritage Auctions Design District Showroom
1518 Slocum Street • Dallas, TX 75207

Friday, September 8 – Saturday, September 9
10:00 AM – 5:00 PM CT

Heritage Auctions, New York
445 Park Avenue • New York, NY 10022
Wednesday, September 13 – Thursday, September 14
10:00 AM – 6:00 PM ET

LOT VIEWING
Heritage Auctions, Beverly Hills
9478 W. Olympic Blvd. • Beverly Hills, CA 90212

Friday, September 22 – Saturday, September 23
10:00 AM – 5:00 PM PT
Sunday, September 24 • 1:00 PM – 5:00 PM PT

View lots & auction results online at HA.com/5312

BIDDING METHODS
HERITAGE Live!®[1] Bidding
Bid live on your computer or mobile, anywhere in the world, during the Auction using our HERITAGELive!® program at HA.com/Live

Live Floor Bidding
Bid in person during the floor sessions.

Live Telephone Bidding (Floor Sessions Only)
Phone bidding must be arranged 24 hours before your session begins. Client Service: 866-835-3243

Internet Absentee Bidding
Proxy bidding ends ten minutes prior to the session start time. Live Proxy bidding continues through the session. HA.com/5312

Fax Bidding
Fax bids must be received 24 hours before your session begins. Fax: 214-409-1425

Phone: 214-528-3500 • 877-HERITAGE (437-4824)
Fax: 214-409-1425
Direct Client Service Line: 866-835-3243
Email: Bid@HA.com

45275

Steve Ivy
CEO
Co-Chairman of the Board

Jim Halperin
Co-Chairman of the Board

Greg Rohan
President

Paul Minshull
Chief Operating Officer
Chief Technology Officer

Todd Imhof
Executive Vice President

Cristiano Bierrenbach
Executive Vice President
International

Mike Haynes
Chief Financial Officer

Kathleen Guzman
Managing Director
New York

Hayley Brigham
Managing Director
Beverly Hills

Alissa Ford
Managing Director
San Francisco

Roberta Kramer
Managing Director
Chicago

Kenneth Yung
Managing Director
Hong Kong

Jacco Scheper
Managing Director
Europe

Fine Jewelry Specialists

Jill Burgum
Sr. Director of Fine Jewelry

Eva Violante
Director of Fine Jewelry
New York

Peter Shemonsky
Director of Fine Jewelry
San Francisco

Gina D'Onofrio
Director of Fine Jewelry
Beverly Hills

Tracy Sherman
Director of Fine Jewelry
Palm Beach

Ruth Thuston
Director of Fine Jewelry
Chicago

Jessica DuBroc
Assistant Director of Fine Jewelry
Dallas

Ana Wroblaski
Assistant Director of Fine Jewelry
Beverly Hills

Worldwide Headquarters
3500 Maple Avenue • Dallas, Texas 75219
Phone 214-528-3500 • 877-HERITAGE (437-4824)
HA.com/Jewelry

Consignment Directors: Jill Burgum, Gina D'Onofrio, Jessica DuBroc, Peter Shemonsky,
Tracy Sherman, Ruth Thuston, Eva Violante, Ana Wroblaski

Cataloged by: Jill Burgum, Gina D'Onofrio, Jessica DuBroc, Haley Giller,
Peter Shemonsky, Ruth Thuston, Ana Wroblaski

Featuring:

- Property of a Wyoming Collector

- From the Estate of Fina Rox

- Property of an Oklahoma Lady

- Property from the Estate of Lupita Tovar and
  Paul Kohner Bel Air, California

- Property of a Private Texas Collector

- Property of a Plano, TX Lady

- Property of a Las Vegas NV Estate

- From the Collection of a San Antonio, TX Lady

- Property of a Collector

Designer Listing

55001

55001
Gold, Silver Pendant-Necklace, Carrera y Carrera
The *Bestiario* leopard's head pendant-necklace is crafted in blackened sterling silver and 18k gold, marked Carrera y Carrera. Gross weight 54.00 grams.
Pendant Dimensions: 2 inches x 2 inches
Chain Length: 18 inches to 20 inches, adjustable

Estimate: $4,000-$6,000
Starting Bid: $2,900

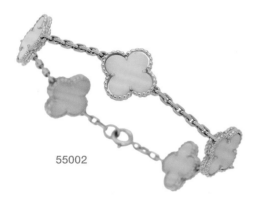

55002

55002
Coral, Gold Bracelet, Van Cleef & Arpels
The five station *Alhambra* bracelet features carved coral, set in 18k gold, marked VCA. Gross weight 11.52 grams.
Dimensions: 7-1/2 inches x 9/16 inch

Estimate: $6,000-$8,000
Starting Bid: $4,000

55003

55003
Diamond, Enamel, Platinum, Gold Bracelet, David Webb
The hinged bangle features full-cut diamonds weighing a total of approximately 3.00 carats, set in platinum, accented by enamel applied on 18k gold, marked Webb. Gross weight 100.40 grams.
Dimensions: 6-1/4 inches x 1-1/8 inches

Estimate: $22,000-$28,000
Starting Bid: $17,000

55004

55004

**Diamond, Multi-Stone, White Gold
Brooches, Vhernier**

The balloon brooches feature lapis lazuli, turquoise,
and yellow chalcedony crowned by rock crystal quartz
cabochons, accented by full-cut diamonds weighing
a total of approximately 1.15 carats, set in 18k white
gold, marked Vhernier. Gross weight 34.00 grams.
Dimensions: 2-1/2 inches x 3/4 inch

Estimate: $4,000-$6,000
Starting Bid: $3,000

55005

55005

Diamond, Gold Ring

The ring features full-cut diamonds weighing
a total of approximately 2.00 carats, set in
18k gold. Gross weight 12.14 grams.
Size: 7 (sizeable)

Property of an Oklahoma Lady

Estimate: $4,000-$6,000
Starting Bid: $3,000

55006

55006

Turquoise, Enamel, Gold Bracelet, Cellino

The hinged bangle features turquoise cabochons,
accented by enamel applied on 18k gold,
marked Cellino. Gross weight 101.90 grams.
Dimensions: 6-1/2 inches x 1 inch

Estimate: $3,000-$5,000
Starting Bid: $1,500

55007

55008

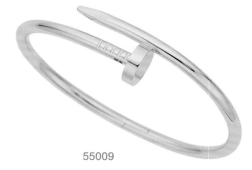

55009

55007
Titanium, Gold Earrings, JAR
The titanium *Morning Glory* earrings are completed by 18k gold omega clips, marked JAR. Gross weight 33.55 grams.
Dimensions: 2-1/4 inches x 2/14 inches
*Note: earrings are designed for non-pierced ears

Estimate: $3,000-$4,000
Starting Bid: $1,500

55008
Diamond, White Gold Bracelet, Cartier
The *Love* bangle features full-cut diamonds weighing a total of approximately 0.35 carat, set in 18k white gold, marked Cartier. Gross weight 31.17 grams.
Dimensions: 6-1/2 inches x 1/4 inch

Estimate: $7,000-$9,000
Starting Bid: $6,500

55009
White Gold Bracelet, Cartier
The 18k white gold *Juste un Clou* bangle weighs 34.30 grams, marked Cartier.
Length: 6-3/8 inches

Estimate: $4,000-$6,000
Starting Bid: $3,000

55010

55010

Glass, Titanium Earrings, JAR
The earrings feature gold flecked glass
beads, enhanced by red titanium wires,
marked JAR. Gross weight 36.60 grams.
Dimensions: 2-1/2 inches x 2 inches
Note: earrings are designed for non-pierced ears

Estimate: $3,000-$4,000
Starting Bid: $1,500

55011

55011

Emerald, Enamel, Gold Brooch, David Webb
The brooch features marquise-shaped emeralds
measuring 7.00 x 3.50 mm and weighing a total of
approximately 0.55 carat, set in 18k gold, marked
David Webb. Gross weight 55.80 grams.
Dimensions: 3 inches x 1-1/2 inches

Estimate: $5,000-$7,000
Starting Bid: $4,000

55012

Gold Bracelet, Van Cleef & Arpels
The 18k gold *Zodiac* bracelet weighs
21.40 grams, marked VCA.
Length: 6-7/8 inches

Estimate: $4,000-$6,000
Starting Bid: $2,500

55012

55013

55013
Gold Jewelry Suite
The 18k gold necklace and matching
earrings weigh 164.97 grams.
Necklace Length: 15-1/4 inches x 7/8 inch
Earring Dimensions: 1-1/2 inches x 7/8 inch
*Note: earrings are designed for pierced ears

Estimate: $7,000-$9,000
Starting Bid: $5,000

55014

55014
Ruby, Gold Zipper Pull, David Webb
The monkey zipper pull features ruby cabochons, set
in 18k gold, marked Webb. Gross weight 30.20 grams.
Dimensions: 1-5/8 inches x 7/8 inch

Estimate: $4,000-$6,000
Starting Bid: $2,000

55015

55015
Diamond, Gold Brooch
The bow brooch features full-cut diamonds weighing a total of approximately 12.00 carats, pavé-set in 18k white and yellow gold. Gross weight 76.20 grams.
Dimensions: 3-5/8 inches x 2-3/4 inches

Estimate: $8,000-$10,000
Starting Bid: $4,000

55016

55016
Diamond, Sapphire, Gold
Bracelet, Golay Fils & Stahl
The bracelet features full-cut diamonds weighing a total of approximately 2.80 carats, enhanced by round-cut sapphires weighing a total of approximately 2.80 carats, set in 18k gold, marked GFS. Gross weight 100.45 grams.
Dimensions: 7-3/4 inches x 3/4 inch

Estimate: $5,000-$7,000
Starting Bid: $3,000

55017
Diamond, Gold Bracelet
The bracelet features full-cut diamonds weighing a total of 7.95 carats, set in 18k gold with white gold accents. Gross weight 81.90 grams.
Dimensions: 7 inches x 3/4 inch

Estimate: $6,000-$8,000
Starting Bid: $3,000

55017

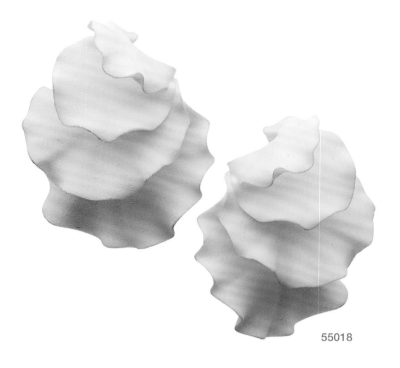

55018

55018
Resin, Gold Earrings, JAR
The resin earrings are completed by 18k gold
clips, marked JAR. Gross weight 17.59 grams.
Dimensions: 2-1/2 inches x 2 inches x 3/4 inch
Note: earrings are designed for non-pierced ears

Estimate: $2,000-$3,000
Starting Bid: $1,000

55019

55019
Opal, Diamond, Ruby, Gold Ring
The ring centers an oval-shaped opal cabochon
measuring 17.00 x 9.50 7.62 mm and weighing
approximately 6.30 carats, framed by pear-
shaped ruby cabochons weighing a total of
approximately 8.00 carats, accented by full-cut
diamonds weighing a total of approximately 0.45
carat, set in 14k gold. Gross weight 14.60 grams.
Size: 7 (sizeable)

Estimate: $4,000-$6,000
Starting Bid: $3,200

55020

55020
Diamond, Gold Bracelet
The double-hinged cuff features full-cut diamonds
weighing a total of approximately 3.50 carats,
set in 18k gold. Gross weight 112.89 grams.
Dimensions: 7 inches x 2 inches

Estimate: $6,000-$8,000
Starting Bid: $4,000

55021

55021
Diamond, Citrine, Gold Jewelry, Kieselstein-Cord
The lot includes a pendant featuring a cushion-shaped citrine measuring 16.10 x 16.10 x 10.65 mm, framed by full-cut diamonds weighing a total of approximately 0.60 carat; a heart pendant enhanced by full-cut diamonds weighing a total of approximately 0.80 carat; together with a necklace accented by full-cut diamonds weighing a total of approximately 0.75 carat; all set in 18k gold and marked Kieselstein-Cord. Gross weight 274.20 grams.
Citrine Pendant Dimensions: 1-1/16 inches x 7/8 inch
Heart Pendant Dimensions: 2-1/8 inches x 1-3/8 inches
Chain Length: 19 inches

Estimate: $8,000-$10,000
Starting Bid: $4,000

55022
Diamond, Gold Bracelet, Kieselstein-Cord
The *Camelot* bracelet features full-cut diamonds weighing a total of approximately 2.40 carats, set in 18k gold, marked Kieselstein-Cord. Gross weight 161.07 grams.
Dimensions: 8-1/4 inches x 1-5/16 inches

Estimate: $6,000-$8,000
Starting Bid: $4,000

55022

55023

55023
Diamond, Gold Jewelry Suite, Kieselstein-Cord
The *Camelot* necklace and earrings feature full-cut diamonds
weighing a total of approximately 10.85 carats, set in 18k gold,
marked B. Keiselstein-Cord. Gross weight 418.80 grams.
Necklace Dimensions: 18 inches x 2-5/8 inches
Earring Dimensions: 2-5/8 inches x 1/2 inch
Note: earrings are designed for pierced ears

Estimate: $12,000-$16,000
Starting Bid: $10,000

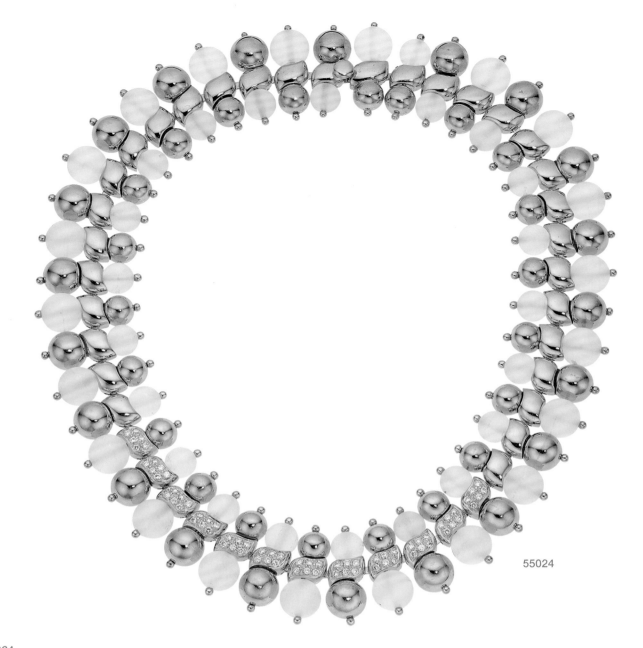

55024

55024
Diamond, Frosted Rock Crystal Quartz, Gold Necklace
The necklace features full-cut diamonds weighing a total of
approximately 1.40 carats, enhanced by frosted rock crystal
quartz beads measuring 8.00 mm and 10.00 mm, set in 18k
rose and yellow gold. Gross weight 201.21 grams.
Dimensions: 16 inches x 1 inch

Estimate: $5,000-$7,000
Starting Bid: $4,000

55025

55025
Amethyst, Diamond, Gold Ring, Piranesi
The ring features an oval-shaped amethyst weighing
20.56 carats, accented by full and single-cut diamonds
weighing a total of 2.00 carats, set in 18k white and yellow
gold, marked Piranesi. Gross weight 20.20 grams.
Size: 7-1/2 (sizeable)

Estimate: $5,000-$7,000
Starting Bid: $3,000

55026

55026

Diamond, Enamel, Platinum, Gold Jewelry, David Webb

The lot includes a ring featuring full-cut diamonds weighing a total of approximately 0.45 carat, together with a pair of earrings enhanced by single-cut diamonds weighing a total of approximately 0.70 carat, set in platinum, both accented by blue and green enamel applied on 18k gold, marked Webb. Gross weight 57.24 grams.
Ring Size: 6-1/2 (sizeable with caution)
Earring Dimensions: 1-1/4 inches x 5/8 inch
*Note: earrings are designed for non-pierced ears

Estimate: $9,000-$10,000
Starting Bid: $8,000

55027

55027

Emerald, Enamel, Gold Ring, David Webb

The panther ring features emerald cabochons, enhanced by black enamel applied on 18k gold, marked Webb. Gross weight 25.89 grams.
Size: 6-1/2 (not sizeable)

Estimate: $4,000-$6,000
Starting Bid: $2,000

55028

55028

Diamond, Platinum, Gold Bracelet, David Webb

The hinged bangle features full-cut diamonds weighing a total of approximately 3.35 carats, set in platinum and 18k gold, marked David Webb. Gross weight 113.58 grams.
Dimensions: 6-1/4 inches x 1-5/16 inches

Estimate: $20,000-$30,000
Starting Bid: $15,000

55029

55029
Enamel, Gold Jewelry Suite, Somenzi
The brooch and earrings feature
enamel applied on 18k gold, marked
Somenzi. Gross weight 68.96 grams.
Brooch Diameter: 1-3/8 inches
Earring Diameter: 1-3/16 inches
*Note: earrings are designed
for non-pierced ears

Estimate: $3,000-$4,000
Starting Bid: $2,000

55030
**Rock Crystal Quartz, Diamond, Gold
Jewelry Suite, Sabbadini**
The suite includes earrings, a bracelet and
matching ring; each featuring carved rock
crystal quartz, set in 18k gold; in addition, the
ring has full-cut diamond accents weighing
a total of approximately 0.70 carat; marked
Sabbadini. Gross weight 155.80 grams.
Bracelet Dimensions: 6 inches x 7/8 inch
Ring Size: 3-3/4 with sizing cleats (sizeable)
Earring Dimensions: 1-1/8 inches x 1 inch
*Note: earrings are designed
for non-pierced ears

Estimate: $8,000-$10,000
Starting Bid: $5,000

55030

55031

55032

55033

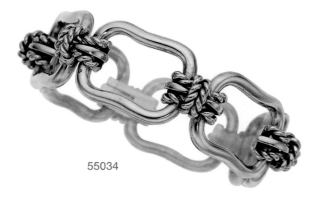

55034

55031
Gold Belt Buckle, David Webb
The 18k gold snake belt buckle weighs
79.50 grams, marked Webb.
Buckle Dimensions: 2-1/16 inches x 2-1/4 inches
Slide Dimensions: 1-11/16 inches x 7/8 inch

Estimate: $4,000-$6,000
Starting Bid: $2,000

55032
Emerald, Opal, Diamond, Gold Earrings
The earrings feature oval-shaped opal cabochons
measuring 14.00 x 10.00 x 4.50 mm and weighing
approximately 7.60 carats, enhanced by full-cut
diamonds weighing a total of approximately 1.90 carats,
suspending pear-shaped emeralds measuring 10.70 x
7.80 x 5.40 mm and weighing a total of approximately
5.00 carats, set in 14k gold. Gross weight 12.00 grams.
Dimensions: 1-3/4 inches x 1 inch
*Note: earrings are designed for pierced ears

Estimate: $4,000-$6,000
Starting Bid: $2,500

55033
Enamel, Gold Ring, David Webb
The shrimp ring features white enamel applied on 18k
gold, marked Webb. Gross weight 16.95 grams.
Size: 5 (not sizeable)

Estimate: $4,000-$6,000
Starting Bid: $2,000

55034
Gold Bracelet
The 18k gold bracelet weighs 65.90 grams.
Dimensions: 7-7/8 inches x 7/8 inch

Estimate: $4,000-$5,000
Starting Bid: $3,000

55035

Diamond, Gold Jewelry Suite, Van Cleef & Arpels
The suite includes a pair of hoop earrings together
with a scarf clip featuring full-cut diamonds weighing
a total of approximately 1.75 carats, set in 18k
gold, marked VCA. Gross weight 52.20 grams.
Scarf Clip Diameter: 1-3/4 inches
Earring Diameter: 1-1/4 inches
*Note: earrings are designed for non-pierced ears

Estimate: $15,000-$20,000
Starting Bid: $13,000

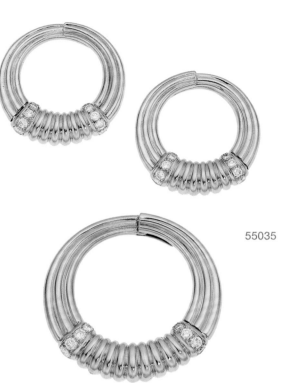

55035

55036

Boulder Opal, Diamond, Gold Bracelet
The bracelet features a boulder opal measuring 35.00
x 30.00 x 9.25 mm, accented by full-cut diamonds
weighing a total of approximately 0.25 carat, set
in 18k gold. Gross weight 62.43 grams.
Length: 6-3/4 inches

Estimate: $4,000-$5,000
Starting Bid: $2,000

55036

55037

Diamond, Colored Diamond, Gold Bracelet
The bow bracelet features pink and near-colorless diamonds
weighing a total of approximately 12.00 carats, set in 18k
rose, white and yellow gold. Gross weight 85.59 grams.
Dimensions: 8 inches x 2-1/2 inches
*Note: colored diamonds not tested for origin of color

Estimate: $9,000-$12,000
Starting Bid: $5,000

55037

55038

55038
Lapis Lazuli, Diamond, Gold Enhancer-Brooch, Robert Wander, French
The brooch features oval and pear-shaped lapis lazuli cabochons, accented by full-cut diamonds weighing a total of approximately 2.00 carats, set in 18k gold, marked Wander. Gross weight 71.20 grams.
Dimensions: 2-15/16 inches x 3-1/8 inches

From the Collection of a San Antonio, TX Lady

Estimate: $6,000-$8,000
Starting Bid: $3,000

55039

55039
Diamond, Gold Ring
The ring features a marquise-shaped diamond measuring 11.00 x 5.00 mm and weighing approximately 1.15 carats, set in 18k gold. Gross weight 12.02 grams.
Size: 6-1/4 (sizeable)

Estimate: $4,000-$6,000
Starting Bid: $2,500

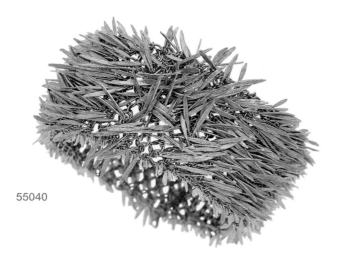

55040

55040
Gold Bracelet, H. Stern
The 18k gold *Feather* bracelet weighs 115.11 grams, marker's mark for H. Stern.
Dimensions: 7-1/4 inches x 1 inch

Estimate: $7,000-$9,000
Starting Bid: $5,000

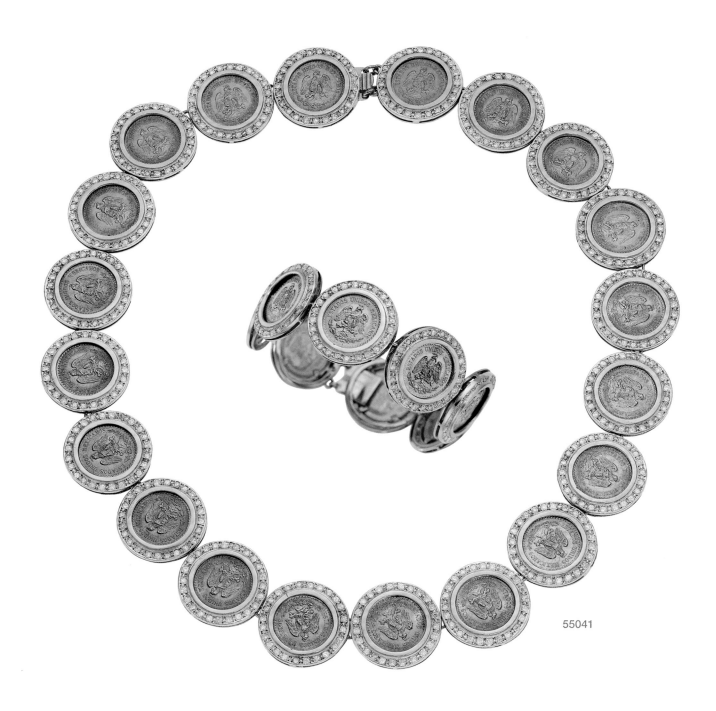

55041

Diamond, Gold Coin, Gold Jewelry Suite
The suite includes a necklace and bracelet featuring
Dos y Medio Pesos gold coins, dated 1945, encircled by
full-cut diamonds weighing a total of approximately
10.00 carats, set in 14k gold. Gross weight 166.20 grams.
Necklace Dimensions: 17-1/2 inches x 7/8 inch
Bracelet Dimensions: 7 inches x 7/8 inch

Property of a Las Vegas, NV Estate

Estimate: $8,000-$10,000
Starting Bid: $4,000

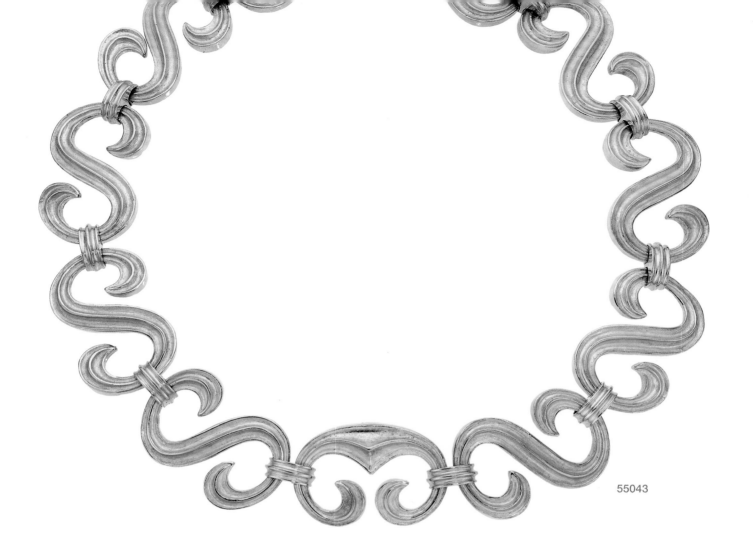

55043

55042

55042
Coral, Diamond, Gold Earrings, Aletto Bros.
The earrings feature carved coral, accented by full-cut diamonds weighing a total of 0.30 carat, set in 18k gold, marked Aletto Bros. Gross weight 31.34 grams.
Dimensions: 1-1/4 inches x 1-1/8 inches
*Note: earrings are designed for non-pierced ears

Estimate: $7,000-$9,000
Starting Bid: $6,000

55043
Gold Necklace, Robert Wander
The 18k gold necklace weighs 131.98 grams, maker's mark for Robert Wander.
Dimensions: 17-1/2 inches x 1 inch

From the Collection of a San Antonio, TX Lady

Estimate: $4,000-$6,000
Starting Bid: $2,000

55044

55044
Diamond, Gold Necklace
The hinged ram's head torque features full-cut
diamonds weighing a total of approximately 0.70
carat, set in 18k gold. Gross weight 98.60 grams.
Dimensions: 15 inches x 1-1/8 inches

Estimate: $4,000-$5,000
Starting Bid: $2,000

55045

55045
Lavender Jadeite Jade, Diamond,
White Gold Pendant
The pendant features a carved lavender jadeite
jade measuring 15.58 x 23.40 x 8.88 mm, accented
by pear-shaped diamonds weighing a total of 0.87
carat, set in 18k white gold. A Mason-Kay report
344549, dated July 17, 2017, stating *Natural
Jadeite Jade, No Dye or Polymer Detected, 'A' Jade,*
accompanies the jadeite. Gross weight 7.00 grams.
Dimensions: 1-7/8 inches x 5/8 inch

Estimate: $8,000-$10,000
Starting Bid: $6,000

55046
Diamond, Multi-Stone, Gold Bracelet
The hinged bangle features carved lapis lazuli animal
heads, enhanced by round-cut emeralds, accented
by full-cut diamonds weighing a total of approximately
1.00 carat, set in 18k gold. Gross weight 137.10 grams.
Dimensions: 7 inches x 7/8 inch

Estimate: $4,000-$6,000
Starting Bid: $2,000

55046

55047

55048

55049

55047
Gold Necklace, Michalis
The 22k gold necklace weighs 133.20
grams, marked Michalis.
Dimensions: 17 inches x 5/8 inch

From the Collection of a San Antonio, TX Lady

Estimate: $4,000-$6,000
Starting Bid: $2,000

55048
**Diamond, Enamel, Platinum, Gold
Earrings, David Webb**
The earrings feature full-cut diamonds weighing a
total of approximately 2.45 carats, set in platinum,
enhanced by black enamel applied on 18k gold,
marked Webb. Gross weight 48.75 grams.
Dimensions: 1-1/4 inches x 7/8 inch
Note: earrings are designed for pierced ears

From the Collection of a San Antonio, TX Lady

Estimate: $4,000-$6,000
Starting Bid: $2,000

55049
Multi-Stone, Diamond, Gold Ring
The ring features a cushion-shaped chrysoprase
cabochon measuring 20.80 x 20.80 x 10.00
mm, enhanced by full-cut diamonds weighing
a total of approximately 1.00 carat, accented
by emerald cabochons and black onyx rods,
set in 18k gold. Gross weight 36.80 grams.
Size: 8 (sizeable)

Estimate: $5,000-$7,000
Starting Bid: $3,500

55050

Colombian Emerald, Diamond, Gold Necklace
The necklace features a square emerald-cut emerald measuring 13.41 x 13.16 x 5.75 mm and a pear-shaped emerald measuring 17.80 x 14.36 x 9.63 mm and weighing a total of 22.10 carats, accented by a round brilliant-cut diamond measuring 5.75 x 3.36 mm and weighing 0.75 carat, set in 18k gold. An AGL report # 1085189, dated July 20, 2017, stating *Origin Colombia, Minor Modern Clarity Enhancement*, accompanies the emeralds. Gross weight 15.52 grams.
Pendant Dimensions: 1-3/4 inches x 3/4 inch
Chain Length: 20 inches

Estimate: $12,000-$16,000
Starting Bid: $9,500

55050

55051

Diamond, Gold Ring
The ring features a rectangular modified brilliant-cut diamond measuring 6.86 x 6.30 x 4.53 mm and weighing 1.57 carats, enhanced by full-cut diamonds weighing a total of approximately 2.00 carats, set in 18k gold. A GIA Laboratory report # 12909138, dated January 11, 2017, stating *J color, VS2 clarity*, accompanies the center diamond. Gross weight 17.25 grams.
Size: 8-1/2 (sizeable)

Estimate: $7,000-$9,000
Starting Bid: $5,000

55051

55052

Diamond, Multi-Stone, Gold Bracelets, Fratelli Coppini
The bracelets feature full-cut diamonds weighing a total of approximately 0.80 carat, with one accented by ruby cabochons and the other by sapphire cabochons; both set in 18k gold, marked Coppini. Gross weight 184.20 grams.
Dimensions: 6-1/2 inches x 5/8 inch

Estimate: $6,500-$8,500
Starting Bid: $4,500

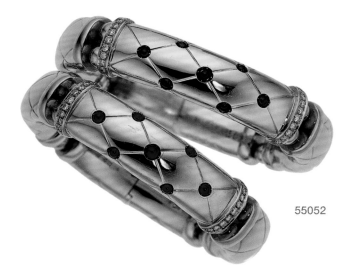

55052

55053

55053
Gold Necklace, Tiffany & Co.
The 18k gold convertible necklace weighs
206.00 grams, marked Tiffany & Co.
Necklace Length: 16-1/2 inches
Bracelet Lengths: 9 inches, 7-1/2 inches

Estimate: $4,500-$5,500
Starting Bid: $3,500

55054

55054
Turquoise, Diamond, Gold Jewelry Suite, Aletto Bros.
The ring and matching earrings feature turquoise beads
ranging in size from 5.50 to 6.50 mm, accented by full-
cut diamonds weighing a total of 1.38 carats, set in 18k
gold, marked Aletto Bros. Gross weight 52.24 grams.
Ring Size: 6-3/4 (sizeable)
Earring Dimensions: 1-1/4 inches x 1 inch
*Note: earrings are designed for non-pierced ears

Estimate: $12,000-$15,000
Starting Bid: $10,000

55055

Black Opal, Diamond, Gold Necklace
The necklace features an oval-shaped black opal
cabochon measuring 19.45 x 13.35 x 6.15 mm, enhanced
by full-cut diamonds weighing a total of approximately
0.25 carat, set in 14k gold. Gross weight 8.87 grams.
Centerpiece Dimensions: 1-11/16 inches x 9/16 inch
Chain Length: 16 inches

Estimate: $5,000-$7,000
Starting Bid: $3,000

55055

55056

**Multi-Stone, Diamond, Gold Earrings,
Temple St. Clair**
The earrings feature pear-shaped aquamarine,
oval-shaped tanzanite, marquise-cut tsavorite
garnets, accented by full-cut diamonds weighing
a total of 0.61 carat, set in 18k gold, maker's mark
for Temple St. Clair. Gross weight 17.50 grams.
Dimensions: 1-3/4 inches x 7/8 inch
Note: earrings are designed for pierced ears

Estimate: $4,000-$6,000
Starting Bid: $3,000

55056

55057

Colombian Emerald, Diamond, Platinum, Gold Ring
The ring features a square emerald-cut emerald
measuring 8.88 x 8.26 x 5.93 mm and weighing
2.77 carats, enhanced by epaulet-shaped diamonds
weighing a total of 0.43 carat, accented by full-cut
diamonds weighing a total of 0.32 carat, set in platinum
and 18k gold. A Gübelin report # 11060056, dated
June 16, 2011, stating *Natural Beryl, Origin Colombia,
Indications of Insignificant Clarity Enhancement*,
accompanies the emerald. Gross weight 5.64 grams.
Size: 6-3/4 (sizeable)

Estimate: $20,000-$30,000
Starting Bid: $16,000

55057

55058

Diamond, Gold Bracelet, Carrera y Carrera
The cherub motif bracelet features full-cut
diamonds weighing a total of approximately 0.40
carat, enhanced by round-cut emeralds and
rubies, set in 18k gold, maker's mark for mark
Carrera y Carrera. Gross weight 76.50 grams.
Dimensions: 7-3/8 inches x 1 inch

Estimate: $5,000-$8,000
Starting Bid: $3,000

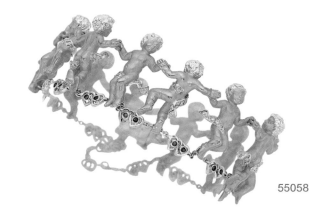

55058

55059

55060

55061

55059
Gold Necklace, Craig Drake
The 18k gold necklace weighs 145.07 grams, maker's mark for Craig Drake.
Dimensions: 16 inches x 11/16 inch

Estimate: $3,000-$4,000
Starting Bid: $2,000

55060
Multi-Stone, Diamond, Gold Ring
The ring features carved black onyx, enhanced by a coral bead measuring 9.75 mm, accented by full-cut diamonds weighing a total of approximately 0.60 carat, completed by round-cut rubies, set in 18k gold with rhodium finish accents. Gross weight 60.20 grams.
Size: 6-3/4 (not sizeable)

Estimate: $3,500-$5,500
Starting Bid: $2,300

55061
Gold Bracelet, Cartier, French
The 18k white, rose and yellow gold *Trinity* bracelet weighs 102.30 grams, marked Cartier with French hallmarks.
Circumference: 7 inches inches

Estimate: $8,000-$10,000
Starting Bid: $7,400

55062

55062
Diamond, Gold Earrings, Kurt Wayne
The earrings feature full-cut diamonds weighing
a total of approximately 2.50 carats, set in
18k gold. Gross weight 26.80 grams.
Dimensions: 1-3/16 inches x 1 inch
Note: earrings are designed for non-pierced ears

Property of an Oklahoma Lady

Estimate: $5,000-$7,000
Starting Bid: $3,500

55063

55063
Citrine, Yellow Beryl, Gold Ring
The ring features a rectangular-shaped citrine
measuring 24.55 x 19.50 x 14.20 mm and weighing
approximately 40.50 carats, enhanced by square-cut
yellow beryl weighing a total of approximately 1.10
carat, set in 18k gold. Gross weight 39.30 grams.
Size: 7 (sizeable)

Estimate: $10,000-$15,000
Starting Bid: $8,500

55064

55064
Amethyst, Chrome Diopside, Gold Ring
The ring features an oval-shaped amethyst measuring
25.50 x 20.10 x 15.20 mm, enhanced by square-shaped
chrome diopside weighing a total of approximately 2.00
carats, set in 18k gold. Gross weight 41.91 grams.
Size: 6-1/2 (sizeable)

Estimate: $8,500-$9,500
Starting Bid: $7,000

55065
Gold Bracelet, Gucci
The 18k gold bracelet weighs 111.60
grams, marked Gucci.
Length: 6-3/4, 7 inches, 7-1/2 inches (adjustable)

Estimate: $5,000-$7,000
Starting Bid: $4,500

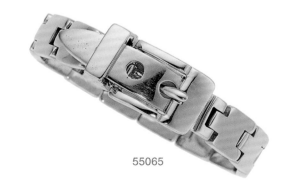

55065

55066
Diamond, Cultured Pearl, Gold Earrings, Chanel
The gardenia earrings feature full-cut diamonds weighing a total of approximately 3.70 carats, accented by cultured pearls measuring 7.90 mm, set in 18k gold, marked Chanel. Gross weight 28.00 grams.
Dimensions: 1-5/16 inches x 13/16 inch
Note: earrings designed for pierced ears

Estimate: $6,000-$8,000
Starting Bid: $3,000

55066

55067
Black Opal, Diamond, Platinum Ring-Dant
The ring centers a black opal measuring 15.80 x 9.70 x 5.14 mm and weighing approximately 4.00 carats, accented by marquise and baguette-cut diamonds weighing a total of approximately 3.90 carats, set in platinum. Gross weight 14.50 grams.
Size: 7 (sizeable)

Estimate: $4,000-$6,000
Starting Bid: $2,000

55067

55068
Diamond, Rock Crystal Quartz, White Gold Ring, Cartier, French
The *Must de Cartier* ring features full-cut diamonds weighing a total of approximately 1.30 carats, enhanced by carved rock crystal quartz, set in 18k white gold, marked Cartier, with French hallmarks. Gross weight 17.66 grams.
Size: 7-1/2 (sizeable)

Estimate: $4,000-$6,000
Starting Bid: $2,000

55068

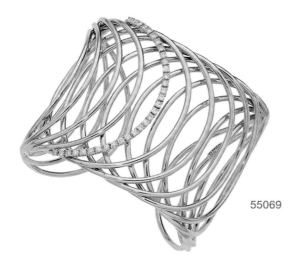

55069
Diamond, Gold Bracelet
The cuff features full-cut diamonds weighing a total of approximately 1.00 carat, set in 18k gold. Gross weight 66.30 grams.
Dimension: 7 inches x 2-1/4 inches

Estimate: $4,000-$6,000
Starting Bid: $3,200

55069

55070
Diamond, Gold Brooch, George Lederman
The articulated brooch features full-cut diamonds weighing a total of approximately 1.20 carats, set in platinum and 18k gold, maker's mark for George Lederman. Gross weight 40.00 grams.
Dimensions: 2-5/8 inches x 1-3/4 inches

From the Collection of a San Antonio, TX Lady

Estimate: $4,000-$6,000
Starting Bid: $2,000

55070

55071
Burma Ruby, Diamond, Platinum, Gold Ring
The ring features a cushion-shaped ruby cabochon measuring 19.61 x 11.60 x 7.25 mm and weighing approximately 17.20 carats, enhanced by baguette and tapered baguette-cut diamonds weighing a total of approximately 1.10 carats, set in platinum and 18k gold. An AGL report # 1084882, dated July 14, 2017, stating *Natural Corundum, Origin Burma, No Gemological Evidence of Heat*, accompanies the ruby. Gross weight 13.52 grams.
Size: 7-1/2 (not easily sized)

Estimate: $6,000-$8,000
Starting Bid: $3,000

55071

55072
Ruby, Diamond, Gold Brooch
The brooch features oval and pear-shaped rubies weighing a total of approximately 2.50 carats, accented by full-cut diamonds weighing a total of approximately 2.20 carats, set in 18k gold with white gold accents. Gross weight 6.40 grams.
Dimensions: 1 inch x 7/8 inch

Estimate: $3,000-$4,000
Starting Bid: $1,500

55072

55073
Diamond, Peridot, Ruby, White Gold Brooch, Assil
The brooch features full-cut diamonds weighing a total of 5.77 carats, enhanced by oval-shaped peridot cabochons weighing a total of 24.97 carats, accented by ruby cabochons weighing a total of 0.14 carat, set in 18k white gold, marked Assil. Gross weight 35.80 grams.
Dimensions: 2-1/4 inches x 1-9/16 inches

Estimate: $6,000-$8,000
Starting Bid: $5,000

55073

55074

Antique Pink Tourmaline, Seed Pearl Pendant, Qing Dynasty
The pink tourmaline carving measures 41.00 x 37.00 x 12.00 mm, suspended from a cord woven with seed pearls and a cylindrical glass bead. Gross weight 30.40 grams.
Dimensions: 4 inches x 1-3/4 inches

Estimate: $9,000-$12,000
Starting Bid: $4,500

55075

Jadeite Jade, Diamond, Gold Earrings
The earrings feature oval-shaped jadeite jade cabochons measuring 10.95 x 14.46 x 4.25 mm and 10.95 x 14.05 x 4.35 mm, accented by full-cut diamonds weighing a total of approximately 3.40 carats, set in 18k gold with rhodium finished accents. A Mason-Kay report # 33372, dated July 17, 2017, stating *Natural Jadeite Jade, No Dye or Polymer Detected, 'A' Jade,* accompanies the jadeite. Gross weight 28.00 grams.
Dimensions: 1-1/16 inches x 7/8 inch
Note: earrings are designed for non-pierced ears

Estimate: $7,000-$9,000
Starting Bid: $5,000

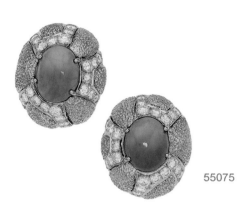

55076

Jadeite Jade, Diamond, Gold Ring
The ring features an oval-shaped jadeite jade cabochon measuring 16.09 x 22.57 x 7.48 mm, accented by full-cut diamonds weighing a total of approximately 2.00 carats, set in 18k gold with rhodium finished accents. A Mason-Kay report # 345294, dated July 17, 2017, stating *Natural Jadeite Jade, No Dye or Polymer Detected, 'A' Jade,* accompanies the stone. Gross weight 27.10 grams.
Size: 5-1/2 (sizeable)

Estimate: $18,000-$20,000
Starting Bid: $16,000

55077

Emerald, Enamel, Gold Ring, Cartier, French
The ring features round-cut emeralds, accented by enamel applied onto 18k gold, marked Cartier, French hallmarks. Gross weight 17.60 grams.
Size: 5-3/4 (sizeable)

Estimate: $5,000-$7,000
Starting Bid: $4,000

55078
Diamond, Coral, Gold Brooch
The brooch features oval-shaped coral cabochons
ranging in size from 17.80 x 15.00 mm to 15.00
x 10.00 mm, accented by full-cut diamonds
weighing a total of approximately 1.00 carat, set
in 18k gold. Gross weight 46.20 grams.
Dimensions: 2-1/2 inches x 2-1/8 inches

Estimate: $4,000-$6,000
Starting Bid: $2,000

55078

55079
South Sea Cultured Pearl, Diamond, Gold Earrings
The starfish earrings feature South Sea cultured
pearls measuring 17.30 x 21.50 mm and 16.90
x 22.00 mm, enhanced by full-cut diamonds
weighing a total of approximately 0.40 carat, set
in 18k gold. Gross weight 35.20 grams.
Dimensions: 1-3/4 inches x 15/16 inch
Note: earrings are designed for pierced ears

Estimate: $8,000-$10,000
Starting Bid: $6,000

55079

55080
Coral, Diamond, Gold Bracelet
The bracelet features oval-shaped coral
cabochons, enhanced by full-cut diamonds
weighing a total of approximately 1.35 carats,
set in 14k gold. Gross weight 85.17 grams.
Dimensions: 7 inches x 3/4 inch

Estimate: $5,000-$7,000
Starting Bid: $3,000

55080

55081

55081
Turquoise, Gold Necklace
The necklace is composed of turquoise
beads measuring 16.70 mm to 17.10 mm,
accented by gold rondelles and a 14k gold
clasp. Gross weight 153.60 grams.
Length: 18 inches

Estimate: $5,000-$7,000
Starting Bid: $2,500

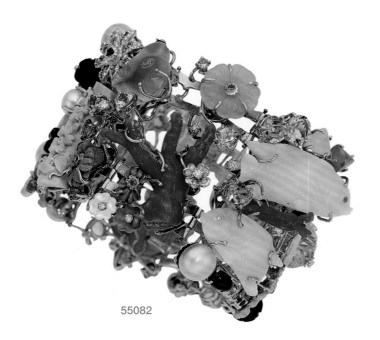

55082

55082
Diamond, Multi-Stone, Gold Bracelet
The bracelet features full-cut diamonds weighing
a total of approximately 0.50 carat, enhanced by
carved chalcedony, fire opal, aquamarine, turquoise,
carnelian, rose quartz, frosted rock crystal quartz,
lapis lazuli and branch coral, further enhanced by
heart-shaped blue topaz and garnets, accented by
round-cut ruby, tsavorite garnet, pink tourmaline
and yellow sapphires, further accented by an oval-
shaped garnet cabochon and pear-shaped tsavorite
garnets, completed by freshwater cultured pearls,
set in 18k gold. Gross weight 141.85 grams.
Dimensions: 7-1/2 inches x 2 inches

Estimate: $5,000-$7,000
Starting Bid: $3,500

55083
Aquamarine, Diamond, Gold Pendant-Necklace
The pendant centers an oval-shaped aquamarine
measuring 35.00 x 19.96 x 11.25 mm and weighing
approximately 44.00 carats, accented by rose and single-
cut diamonds, set in 14k gold. Gross weight 30.10 grams.
Pendant Dimensions: 1-7/8 inches x 1-1/4 inches
Chain Length: 20 inches

Estimate: $5,000-$7,000
Starting Bid: $4,000

55083

55084
Multi-Stone, Diamond, Gold Ring
The ring features a cushion-shaped kunzite measuring
21.25 x 20.95 x 14.45 mm and weighing approximately
43.50 carats, enhanced by oval and pear-shaped amethyst
weighing a total of approximately 6.00 carats, accented
by pear-shaped peridot weighing a total of approximately
5.50 carats, set in 18k gold. Gross weight 21.66 grams.
Size: 6-1/2 (sizeable)

Estimate: $4,000-$6,000
Starting Bid: $2,000

55084

55085
**Multi-Stone, Diamond, South Sea
Cultured Pearl, Gold Bracelet**
The starfish bracelet features a variety of
carved and faceted gemstones and South Sea
cultured pearls, accented by full-cut diamonds
weighing a total of approximately 0.15 carat, set
in 18k gold. Gross weight 122.55 grams.
Dimensions: 7-1/2 inches x 1-1/2 inches

Estimate: $4,000-$6,000
Starting Bid: $3,000

55085

55086

55086
Gentleman's Diamond, Gold Ring
The ring features a European-cut diamond measuring
8.34 - 8.53 x 5.48 mm and weighing 2.46 carats, set
in 14k gold. A GIA report # 5181630001, dated July
25, 2017, stating *L color, SI1 clarity*, accompanies
the diamond. Gross weight 8.65 grams.
Size: 10 (sizeable)

Property of a Wyoming Collector

Estimate: $4,000-$6,000
Starting Bid: $2,000

55087

55087
Gentleman's Colombian Emerald, Diamond, Gold Ring
The ring features an emerald-cut emerald measuring
6.30 x 6.30 x 4.15 mm and weighing approximately 1.00
carat, accented by full-cut diamonds weighing a total
of approximately 1.75 carats, set in 14k gold. An AGL
report # 1085623, dated July 27, 2017, stating *Origin
Colombia, Minor Traditional Clarity Enhancement*,
accompanies the emerald. Gross weight 27.50 grams.
Size: 10-3/4 (sizeable)

Estimate: $4,000-$6,000
Starting Bid: $2,000

55088

55088
Gentleman's Diamond, Gold Ring
The ring centers a round brilliant-cut diamond
measuring 11.23 - 11.35 x 6.58 mm and weighing
5.19 carats, set in 14k gold. Accompanied by GIA
report # 1186506210, dated June 14, 2017, stating *N
color, VVS2 clarity*. Gross weight 13.21 grams.
Size: 8 (sizeable)

Estimate: $15,000-$20,000
Starting Bid: $12,000

55089

55089
Gianni Versace Unisex Gold Watch
Case: 35 mm, round, 18k gold, 00009,
reference 800801 Swiss
Dial: Gold with raised image of Medusa,
Dauphine minute and hour hands
Movement: Quartz
Bracelet: four round links with the raised image
of Medusa surrounded by a beaded edge with
Greek key border; 7-1/2 inches x 3/8 inch
Signed: Gianni Versace on the caseback
Gross weight: 177.10 grams
Note: watch is currently in working order

Estimate: $8,000-$10,000
Starting Bid: $7,500

55090

Gentleman's Diamond, White Gold Ring
The ring features a round brilliant-cut diamond measuring 11.26 - 11.33 x 7.00 mm and weighing 5.56 carats, enhanced by radiant-cut diamonds weighing a total of approximately 2.25 carats, accented by full and baguette-cut diamonds weighing a total of approximately 1.75 carats, set in 18k white gold. A GIA report # 2185605361, dated July 17, 2017, stating *M color, VS2 clarity*, accompanies the center stone. Gross weight 26.71 grams.
Size: 10 (not easily sized)

Estimate: $20,000-$30,000
Starting Bid: $15,000

55090

55091

Gentleman's Sapphire, Diamond, White Gold Dress Set, Assil
The set includes a pair of cuff links and four matching shirt studs featuring square-cut sapphires weighing a total of 5.15 carats, enhanced by full-cut diamonds weighing a total of 2.08 carats, set in 18k white gold, marked Assil. Gross weight 20.84 grams.
Cuff Link Dimensions: 1/2 inch x 3/8 inch x 15/16 inch
Shirt Stud Dimensions: 3/8 inch x 5/16 inch

Estimate: $6,000-$8,000
Starting Bid: $5,000

55091

55092

Gentleman's Diamond, White Gold Bracelet
The bracelet features radiant-cut diamonds weighing a total of approximately 4.00 carats, set in 18k white gold. Gross weight 68.75 grams.
Dimensions: 7-1/4 inches x 1/2 inch

Estimate: $5,000-$7,000
Starting Bid: $2,500

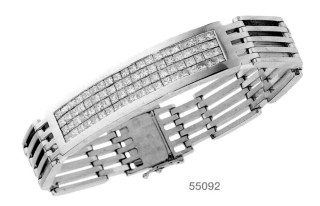

55092

55093

55093
Diamond, White Gold Cuff Links
The cuff links feature emerald and tapered baguette-cut diamonds weighing a total of 2.30 carats, set in 18k white gold. Gross weight 7.28 grams.
Dimensions: 1/2 inch x 3/8 inch x 3/4 inch

Estimate: $16,000-$20,000
Starting Bid: $14,000

55094

55094
Emerald, Black Onyx, White Gold Cuff Links, Cartier
The cuff links feature pear-shaped emeralds, accented by carved black onyx, set in 18k white gold, marked Cartier 631333. Gross weight 23.64 grams.
Dimensions: 9/16 inch x 5/8 inch x 1-1/8 inches

Estimate: $7,000-$9,000
Starting Bid: $6,500

55095
Gentleman's Diamond, Ruby, Platinum, White Gold Dress Set
The set includes a pair of cuff links and four matching shirt studs featuring calibé-cut rubies weighing a total of 6.10 carats, enhanced by full-cut diamonds weighing a total of 0.88 carat, set in platinum and 18k white gold. Gross weight 20.37 grams.
Cuff Link Dimensions: 1/2 inch x 1 inch
Shirt Stud Diameter: 7/16 inch

Estimate: $8,000-$10,000
Starting Bid: $7,000

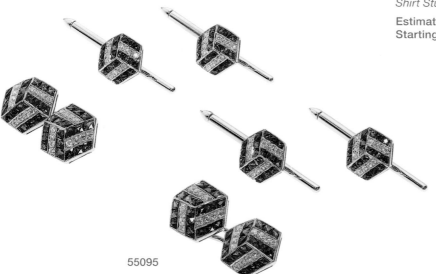

55095

55096
Jacob & Co. Women's Diamond, Colored Diamond, Stainless Steel Five Time Zone Watch
Case: 40 mm, round, stainless steel, diamond set bezel, No. S2625, water resistant 100M/330FT
Dial: irradiated blue and yellow diamond pavé-set depicting a map of the world, with four subsidiary dials for Los Angeles, New York, Paris and Tokyo, with gold luminous Baton hour and minute hands, gold Baton sweep seconds, gold luminous Dauphine hour and minute hands for additional time zones, sapphire crystal
Movement: Swiss Quartz ETA
Stones: full-cut colored diamonds weigh a total of approximately 2.00 carats; full-cut near colorless diamonds weigh a total of approximately 2.10 carats
Band: aquamarine blue alligator with stainless steel Seiko buckle & tang; 8-1/2 inches (adjustable)
Signed: Jacob & Co. on the case, crystal, sweep seconds, and strap
Gross Weight: 81.60 grams
Note: watch is currently in working order

Estimate: $8,000-$10,000
Starting Bid: $7,000

55096

55097
Cartier Lady's White Gold La Dona Watch
Case: 22 mm x 22 mm, 18k white gold, model 2905, 94501 LX, two body, water resistant back secured with four screws, sapphire crystal, sapphire crown
Dial: sunray engine turned silver, black Roman numerals, black minute track, blue batons
Movement: Swiss quartz
Bracelet: 18k white gold S-link with double deployant clasp; 6 inches
Signed: Cartier on the dial, clasp, case back
Gross weight: 125.43 grams
Note: watch is currently in working order

Estimate: $3,500-$4,500
Starting Bid: $2,750

55097

55098
Franck Muller Lady's White Gold Color Dreams Master of Complications Watch
Case: 28 x 38 mm, curved tonneau, 18k white gold, two body, back secured by screws, Master of Complications No 793, Ref. 7502 QZ
Dial: black, unconventional and arbitrary placement of multi colored Arabic numeral hour markers, blue Feuille luminescent hands, sapphire crystal
Movement: quartz
Bracelet: red leather with 18k white gold buckle; 6 inches to 7-1/4 inches adjustable
Signed: Franck Muller on the case and dial
Gross Weight: 52.71 grams
Notes: watch is currently in working order

Estimate: $4,000-$6,000
Starting Bid: $2,000

55098

55099

55099
Rolex Lady's Diamond, White Gold Pearlmaster Watch
Case: 29 mm, round, 18k white gold, case # D800485, three body, screw down case back and crown, diamond bezel, sapphire crystal
Dial: single-cut diamonds, date aperture at three with cyclops, gold baton hands
Movement: automatic, caliber 2235, 31 jewels
Band: 18k white gold, hidden deployant clasp, diamonds; 6-3/4 inches
Stones: full and single-cut diamonds weigh a total of approximately 5.80 carats
Signed: Rolex on dial, case back, clasp, movement
Gross weight: 110.09 grams
Note: watch is currently in working order

Estimate: $10,000-$15,000
Starting Bid: $5,000

55100
Cartier Lady's Rose Gold La Dona Watch
Case: 20 x 26 mm, 18k rose gold, model 2896, serial 120673LX, water resistant back secured with screws, sapphire crystal, sapphire set crown
Dial: sunray engine turned silver, black Roman numerals, black minute track, blue baton hour and minute hands
Movement: quartz, 8 jewels, caliber 690
Bracelet: 18k gold, S-link with double deployant clasp; 6-1/4 inches
Signed: Cartier on the dial, case back and clasp
Gross weight: 171.77 grams
Note: watch is currently in working order

Estimate: $6,000-$8,000
Starting Bid: $4,500

55100

55101

55101
Patek Philippe Lady's Diamond, Gold La Flamme Watch
Case: 21 x 25 mm, 18k gold diamond bezel, sapphire crystal, Ref. 4815/003
Dial: champagne, applied diamond hour markers, gold twisted baton hour and minute hands
Movement: quartz, 1.603.020, caliber E-15
Bracelet: 18k gold integral bracelet, diamond set links; 6 inches to 6-3/8 inches
Stones: full and single-cut diamonds weigh a total of 1.11 carats
Signed: Patek Philippe on dial and clasp
Gross Weight: 68.49 grams
Note: watch is currently not in working order

Estimate: $6,000-$8,000
Starting Bid: $3,000

55102

Harry Winston Lady's Gold Classique Watch
Case: 30 mm, round, 18k gold, smooth bezel,
water resistant, 01020060, Swiss made
Dial: textured champagne with applied gold o
and circular hour indexes and Arabic markers at
3 & 9 o'clock positions, gold Baton hour, minute
and sweep seconds hands, date aperture at 6
Movement: quartz
Bracelet: 18k gold circular links, completed
by a double deployant clasp; 7 inches
Signed: Harry Winston on the case and dial
Gross Weight: 104.00 grams
Note: watch is currently in working order

Estimate: $5,000-$7,000
Starting Bid: $4,000

55102

55103

**Rolex Lady's Diamond, Gold Oyster
Perpetual DateJust Watch, circa 1981**
Case: 26 mm, 18k gold, three body, screw
back, screw down crown, diamond set
bezel, case # 6518974, ref. 6917
Dial: gold, applied single-cut diamond hour
markers, gold baton hour, minute, and center
center sweep seconds hands, date aperture
at 3 o'clock with Cyclops, sapphire crystal
Movement: automatic, caliber 2030, 28 jewels
Bracelet: 18k gold Presidential links, concealed
deployant clasp; 6-1/2 inches
Stones: full and single-cut diamonds weigh
a total of approximately 0.90 carat
Signed: Rolex on the case, dial, movement, and clasp
Gross weight: 70.51 grams
Note: watch is currently in working order

Property of a Las Vegas, NV Estate

Estimate: $4,000-$6,000
Starting Bid: $2,000

55103

55104

Tourmaline, Diamond, Gold Earrings
The earrings feature oval-shaped green tourmaline
weighing a total of approximately 15.60 carats, accented
by full-cut diamonds weighing a total of approximately
0.45 carat, set in 18k gold. Gross weight 39.20 grams.
Dimensions: 2-1/4 inches x 5/8 inch
Note: earrings designed for non-pierced ears

Estimate: $4,000-$5,000
Starting Bid: $2,000

55104

55105

55105
Amber, Cultured Pearl, Gold Necklace, Bvlgari
The necklace features tumbled amber, enhanced by cultured pearls measuring 5.00 mm to 6.50 mm, accented by 18k gold charms, set in 18k gold, maker's mark for Bvlgari. Gross weight 94.60 grams.
Length: 17 inches

Estimate: $4,500-$5,500
Starting Bid: $3,500

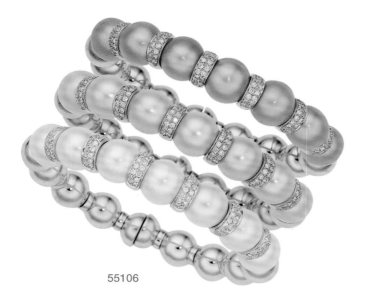

55106

55106
Cultured Pearl, Diamond, Gold Bracelets
The trio of 18k white, yellow and rose gold bangles feature cultured pearls ranging in size from 11.00 - 11.60 mm, enhanced by full-cut diamonds weighing a total of approximately 2.80 carats. Gross weight 132.03 grams.
Dimensions: 6 inches (adjustable)

Estimate: $6,000-$9,000
Starting Bid: $3,000

55107

55107
Multi-Stone, Diamond, White Gold Suite
The necklace and bracelet feature oval-shaped
chalcedony cabochons, enhanced by rose
quartz and green tourmaline, alternating with
diamonds weighing a total of 3.16 carats, set
in 18k gold. Gross weight 143.00 grams.
Necklace Dimensions: 17 inches x 1/2 inch
Bracelet Dimensions: 7-1/4 inches

Estimate: $6,000-$8,000
Starting Bid: $4,000

55108

55108
Diamond, White Gold Eternity Band
The ring features round brilliant-cut diamonds weighing
6.03 carats, continuously set in 18k white gold.
Gross weight 6.65 grams.
Size: 6-1/4 (not sizeable)

Estimate: $5,500-$7,500
Starting Bid: $3,500

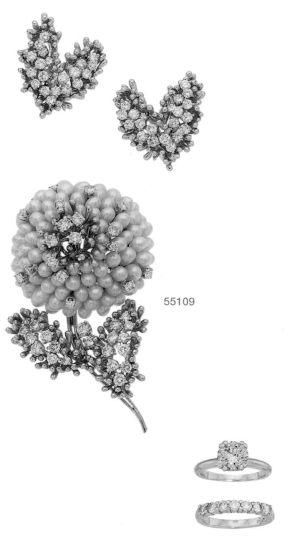

55109

55109
Diamond, Freshwater Pearl, Platinum, Gold Jewelry Suite
The brooch and matching earrings feature full-cut diamonds weighing a total of approximately 5.00 carats, set in platinum and 18k gold, the brooch is enhanced by freshwater cultured pearls, marked KW for Kurt Wayne. Gross weight 69.80 grams.
Brooch Dimensions: 2-3/4inches x 1-1/2 inches
Earring Dimensions: 1-1/8 inches x 1 inch
*Note: earrings are designed for non-pierced ears

Estimate: $4,000-$6,000
Starting Bid: $2,500

55110
Diamond, Platinum Ring Set
The set includes one ring featuring a round brilliant-cut diamond measuring 6.23 - 6.30 x 4.05 mm and weighing 1.01 carats, set in platinum; together with a band featuring full-cut diamonds weighing a total of approximately 0.55 carat, set in platinum. A GIA report # 2107383805, dated June 22, 2009, stating *I color, SI1 clarity,* accompanies the center diamond. Gross weight 9.40 grams.
Size: 5 (sizeable)

Estimate: $4,000-$6,000
Starting Bid: $2,000

55110

55111
Diamond, Platinum Ring
The ring features a pear-shaped diamond measuring 10.88 x 7.64 x 5.04 mm and weighing 2.37 carats, enhanced by tapered baguette-cut diamonds, set in platinum. A GIA report # 2181551806, dated June 23, 2017, stating *D color, VVS1 clarity*, accompanies the center stone. Gross weight 9.15 grams.
Size: 7-3/4 (sizeable)

Estimate: $20,000-$30,000
Starting Bid: $12,000

55111

55112

55112
Diamond, White Gold Bracelet, Cartier, France
The *Maillon Panthere* bracelet features full-cut diamonds weighing a total of approximately 7.50 carats, set in 18k white gold, marked Cartier, having French hallmarks. Gross weight 32.20 grams.
Dimensions: 7-1/4 inches x 3/8 inch

Estimate: $12,000-$14,000
Starting Bid: $10,000

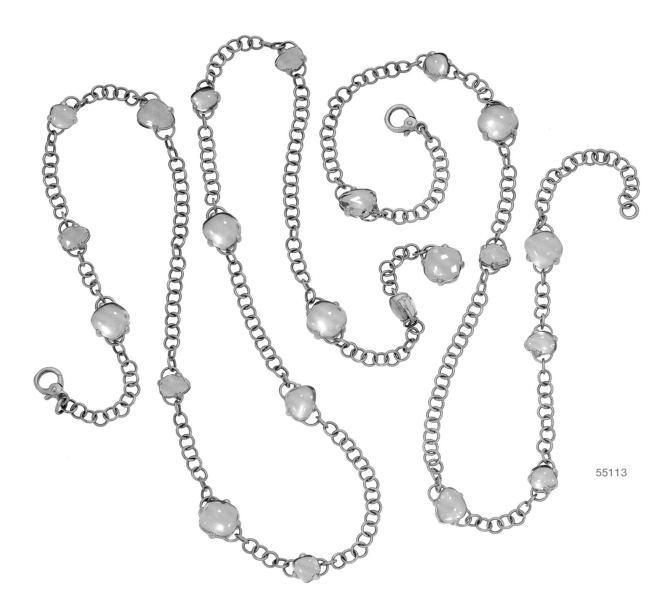

55113

55113
Rose Gold Necklaces, Pomellato
The necklaces feature rose quartz cabochons and
rose-cut rock crystal quartz, set in 18k rose gold,
marked Pomellato. Gross weight 46.30 grams.
Lengths: 25 inches, 16-1/2 inches

Estimate: $6,000-$8,000
Starting Bid: $5,000

55114

55114
Enamel, Gold Bracelets
The hinged bangles feature enamel applied
on 18k gold. Gross weight 62.00 grams.
Inner Circumference: 6-1/4 inches

Estimate: $4,000-$5,000
Starting Bid: $3,500

55115

55115
Aquamarine, Peridot, Gold Necklace, Frank Ancona
The torsade is composed of peridot beads measuring
4.50 mm, forming fifteen strands, completed by an
18k gold clasp centering an oval-shaped aquamarine
cabochon measuring 35.00 x 25.00 x 14.00 mm and
weighing approximately 90.00 carats, marked FA
for Frank Ancona. Gross weight 341.50 grams.
Dimensions: 18-1/2 inches (untwisted)

Estimate: $15,000-$20,000
Starting Bid: $12,000

55116

55116
Diamond, Gold Bracelet, Leslie Greene
The hinged cuff features full-cut diamonds weighing a
total of approximately 1.75 carats, set in 18k gold, maker's
mark for Leslie Greene. Gross weight 43.40 grams.
Dimensions: 6-1/4 inches x 1-5/8 inches

Estimate: $4,000-$6,000
Starting Bid: $2,500

55117

55117
Diamond, Cultured Pearl, Gold Necklace, French
The necklace features cultured pearls ranging in size from 3.00 mm to 6.75 mm, enhanced by full-cut diamonds weighing a total of approximately 0.40 carat, set in 18k gold, having French hallmarks. Gross weight 60.48 grams.
Length: 15-1/2 inches

Estimate: $4,000-$5,000
Starting Bid: $2,600

55118

55118
Diamond, Gold Pendant
The pendant features a round brilliant-cut diamond measuring 8.00 - 8.06 x 5.08 mm and weighing 1.95 carats, enhanced by full-cut diamonds, set in 14k gold. A GIA report # 1186625186, dated July 24, 2017, stating *I color, VVS2 clarity*, accompanies the center stone. Gross weight 3.28 grams.
Dimensions: 7/8 inch x 5/8 inch

Estimate: $7,000-$9,000
Starting Bid: $5,000

55119

55119
Multi-Stone, White Gold Ring, Assil
The ring features oval and round-cut blue sapphires weighing a total of 6.44 carats, enhanced by round-cut tsavorite garnets weighing a total of 2.14 carats, accented by round-cut yellow sapphires weighing a total of 2.50 carats, set in 18k white gold, marked Assil. Gross weight 18.60 grams.
Size: 6-1/2 (sizeable)

Estimate: $4,000-$6,000
Starting Bid: $2,000

55120

55120

Fire Opal, Sapphire, Gold Earrings

The earrings feature pear and cushion-shaped fire opals weighing a total of 14.12 carats, enhanced by cut-cornered rectangular-shaped yellow sapphires weighing a total of 2.36 carats, set in 18k gold. Gross weight 20.61 grams.
Dimensions: 1-7/8 inches x 1/2 inch
Note: earrings are designed for non-pierced ears

Estimate: $8,000-$10,000
Starting Bid: $6,000

55121

55121

Diamond, White Gold Pendant

The pendant features a round brilliant-cut diamond measuring 9.84 - 9.98 x 5.76 mm and weighing 3.48 carats, set in 14k white gold. A GIA report # 1182607076, dated July 19, 2017, stating *M color, VS1 clarity*, accompanies the diamond. Gross weight 1.23 grams.
Dimensions: 3/8 inch x 3/8 inch

Property from the Estate of Wanda Lee Lofton

Estimate: $10,000-$15,000
Starting Bid: $5,000

55122

55122

Ruby, Diamond, Gold Ring, Cartier, French

The ring features an oval-shaped ruby cabochon measuring 7.80 x 6.30 x 4.75 mm and weighing approximately 2.25 carats, enhanced by full-cut diamonds weighing a total of approximately 1.30 carats, set in 18k gold, marked Cartier 614340, having French hallmarks. Gross weight 13.89 grams.
Size: 6 (sizeable)

Estimate: $8,000-$10,000
Starting Bid: $6,500

55123

55123

South Sea Cultured Pearl, Sapphire, Diamond, Gold Bracelet, Zorab

The bracelet features South Sea cultured pearls measuring 17.50 x 16.60 mm to 18.30 x 16.70 mm, enhanced by round-cut orange, pink, blue and red sapphires weighing a total of 28.69 carats, accented by full-cut diamonds weighing a total of 1.16 carats, marked Zorab. Gross weight 59.52 grams.
Length: 8 inches

Estimate: $4,000-$6,000
Starting Bid: $2,000

55124
Diamond, Rose Gold Earrings
The hoops feature full-cut diamonds
weighing a total of 5.08 carats, set in 18k
rose gold. Gross weight 12.98 grams.
Dimensions: 1-1/2 inches x 1/8 inch
*Note: earrings are designed for pierced ears

Estimate: $4,000-$6,000
Starting Bid: $2,700

55124

55125
Diamond, Tsavorite Garnet, Rose Gold Ring
The ring features full-cut diamonds weighing
a total of 4.07 carats, accented by round-cut
tsavorite garnets weighing a total of 0.11 carat, set
in 18k rose gold. Gross weight 24.50 grams.
Size: 6-1/2 (sizeable)

Estimate: $5,000-$7,000
Starting Bid: $3,500

55125

55126
Diamond, Platinum Ring, Precision Set
The *FlushFit™* ring features a round brilliant-cut
diamond measuring 7.37 - 7.47 x 4.38 mm and
weighing 1.50 carats, flanked by round brilliant-cut
diamonds measuring 5.78 - 5.80 x 3.56 mm and
5.76 x 5.79 x 3.64 mm and weighing a total of 1.468
carats, set in platinum. Gross weight 8.60 grams.
Size: 5-1/2 (sizeable)

Three gemological reports accompany the diamonds:

GIA report # 11542318, dated May 22,
2001, stating *E color, VVS1 clarity*

AGS report # 0004311305, dated August
12, 2003 stating *E color, VVS2 clarity*

AGS report # 0004522106 dated November
3, 2003 stating *F color, VVS1 clarity*

Estimate: $15,000-$20,000
Starting Bid: $10,000

55126

55127
Diamond, Rose Gold Bracelet
The hinged bangle features full and rose-cut diamonds
weighing a total of approximately 16.00 carats, set
in 18k rose gold. Gross weight 57.20 grams.
Interior Circumference: 6-1/2 inches

Estimate: $6,000-$8,000
Starting Bid: $4,500

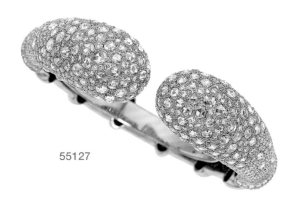

55127

55128

55129

55128
South Sea Cultured Pearl, White Gold Necklace
The necklace is composed of black South Sea cultured pearls ranging in size from 11.00 - 14.60 mm, forming a graduated single knotted strand, completed by a 14k white gold clasp. Gross weight 103.70 grams.
Length: 21 inches

Estimate: $5,000-$7,000
Starting Bid: $2,500

55129
Emerald, South Sea Cultured Pearl, Gold Earrings
The earrings feature silver South Sea cultured pearls measuring 17.05 and 16.70 mm, enhanced by rose-cut emeralds, set in 18k gold. Gross weight 28.35 grams.
Dimensions: 1-5/8 inches x 5/8 inch
*Note: earrings are designed for pierced ears

Estimate: $9,000-$12,000
Starting Bid: $7,000

55130

Diamond, Green Tourmaline, Green Quartz, White Gold Earrings

The earrings feature pear-shaped green quartz briolette measuring 25.00 x 20.00 x 10.00 mm and weighing a total of approximately 60.00 carats, enhanced by full-cut diamonds weighing a total of approximately 1.80 carats, accented by rectangular-cut green tourmaline weighing a total of approximately 3.60 carats, set in 18k white gold. Gross weight 32.30 grams.
Dimensions: 3 inches x 3/4 inch
*Note: earrings are designed for pierced ears

Estimate: $5,000-$7,000
Starting Bid: $3,500

55130

55131

Diamond, Platinum, Gold Ring

The ring features round brilliant-cut diamonds weighing a total of approximately 3.25 carats, enhanced by full-cut diamonds weighing a total of approximately 2.60 carats, set in platinum and 18k gold. Gross weight 10.10 grams.
Size: 5 (sizeable)

Estimate: $10,000-$15,000
Starting Bid: $7,500

55131

55132

Diamond, White Gold Bracelet

The bracelet features full-cut diamonds weighing a total of 10.44 carats, set in 18k white gold. Gross weight 53.70 grams.
Dimensions: 7-1/8 inches x 7/8 inch

Estimate: $4,500-$6,500
Starting Bid: $3,700

55132

55133

55133
Antique Garnet, Diamond, Silver-Topped Gold
Jewelry Suite, 18th Century
The suite features a brooch and pair of earrings set with
pear and rectangular-shaped faceted garnet, surrounded
by Mazarin-cut diamonds, accented by mine-cut diamonds,
set in silver and gold. Gross weight 40.90 grams.
Brooch Dimensions: 3 inches x 1-1/4 inches
Earring Dimensions: 2 inches x 1 inches
*Note: earrings are designed for non-pierced ears

Estimate: $3,000-$4,000
Starting Bid: $1,500

55134

55134
Antique Diamond, Garnet, Enamel,
Silver-Topped Gold Bracelet
The bracelet features an oval-shaped garnet measuring 22.00
x 19.00 x 10.00 mm, enhanced by rose-cut diamonds and
rectangle-shaped garnet cabochons, accented by enamel
applied on silver-topped gold. Gross weight 41.16 grams.
Dimensions: 7-1/2 inches x 1-1/8 inches

Estimate: $4,000-$6,000
Starting Bid: $2,000

55135

55135

Edwardian Topaz, Diamond, Pearl, Platinum, Gold Jewelry Suite
The suite includes a necklace with oval-shaped topaz ranging
in size from 9.60 x 6.20 x 3.60 mm to 22.00 x 9.40 x 6.30 mm
and weighing a total of approximately 27.50 carats, set in
14k gold, enhanced by rose-cut diamonds and pearls, set in
platinum; together with a pair of earrings set with oval-shaped
topaz measuring 13.10 x 7.75 x 3.90 mm and weighing a total
of approximately 5.70 carats, highlighted by European and
baguette-cut diamonds weighing a total of approximately 1.40
carats, set in platinum and 14k gold. Gross weight 33.10 grams.
Necklace Dimensions: 15 inches x 2 inches
Earring Dimensions: 2-1/4 inches x 5/16 inch
*Note: earrings are designed for pierced ears

Estimate: $4,000-$6,000
Starting Bid: $2,500

55136

55136

Antique Diamond, Silver-Topped Gold Bracelet, French
The bracelet features mine-cut diamonds weighing a total of
approximately 4.50 carats, accented by rose-cut diamonds,
set in silver-topped gold. Gross weight 23.00 grams.
Dimensions: 6-3/4 inches x 5/8 inch

Property of a Wyoming Collector

Estimate: $4,000-$6,000
Starting Bid: $2,000

55137

55137
Antique Diamond, Silver-Topped
Gold Bracelets
The matching bracelets feature rose and
mine-cut diamonds ranging in size from
1.00 mm to 6.60 mm, set in silver-topped
18k gold. Gross weight 269.18 grams.
Dimensions: 6 - 7 inches (tapered) x 2-7/8 inches

Estimate: $8,000-$10,000
Starting Bid: $5,000

55138

55138
Diamond, White Gold Ring
The ring features a rose-cut diamond
measuring 11.00 x 10.50 mm, enhanced
by single-cut diamonds weighing a total
of approximately 0.80 carat, set in 14k
white gold. Gross weight 7.20 grams.
Size: 5-1/4 (sizeable)

Estimate: $4,000-$5,000
Starting Bid: $2,000

55139
Victorian Hardstone Cameo, Diamond, Gold Jewelry Suite, circa 1880
The suite includes a pendant, brooch and single earring, each featuring a hardstone cameo, enhanced by mine-cut diamonds weighing a total of approximately 6.45 carat, set in 14k gold. Gross weight 56.40 grams.
Pendant Dimensions: 1-3/4 inches x 3 inches
Brooch Dimensions: 7/8 inch x 1-1/2 inches
Earring Dimensions: 7/8 inch x 1-1/2 inches
Chain Length: 15-1/4 inches

Estimate: $4,000-$6,000
Starting Bid: $2,500

55139

55140
Ruby, Ebony, Gold Brooch, Nardi
The blackamoor brooch features carved ebony, enhanced by pear-shaped rubies weighing a total of approximately 2.50 carats, set in 18k gold, marked Nardi. Gross weight 24.70 grams.
Dimensions: 2-1/2 inches x 1 inch

Estimate: $4,000-$5,000
Starting Bid: $2,000

55140

55141

55142

55141
Antique Diamond, Platinum Necklace
The graduated rivière necklace features European-cut diamonds weighing a total of approximately 25.00 carats, set in platinum. Gross weight 34.17 grams.
Length: 15 inches

Estimate: $20,000-$30,000
Starting Bid: $15,000

55142
Antique Opal, Diamond, Gold Ring
The ring features an oval-shaped opal measuring 10.55 x 8.45 x 5.70 mm and weighing approximately 2.65 carats, accented by European-cut diamonds weighing a total of approximately 2.60 carats, set in 14k gold. Gross weight 4.20 grams.
Size: 7 (sizeable)

Estimate: $5,000-$7,000
Starting Bid: $4,000

55143

55143
Antique Diamond, Platinum-Topped Gold Necklace
The necklace features mine, rose, and pear-shaped
diamonds weighing a total approximately 14.50 carats,
set in platinum-topped gold. Gross weight 48.06 grams.
Length: 18-1/2 inches
Drop Length: 3-1/2 inches

Estimate: $25,000-$30,000
Starting Bid: $20,000

55144
Victorian Diamond, Platinum-Topped Gold Ring
The ring features European-cut diamonds weighing
a total of approximately 3.20 carats, set in platinum-
topped 18k gold. Gross weight 6.12 grams.
Size: 7 (sizeable)

Estimate: $4,000-$6,000
Starting Bid: $2,000

55144

55145
55145

Arts and Crafts Black Opal, Diamond, Enamel, Gold Necklace, Marcus & Co.
The necklace features a pear-shaped black opal cabochon measuring 17.10 x 9.00 x 3.05 mm, enhanced by European-cut diamonds, accented by blue and green enamel applied on 14k gold, marked Marcus & Co, 05545. Gross weight 6.92 grams.
Pendant Dimensions: 1-1/4 inches x 7/8 inch
Chain Length: 15 inches

Estimate: $4,000-$5,000
Starting Bid: $2,000

55146

55146
Fancy Yellow Diamond, Diamond, Gold Ring
The ring centers a mine-cut diamond measuring 10.05 x 9.54 x 4.32 mm and weighing 2.91 carats, surrounded by mine-cut diamonds weighing a total of approximately 1.20 carats, set in 18k gold. A GIA report # 518244830, dated June 8, 2017, stating *Natural, Fancy Yellow color, Even, VS2 clarity,* accompanies the center diamond. Gross weight 5.00 grams.
Size: 6-1/2 (sizeable)

Estimate: $25,000-$30,000
Starting Bid: $20,000

55147

55147
Victorian Diamond, Demantoid Garnet, Ruby, Silver-Topped Gold Brooch
The salamander brooch features European-cut diamonds weighing a total of approximately 0.30 carat, enhanced by round-cut demantoid garnets weighing a total of approximately 0.80 carat, accented by cabochon-cut rubies, set in silver-topped gold. Gross weight 9.30 grams.
Dimensions: 2-3/8 inches x 11/16 inch

Estimate: $5,000-$7,000
Starting Bid: $4,000

55148
Art Deco C.H. Meylan Lady's Diamond, Platinum Pendant-Lapel Watch, retailed by Tiffany & Co.
Case: 24 x 13 mm, rectangle, hinged platinum with engraved side panels
Dial: silvered with black Arabic numerals, black Moon hour and minute hands, mineral crystal
Movement: manual wind, 18 jewels, 5 adjustments, # 35290
Stones: marquise, full and single-cut diamonds weigh a total of approximately 1.50 carats
Signed: Tiffany & Co. on the dial and C. H. Meylan on the movement
Gross Weight: 21.30 grams
Note: watch is currently in working order

55148

Estimate: $5,000-$7,000
Starting Bid: $3,000

55149
Diamond, Sapphire, Platinum Ring
The ring features a round brilliant-cut diamond measuring 7.80 x 8.00 x 4.78 mm and weighing 1.86 carats, enhanced by round brilliant and full-cut diamonds weighing a total of 1.54 carats, accented by calibré-cut sapphires, set in platinum. Gross weight 7.15 grams.
Size: 6-1/2 (sizeable)

55149

Estimate: $6,000-$8,000
Starting Bid: $4,000

55150
Art Deco Diamond, Platinum Ring
The ring features a marquise-shaped diamond measuring 15.26 x 6.42 x 4.20 mm weighing 2.45 carats, accented by single-cut diamonds weighing a total of approximately 0.15 carat, set in platinum. A GIA report # 2183632308, dated July 25, 2017, stating *I color, VS2 clarity*, accompanies the center stone. Gross weight 3.95 grams.
Size: 5-1/2 (sizeable)

55150

Estimate: $15,000-$20,000
Starting Bid: $7,500

55151
Diamond, Demantoid Garnet, Ruby, Platinum Pendant-Brooch
The pendant-brooch features European-cut diamonds weighing a total of approximately 6.95 carats, enhanced by demantoid garnets weighing a total of approximately 0.80 carat, accented by round-cut rubies, set in platinum. Gross weight 18.10 grams.
Dimensions: 2 inches x 7/8 inch

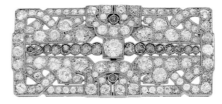

55151

Estimate: $7,000-$9,000
Starting Bid: $6,000

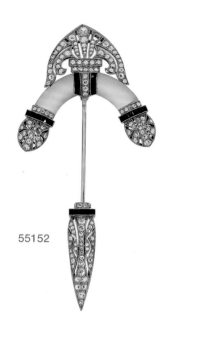

55152

55152

Art Deco Diamond, Frosted Rock Crystal Quartz, Black Onyx, Platinum, Gold Jabot Brooch
The jabot brooch features a frosted rock crystal crescent, accented by rose-cut diamonds and calibre-cut black onyx, set in 18k white gold. Gross weight 15.70 grams.
Dimension: 3-1/2 inches x 1-3/4 inches

Estimate: $4,000-$6,000
Starting Bid: $2,800

55153

55153

Diamond, Ruby, Platinum Ring
The ring features a round brilliant-cut diamond weighing 1.51 carats, enhanced with a calibré-cut ruby surround, further accented with full-cut diamond accents, set in platinum. Gross weight 5.58 grams.
Size: 6-3/4 (sizeable)

Estimate: $4,000-$6,000
Starting Bid: $2,000

55154

55154

Diamond, Platinum Ring
The ring features a European-cut diamond weighing approximately 1.00 carat, accented by European-cut diamonds weighing a total of approximately 1.10 carat, set in platinum. Gross weight 3.80 grams.
Size: 5-1/4 (sizeable)

Estimate: $4,000-$6,000
Starting Bid: $3,000

55155

55155

Art Deco Diamond, Platinum Bracelet
The bracelet features marquise, baguette, European and single-cut diamonds weighing a total of approximately 13.50 carats, set in platinum. Gross weight 76.60 grams.
Dimensions: 8 inches x 5/8 inch

Estimate: $10,000-$15,000
Starting Bid: $5,000

55156

55156
Art Deco Synthetic Sapphire, Gold Purse
Designed in 14k gold, the purse features a patterned frame
supporting gold mesh, crowned by synthetic sapphire
cabochon thumbpushes. Gross weight 204.70 grams.
Dimensions: 4-3/4 inches x 5-1/4 inches
Length of of handle: 12 inches

Estimate: $4,000-$5,000
Starting Bid: $3,500

55157

55157
Diamond, Colored Diamond, Platinum, Gold Brooch, French
The swan brooch features mine-cut diamonds weighing a total of approximately 12.85 carats, enhanced by yellow mine and single-cut diamonds weighing a total of approximately 1.80 carats, accented by a black onyx beak, set in platinum and 18k gold, with French marks. Gross weight 37.30 grams.
Dimensions: 2-1/2 inches x 1-3/4 inches
Note: yellow diamonds not tested for origin of color

Estimate: $10,000-$15,000
Starting Bid: $7,000

55158

55158
Diamond, Platinum Ring
The ring features a circular-cut diamond measuring 7.12 x 7.22 x 4.12 mm and weighing 1.29 carats, accented by baguette and single-cut diamonds weighing a total of approximately 0.45 carat, set in platinum. A GIA report # 2185610175, dated July 18, 2017, stating *G color, I1 clarity,* accompanies the center stone. Gross weight 4.70 grams.
Size: 6-1/2 (sizeable)

Estimate: $4,000-$6,000
Starting Bid: $2,000

55159
Art Deco Diamond, Sapphire, Platinum, Gold Case
The case features single-cut diamonds weighing a total of approximately 0.35 carat, set in platinum, accented by square-cut sapphires weighing a total of approximately 5.25 carats, set in 14k gold. Gross weight 119.10 grams.
Dimensions: 4 inches x 3 inches x 5/16 inch

Estimate: $4,000-$6,000
Starting Bid: $3,500

55159

55160

Art Deco Jadeite Jade, Ruby, Gold Necklace
The necklace features jadeite-jade cabochons, accented by round-cut rubies weighing a total of approximately 0.20 carat, set in 18k gold. A Mason Kay Report # 170731-2, dated July 31, 2017, stating *Natural Jadeite Jade, No Dye or Polymer Detected*, accompanies the jade. Gross weight 13.40 grams.
Length: 16-1/8 inches
Drop Length: 2-1/4 inches

Property of a Wyoming Collector

Estimate: $4,000-$6,000
Starting Bid: $2,000

55160

55161

Ruby, Diamond, Platinum Ring
The ring features a ruby cabochon measuring 12.55 x 9.80 x 6.09 mm and weighing approximately 4.50 carats, accented by full and baguette-cut diamonds weighing a total of approximately 0.25 carat, set in platinum. An AGL report #1084884, dated July 14, 2017, stating *Natural Corundum, Ruby, Origin Burma (Myanmar), No Evidence of Heat,* accompanies the ruby. Gross weight 6.10 grams.
Size: 5-3/4 (sizeable)

Estimate: $4,000-$6,000
Starting Bid: $2,000

55161

55162

Art Deco Diamond, Platinum Bracelet
The bracelet centers an emerald-cut diamond measuring 7.00 x 5.00 x 3.30 mm and weighing approximately 1.00 carat, enhanced by full and single-cut diamonds weighing a total of approximately 3.15 carats, accented by baguette-cut diamonds weighing a total of approximately 1.85 carats, set in platinum. Gross weight 25.04 grams.
Dimensions: 6 inches x 3/4 inch

Estimate: $6,000-$8,000
Starting Bid: $4,000

55162

55163

55164

55165

55163

Diamond, Platinum Necklaces
The pair of necklaces feature European and single-cut diamonds weighing a total of approximately 9.50 carats, set in platinum. Gross weight 19.81 grams.
Lengths: 16 inches, 16-1/8 inches

Estimate: $8,000-$10,000
Starting Bid: $6,500

55164

Diamond, Ruby, Platinum Earrings
The earrings feature round brilliant-cut diamonds each weighing 1.60 and 1.71 carats, trimmed in calibré-cut rubies, accented by full-cut diamonds, set in platinum. Gross weight 8.05 grams.
Dimensions: 1-1/4 inches x 5/8 inch
Note: earrings are designed for pierced ears

Estimate: $7,000-$9,000
Starting Bid: $6,000

55165

Art Deco Diamond, Ruby, Platinum Bracelet
The bracelet features full-cut diamonds weighing a total of 2.00 carats, accented by rectangle-shaped rubies weighing a total of approximately 8.25 carats, set in platinum. Gross weight 16.40 grams.
Length: 7-1/4 inches

Estimate: $8,000-$10,000
Starting Bid: $7,000

55166

Art Deco Diamond, Platinum-Topped Gold Ring
The ring centers a mine-cut diamond measuring 7.16 x 6.22 x 4.25 mm and weighing 1.60 carats, enhanced by European, full and single-cut diamonds weighing a total of approximately 2.00 carats, set in platinum-topped 14k gold. Gross weight 14.97 grams.
Size: 3-3/4 (sizeable)

Estimate: $5,000-$7,000
Starting Bid: $2,500

55166

55167

Star Sapphire, Diamond, Platinum Ring
The ring features an oval-shaped star sapphire measuring 18.74 x 16.70 x 11.20 mm and weighing approximately 34.00 carats, enhanced by baguette and single-cut diamonds weighing a total of approximately 0.90 carat, set in platinum. Gross weight 18.50 grams.
Size: 6 (sizeable)

Estimate: $4,500-$6,500
Starting Bid: $2,200

55167

55168

Aquamarine, Diamond, Platinum Ring
The ring features an emerald-cut aquamarine measuring 19.30 x 16.31 x 13.55 mm and weighing approximately 28.20 carats, enhanced by full-cut diamonds weighing a total of approximately 0.40 carat, set in platinum. Gross weight 20.51 grams.
Size: 7-1/2 (sizeable)

Estimate: $5,000-$7,000
Starting Bid: $2,500

55168

55169

Art Deco Diamond, Synthetic Sapphire, Platinum Bracelet
The bracelet features European and single-cut diamonds weighing a total of approximately 11.50 carats, accented by synthetic sapphires, set in platinum. Gross weight 59.51 grams.
Dimensions: 7 inches x 3/4 inch

Estimate: $7,000-$10,000
Starting Bid: $4,000

55169

55170

55170

Multi-Stone, Diamond, Platinum Ring, Raymond Yard

The ring features emerald and square-cut aquamarines weighing a total of approximately 9.00 carats, enhanced by round-cut sapphires weighing a total of approximately 1.80 carats, accented by marquise, baguette and single-cut diamonds weighing a total of approximately 0.70 carat, set in platinum, marked Yard. Gross weight 16.90 grams. *Size: 6-3/4 (sizeable)*

Estimate: $5,000-$7,000
Starting Bid: $3,000

55171

55171

Star Sapphire, Diamond, White Gold Ring

The ring features an oval-shaped star sapphire measuring 14.55 x 13.80 mm, enhanced by triangle-cut diamonds weighing a total of approximately 0.90 carat, set in 18k white gold. Gross weight 16.82 grams. *Size: 6 (sizeable)*

Property of a Collector

Estimate: $4,000-$6,000
Starting Bid: $2,500

55172

55172

Retro Gold Bracelet

The 18k rose and yellow gold bracelet weighs 245.74 grams.
Dimensions: 7-5/8 inches x 2-/12 inches

Estimate: $7,000-$9,000
Starting Bid: $4,000

55173

**Diamond, Platinum, White Gold
Double-Clip-Brooch**
The pair of brooches feature full and tapered
baguette-cut diamonds weighing a total of
approximately 8.60 carats, set in platinum,
accompanied by an 18k white gold armature and
14k white gold clasp. Gross weight 50.30 grams.
Dimensions: 3 inches x 1-1/2 inches

Estimate: $4,000-$6,000
Starting Bid: $2,000

55173

55174

Sapphire, Diamond, Platinum, Gold Brooch, Ruser
The brooch features European and full-cut
diamonds weighing a total of approximately 4.15
carats, accented by emerald and cushion-shaped
pink and yellow sapphires weighing a total of
approximately 14.00 carats, set in platinum and 18k
gold, marked Ruser. Gross weight 17.90 grams.
Dimensions: 1-13/16 inches x 1-1/2 inches

Estimate: $4,000-$6,000
Starting Bid: $2,000

55174

55175

Diamond, Platinum Pendant-Brooch
The pendant-brooch features a pear-shaped diamond
measuring 9.00 x 5.30 x 3.25 mm and weighing
approximately 0.90 carat, enhanced by pear-
shaped diamonds weighing a total of approximately
3.50 carats, accented by full and baguette-cut
diamonds weighing a total of approximately 3.50
carats, set in platinum. Gross weight 18.20 grams.
Dimensions: 2-1/8 inches x 1-1/4 inches

Estimate: $4,000-$6,000
Starting Bid: $2,500

55175

55176

55176
Diamond, Platinum Clip-Brooch
The diamond spray brooch features round brilliant-cut diamonds measuring 5.10 and 5.39 mm and weighing a total of approximately 1.00 carat, enhanced by full and single-cut diamonds weighing a total of approximately 8.70 carats, set in platinum. Total diamond weight is approximately 9.70 carats. Gross weight 28.50 grams. *Dimensions: 2 inches x 2-1/8 inches*

Estimate: $4,000-$6,000
Starting Bid: $2,000

55177

55177
Aquamarine, Diamond Platinum Ring
The ring centers an emerald-cut aquamarine measuring 23.59 x 20.28 x 12.64 mm and weighing approximately 42.00 carats, flanked by marquise-cut diamonds weighing a total of approximately 2.00 carats, set in platinum. Gross weight 23.40 grams. *Size: 8 (sizeable)*

Estimate: $8,000-$12,000
Starting Bid: $4,000

55178

55178
Freshwater Cultured Pearl, Black Onyx, White Gold Brooch, Ruser
The poodle brooch features freshwater cultured pearls, accented by black onyx, set in 18k white gold, marked Ruser. Gross weight 24.40 Grams. *Dimensions: 1-1/4 inches x 1-5/8 inches*

Estimate: $3,000-$5,000
Starting Bid: $1,500

55179

55179
Burma Ruby, Diamond, Platinum Ring
The ring features a star ruby measuring 10.10 x 9.70 x 8.85 mm and weighing 9.75 carats, enhanced by marquise and baguette-cut diamonds weighing a total of 2.34 carats, set in platinum. An AGL report # 2173432795, dated January 15, 2016, stating *Natural Corundum, Displaying Asterism, Origin Burma (Myanmar), No Indications of Heating*, accompanies the ruby. Gross weight 16.05 grams. *Size: 6-1/4 (sizeable)*

Estimate: $7,000-$9,000
Starting Bid: $3,500

55180
Diamond, Platinum-Topped Gold Brooch
The brooch features European-cut diamonds weighing a total of approximately 11.50 carats, enhanced by baguette-cut diamonds weighing a total of approximately 1.30 carats, set in platinum-topped 14k gold. Gross weight 34.17 grams.
Dimensions: 2-1/4 inches x 1-3/4 inches

Estimate: $6,000-$8,000
Starting Bid: $4,000

55180

55181
Star Sapphire, Diamond, Platinum Ring
The ring centers an oval-shaped light purple star sapphire measuring 17.90 x 13.75 x 12.90 mm and weighing approximately 32.00 carats, flanked tapered baguette-cut diamonds weighing a total of approximately 1.30 carats, set in platinum. Gross weight 18.80 grams.
Size: 9-1/4 (sizeable)

Estimate: $4,000-$6,000
Starting Bid: $2,200

55181

55182
Diamond, South Sea Cultured Pearl, Platinum Ring
The ring features a South Sea cultured pearl measuring 16.50 mm, enhanced by marquise-shaped diamonds weighing a total of approximately 3.15 carats, accented by baguette-cut diamonds, set in platinum. Total diamond weight is approximately 3.65 carats. Gross weight 15.40 grams.
Size: 7 (sizeable)

Estimate: $4,000-$5,000
Starting Bid: $2,000

55182

55183
Diamond, Platinum Earrings
The earrings feature European-cut diamonds measuring 7.00 x 4.20 mm and 7.00 x 3.97 mm and weighing approximately 1.25 carats and 1.15 carats, enhanced by European and single-cut diamonds weighing a total of approximately 4.70 carats, set in platinum. Gross weight 17.40 grams.
Dimensions: 2-3/8 inches x 1/2 inch
Note: earrings are designed for pierced ears

Estimate: $10,000-$15,000
Starting Bid: $7,000

55183

55184

55184
Diamond, Platinum, White Gold Earrings, Harry Winston
The earrings feature full-cut diamonds weighing a total of approximately 3.00 carats, enhanced by pear-shaped diamonds weighing a total of approximately 2.40 carats, accented by marquise-cut diamonds weighing a total of approximately 0.90 carat, set in platinum, completed by 18k white gold clip backs, made by Harry Winston. Total diamond weight is approximately 6.00 carats. Gross weight 11.90 grams. *Dimensions: 1 inch x 1/2 inch*
Note: earrings are designed for pierced ears, and are easily converted

Estimate: $7,000-$9,000
Starting Bid: $5,000

55185

55185
Kashmir Sapphire, Sapphire, Diamond, Platinum, White Gold Brooch
The insect brooch features oval and cushion-shaped sapphires weighing a total of approximately 15.00 carats, enhanced by full and baguette-cut diamonds weighing a total of approximately 3.85 carats, set in platinum. A GIA report # 2155987468, dated October 20, 2014, stating *Natural Corundum, Origin Kashmir, No Indications of Heating*, accompanies one sapphire weighing 1.56 carats. Gross weight 37.28 grams. *Dimensions: 2-1/2 inches x 1-7/8 inches*

Estimate: $12,000-$16,000
Starting Bid: $10,000

55186

55186
Diamond, Platinum, White Gold Brooch, French
The brooch features European, full and single-cut diamonds weighing a total of approximately 7.75 carats, enhanced by baguette-cut diamonds weighing a total of approximately 4.00 carats, set in platinum, completed by an 18k white gold pinstem. Gross weight 51.98 grams. *Dimensions: 3-7/8 inches x 1-1/4 inches*

Estimate: $4,000-$6,000
Starting Bid: $2,500

55187

55187
Diamond, White Gold Necklace
The necklace features full-cut diamonds
weighing a total of approximately 15.00 carats,
set in 18k white gold. Gross weight 34.00 grams.
Dimensions: 16-1/2 inches x 3/16 inch

Estimate: $11,000-$13,000
Starting Bid: $9,500

55188
Diamond, White Gold Earrings
The chandelier earrings feature pear, rectangular,
square and full-cut diamonds weighing a
total of approximately 17.00 carats, set in
18k white gold. Gross weight 29.50 grams.
Dimensions: 3 inches x 3/4 inch
*Note: earrings are designed for pierced ears

Estimate: $12,000-$15,000
Starting Bid: $10,000

55188

55189

55189
Sapphire, Diamond, Platinum Earrings, Jacques Timey for Harry Winston
The earrings feature pear-shaped sapphires, one measuring 11.81 x 8.96 x 6.45 mm and weighing 5.02 carats, and one measuring 11.33 x 9.07 x 5.99 mm and weighing 4.71 carats, enhanced by tapered baguette and full-cut diamonds weighing a total of approximately 4.40 carats set in platinum, marked "JT" for Jacques Timey - workshop for Harry Winston. An AGL report # 1085034 A and B, dated July 19, 2017, stating *Natural Corundum, Origin Sri Lanka (Ceylon), Enhancement Heat, Color Stability Excellent*, accompanies the sapphires. Gross weight 17.50 grams.
Dimensions: 1-1/2 inches x 5/8 inch
Note: earrings are designed for pierced ears

Property of a Collector

Estimate: $15,000-$18,000
Starting Bid: $10,000

55190

55190
Diamond, White Gold Ring
The ring features a long hexagon-shaped diamond weighing 1.75 carats, accented by baguette-cut diamonds weighing a total of 1.05 carats, set in 18k white gold. Gross weight 5.80 grams.
Size: 6-1/4 (sizeable)

Estimate: $4,000-$6,000
Starting Bid: $3,000

55191

55191
Diamond, White Gold Bracelet
The bracelet features full-cut diamonds weighing 19.38 carats set in 18k white gold. Gross weight 20.43 grams.
Length: 7 inches

Estimate: $18,000-$25,000
Starting Bid: $13,000

55192

55192
Emerald, Diamond, Platinum Bracelet
The bracelet features oval-shaped emeralds weighing a total of 5.72 carats, accented by full and baguette-cut diamonds weighing a total of 7.21 carats, set in platinum. Gross weight 42.00 grams.
Length: 6-3/4 inches

Property of a Collector

Estimate: $10,000-$15,000
Starting Bid: $5,000

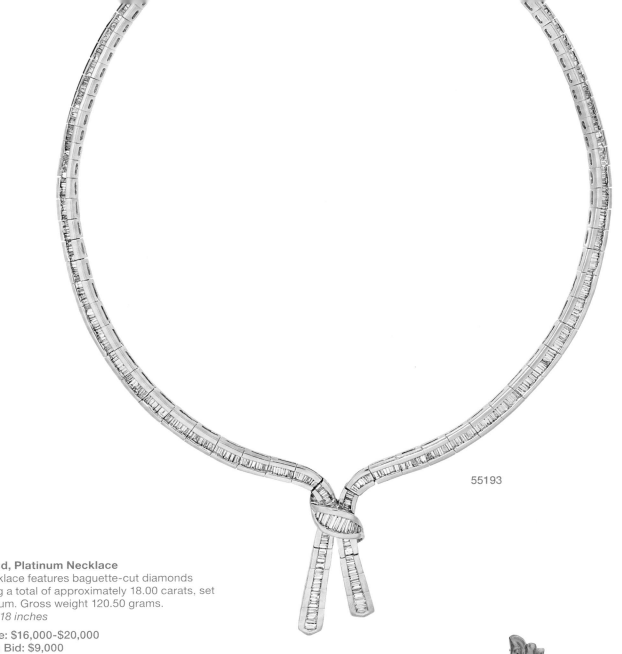

55193

55193
Diamond, Platinum Necklace
The necklace features baguette-cut diamonds
weighing a total of approximately 18.00 carats, set
in platinum. Gross weight 120.50 grams.
Length: 18 inches

Estimate: $16,000-$20,000
Starting Bid: $9,000

55194
Jadeite Jade, Diamond, White Gold Brooch
The brooch features a carved jadeite jade measuring 25.72
x 39.64 x mm, enhanced by full, marquise and baguette-cut
diamonds weighing a total of approximately 2.35 carats, set in
18k white gold. A Mason-Kay report # 170711-1, dated July 11,
2017, stating *Natural Jadeite Jade, No Dye or Polymer Detected,
'A' Jade*, accompanies the jade. Gross weight 31.26 grams.
Dimensions: 2-1/2 inches x 2 inches

Estimate: $10,000-$15,000
Starting Bid: $7,000

55194

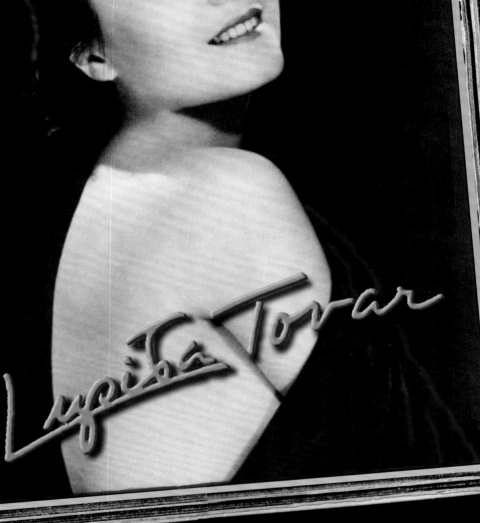

A Memoir

Lupita Tovar

THE SWEETHEART OF MÉXICO

Pancho Kohner

We are excited to offer highlights from the jewelry collection of groundbreaking Mexican - American actress Lupita Tovar (1910 – 2016). Tovar, who began her career in silent films, went on to make more than 30 pictures during her career.

Most notably, she starred in the Spanish-language version of the 1931 horror cult classic "Dracula." Her future husband and legendary agent Paul Kohner cast Tovar as the heroin, "Eva Steward." It was around this time that she began to acquire pieces of the eclectic jewelry collection presented here.

Born to an impoverished family in 1910, Lupita was the eldest of nine siblings living in Matías Romero, a pueblo far from Hollywood in southwest Mexico.

In 2006, honored by the Academy of Motion Picture Arts and Sciences, "The Sweetheart of Mexico" summed up her career simply,

"Listen, I never dreamed it would happen."

55195

55195
Diamond, Ruby, Platinum Double-Clip-Brooch
The brooch features European, full, single, and marquise-cut diamonds weighing a total of approximately 4.00 carats, enhanced by square step-cut rubies, set in platinum. Gross weight 20.50 grams.
Dimensions: 2-1/4 inches x 7/8 inch

Estimate: $7,000-$9,000
Starting Bid: $4,000

55196

55196
Diamond, Platinum Ring
The ring features a European-cut diamond measuring 7.83 - 7.86 x 4.70 mm and weighing approximately 1.70 carats, set in platinum. Gross weight 4.70 grams.
Size: 7 (sizeable)

Estimate: $10,000-$15,000
Starting Bid: $7,000

55197

55197
Ruby, Diamond, Platinum Ring
The ring features an oval-shaped ruby measuring 8.85 x 6.00 x 3.62 mm and weighing approximately 1.40 carats, accented by baguette-cut diamonds weighing a total of approximately 0.80 carat, set in platinum. Gross weight 2.80 grams.
Size: 4 (sizeable)

Estimate: $8,000-$12,000
Starting Bid: $5,000

55198

55198
Art Deco Diamond, Ruby, Platinum Bracelet
The bracelet features oval and pear-shaped rubies, enhanced by calibre-cut rubies, accented by single and rose-cut diamonds weighing a total of approximately 2.65 carats, set in platinum. Total ruby weight is approximately 3.60 carats. Gross weight 18.40 grams.
Dimensions: 6-1/8 inches x 1/4 inch

Estimate: $10,000-$15,000
Starting Bid: $7,000

55199

Diamond, White Gold Pendant
The pendant features a pear-shaped diamond measuring 10.70 x 6.22 x 3.90 mm and weighing approximately 1.50 carats, set in 14k white gold. Gross weight 3.20 grams.
Pendant Dimensions: 11/16 inch x 1/4 inch
Chain length: 18 inches

Estimate: $5,000-$7,000
Starting Bid: $3,000

55199

55200

Diamond, Platinum Earrings
The earrings feature pear-shaped diamonds, one measuring 8.50 x 5.90 x 2.60 mm and weighing approximately 0.75 carat, and one measuring 8.40 x 6.20 x 2.60 mm and weighing approximately 0.80 carat, enhanced by marquise, pear and full-cut diamonds weighing a total of approximately 2.75 carats, set in platinum. Gross weight 11.80 grams.
Dimensions: 2 inches x 1/2 inch
Note: earrings are designed for pierced ears, and are easily converted

Estimate: $10,000-$15,000
Starting Bid: $6,000

55200

55201

Sapphire, Platinum Bracelet
The bracelet features square-cut sapphires weighing a total of approximately 10.00 carats, set in platinum. Gross weight 27.03 grams.
Length: 7 inches

Estimate: $10,000-$12,000
Starting Bid: $5,000

55201

55202

55203

55204

55202
Diamond, Platinum Ring, Van Cleef & Arpels
The ring features a marquise-shaped diamond measuring 12.13 x 6.84 x 3.81 mm and weighing 1.87 carats, enhanced by tapered baguette-cut diamonds weighing a total of approximately 0.30 carat, set in platinum, marked Van Cleef & Arpels. A GIA report # 1186639853, dated July 31, 2017, stating *D color, VS1 clarity*, accompanies the center stone. Gross weight 4.04 grams.
Size: 5-3/4 (sizeable)

Estimate: $10,000-$15,000
Starting Bid: $7,000

55203
Diamond, Platinum Brooches, Tiffany & Co.
The seagull brooches feature full-cut diamonds weighing a total of approximately 2.40 carats, set in platinum, marked Tiffany & Co. Gross weight 11.73 grams.
Dimensions: 1-5/8 inches x 1/2 inch

Estimate: $4,000-$5,000
Starting Bid: $2,000

55204
Cultured Pearl, Diamond, Platinum Bracelet, Tiffany & Co.
The *Aria* bracelet features cultured pearls measuring 6.50 - 7.00 mm, enhanced by full-cut diamonds weighing a total of 2.18 carats, set in platinum, marked Tiffany & Co. Gross weight 26.09 grams.
Dimensions: 7 inches x 1/4 inch

Estimate: $8,000-$10,000
Starting Bid: $4,000

55205
Diamond, Ruby, Platinum, Gold Ring,
Van Cleef & Arpels
The ring features full-cut diamonds weighing a total
of approximately 1.30 carats, enhanced by round-
cut rubies weighing a total of approximately 0.95
carat, set in platinum and 18k gold, marked VCA for
Van Cleef & Arpels. Gross weight 4.51 grams.
Size: 4-1/2 (sizeable)

Estimate: $4,000-$6,000
Starting Bid: $2,000

55205

55206

55206
Ruby, Diamond, Platinum, Gold Brooch,
Van Cleef & Arpels
The brooch features full-cut diamonds weighing a
total of approximately 1.75 carats, set in platinum,
enhanced by round-cut rubies weighing a total
of approximately 11.00 carats, set in 18k gold,
marked VCA. Gross weight 45.40 grams.
Dimensions: 4-1/2 inches x 1-3/4 inches

Estimate: $12,000-$15,000
Starting Bid: $7,000

55207
Ruby, Diamond, Platinum, Gold Earrings,
Van Cleef & Arpels
The earrings feature round-cut rubies weighing a
total of approximately 9.00 carats, set in 18k gold,
enhanced by full-cut diamonds weighing a total of
approximately 1.00 carat, set in platinum, marked
Van Cleef & Arpels. Gross weight 21.05 grams.
Dimensions: 1-1/4 inches x 3/4 inch
Note: earrings are designed for non-pierced ears

Estimate: $7,000-$9,000
Starting Bid: $4,000

55207

55208
Retro Diamond, Synthetic Ruby, Platinum,
Rose Gold Ring
The bypass ring features a European-cut diamond
measuring approximately 10.00 x 10.00 x 5.75 mm and
weighing approximately 3.55 carats, enhanced by a
round-cut synthetic ruby measuring 10.00 mm, set in
platinum-topped 14k rose gold. Gross weight 12.20 grams.
Size: 3-3/4 (sizeable)

Estimate: $15,000-$18,000
Starting Bid: $8,000

55208

55209
Unmounted Diamond
The *Crown of Light*-cut © diamond measures 9.54 - 9.60 x 7.80 mm and weighs 4.49 carats. An AGS report # 104085059083, dated February 26, 2016, stating, *I color, VS1 clarity,* accompanies the diamond.

Estimate: $40,000-$50,000
Starting Bid: $30,000

55210
Unmounted Diamond
The *Crown of Light*-cut © diamond measures 7.49 - 7.53 x 6.25 mm and weighs 2.275 carats. An AGS report # 104084640063, dated February 05, 2016, stating *K color, IF clarity,* accompanies the diamond.

Estimate: $8,000-$10,000
Starting Bid: $6,000

55211
Unmounted Fancy Yellow Diamond
The square modified brilliant-cut diamond measures 9.24 x 8.77 x 6.09 mm and weighs 4.02 carats. A GIA Laboratory report # 1182203946, dated March 06, 2017 stating *Fancy Yellow color, Even, VS1 clarity,* accompanies the diamond.

Estimate: $15,000-$20,000
Starting Bid: $10,000

55212
Unmounted Diamond
The round brilliant-cut diamond measures 10.22 - 10.49 x 6.79 mm and weighs 4.49 carats. A GIA report # 5181380585, dated May 04, 2017, stating *L color, VS1 clarity,* accompanies the diamond.

Estimate: $14,000-$18,000
Starting Bid: $10,000

55213
Unmounted Diamond
The round brilliant-cut diamond measures 7.64 - 7.73 x 4.81 mm and weighs 1.72 carats. A GIA report # 2155663138, dated October 03, 2013, stating *F color, Internally Flawless clarity,* accompanies the diamond.

Estimate: $12,000-$14,000
Starting Bid: $9,000

55214
Unmounted Diamond
The round brilliant-cut diamond measures 9.50 - 9.61 x 5.52 mm and weighs 3.03 carats. A GIA report # 1182509671, dated June 14, 2017, stating *K color, VS2 clarity,* accompanies the diamond.

Estimate: $10,000-$12,000
Starting Bid: $7,000

55215
Unmounted Diamond
The marquise-shaped diamond measures 12.95 x 6.13 x 3.90 mm and weighs 1.85 carats. A GIA report # 1166361321, dated July 15, 2014, stating *G color, VS2 clarity,* accompanies the diamond.

Estimate: $5,000-$7,000
Starting Bid: $4,000

55216
Unmounted Diamond
The round brilliant-cut diamond measures 8.31 - 8.40 x 5.10 mm and weighs 2.18 carats. A GIA report # 1182511282, dated June 14, 2017, stating *L color, VS2 clarity,* accompanies the diamond.

Estimate: $5,000-$7,000
Starting Bid: $2,500

55217
Unmounted Colombian Emerald
The pear-shaped emerald measures 18.94 x 12.56 x 6.98 mm and weighs 9.31 carats. An AGL report # 1084881, dated July 14, 2017, stating *Natural Beryl, Origin Colombia, Minor, Modern Clarity Enhancement,* accompanies the emerald.

Estimate: $8,000-$10,000
Starting Bid: $4,000

55218

South Sea Cultured Pearl, Diamond, Gold Necklace
The necklace is composed of South Sea cultured pearls ranging in size from 13.00 mm to 16.30 mm, forming a single knotted strand, completed by an 18k gold clasp accented by full-cut diamonds. Gross weight 120.56 grams.
Length: 17-1/2 inches

Estimate: $4,000-$6,000
Starting Bid: $2,000

55219

Spessartine Garnet, Orange Sapphire, Gold Ring
The ring features an oval-shaped garnet cabochon measuring 13.40 x 11.30 x 6.45 m and weighing approximately 11.00 carats, accented by round-cut orange sapphires weighing a total of approximately 1.35 carats, set in 18k gold. Gross weight 14.40 grams.
Size: 6-1/2 (sizeable)

Estimate: $6,000-$8,000
Starting Bid: $4,000

55220

Diamond, Freshwater Cultured Pearl, Cultured Pearl, Multi-Stone, Enamel, Platinum, Gold Brooch
The swan and cygnets brooch features full-cut diamonds weighing a total of approximately 4.00 carats, enhanced by a freshwater cultured pearl measuring 26.00 x 12.35 mm, accented by cultured pearls, coral and black onyx, set in platinum and 18k gold with applied enamel. Gross weight 23.90 grams.
Dimensions: 2-1/4 inches x 2 inches

Estimate: $5,000-$6,000
Starting Bid: $4,000

55218

55219

55220

55221

55221
Diamond, South Sea Cultured Pearl, White Gold Necklace
The opera length strand is composed of cultured pearls measuring from 12.00 mm to 13.00 mm, forming a single knotted strand, completed by a pavé-set 18k white gold ball clasp, accented by full-cut diamonds weighing a total of approximately 2.00 carats. Gross weight 183.50 grams.
Length: 36 inches

Estimate: $10,000-$15,000
Starting Bid: $8,000

55222

55222
Black South Sea Cultured Pearl, Diamond, White Gold Ring, Ambrosi
The ring features a black South Sea cultured pearl measuring 14.85 mm, enhanced by full-cut diamonds weighing a total of approximately 1.15 carats, set in 18k white gold, marked Ambrosi. Gross weight 10.10 grams.
Size: 7-1/4 (not sizeable)

Estimate: $4,000-$6,000
Starting Bid: $2,000

55223

55223
Moonstone, Diamond, Ruby, White Gold Brooch, Assil
The brooch features an oval-shaped moonstone cabochon measuring 24.55 x 18.85 mm and weighing 44.49 carats, enhanced by full-cut diamonds weighing a total of 5.61 carats, accented by ruby cabochons weighing a total of 0.09 carat, set in 18k white gold, marked Assil. Gross weight 38.20 grams.
Dimensions: 2 inches x 1-1/4 inches

Estimate: $5,000-$7,000
Starting Bid: $4,000

55224

55224

Diamond, Gold Necklace
The necklace features full-cut diamonds weighing
a total of approximately 14.85 carats, set
in 18k gold. Gross weight 99.00 grams.
Length: 14-1/2 inches

Estimate: $10,000-$12,000
Starting Bid: $8,500

55225

Emerald, Diamond, Platinum, Gold Brooch
The brooch features full and single-cut diamonds
weighing a total of approximately 4.75 carats, set
in platinum, enhanced by round-cut emeralds
weighing a total of approximately 9.50 carats,
set in 18k gold. Gross weight 36.00 grams.
Dimensions: 2-3/4 inches x 1-7/8 inches

Estimate: $4,000-$6,000
Starting Bid: $3,000

55225

55226

Diamond, White Gold Bracelet
The bracelet features full-cut diamonds weighing
a total of approximately 11.50 carats, set in 18k
white gold. Gross weight 22.39 grams.
Length: 7-1/4 inches

Estimate: $6,000-$8,000
Starting Bid: $4,000

55226

55227

55227
Diamond, Platinum Necklace
The necklace features marquise-shaped diamonds
weighing a total of approximately 19.20 carats,
set in platinum. Gross weight 36.10 grams.
Length: 16 inches

Estimate: $12,000-$16,000
Starting Bid: $6,000

55228

55228
**South Sea Cultured Pearl, Diamond,
White Gold Earrings**
The earrings feature white South Sea cultured pearls
measuring 15.30 mm and 12.20 mm, enhanced by
gray South Sea cultured pearls measuring 15.30
mm and 12.30 mm, accented by full-cut diamonds
weighing a total of approximately 0.35 carat, set
in 18k white gold. Gross weight 18.00 grams.
Length: 1-1/4 inches
Note: earrings are designed for pierced ears

Estimate: $4,000-$6,000
Starting Bid: $3,000

55229

55229
Aquamarine, Diamond, White Gold Ring
The ring features an emerald-cut aquamarine
measuring 16.43 x 14.02 x 9.60 mm and
weighing 16.04 carats, accented by baguette-
cut diamonds weighing a total of 1.32 carats, set
in 18k white gold. Gross weight 19.90 grams.
Size: 7-1/4 (sizeable)

Estimate: $6,000-$8,000
Starting Bid: $3,000

55230

55230
Diamond, White Gold Bracelet
The line bracelet features square-cut diamonds
weighing a total of 10.53 carats, set in 18k
white gold. Gross weight 17.50 grams.
Length: 7-1/8 inches

Estimate: $9,000-$12,000
Starting Bid: $7,000

55231

55231
Aquamarine, Blue Topaz, Diamond,
Gold Necklace, Frank Ancona
The necklace is composed of aquamarine and blue
topaz beads, forming six strands, completed by
an 18k gold butterfly clasp accented by full-cut
diamonds weighing a total of approximately 0.60
carat, set in 18k gold. Gross weight 266.80 grams.
Length: 18-1/2 inches

Estimate: $6,000-$8,000
Starting Bid: $5,500

55232
Diamond, Gold Bracelet
The bracelet features full and baguette-cut
diamonds weighing a total of 10.00 carats, set
in 14k gold. Gross weight 62.70 grams.
Dimensions: 6 inches x 5/8 inch

Estimate: $8,000-$10,000
Starting Bid: $6,000

55232

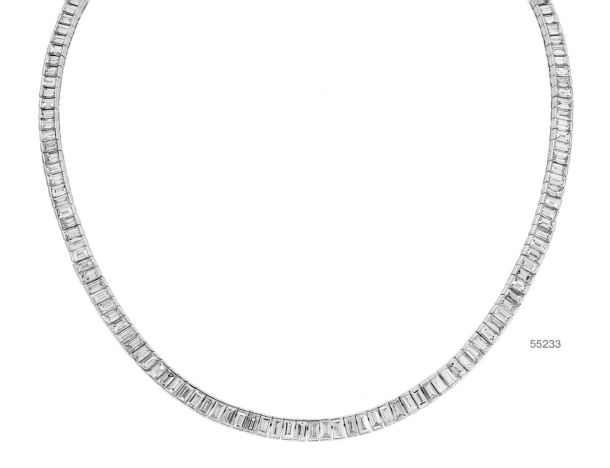

55233

55234

55235

55233
Diamond, Platinum Necklace
The necklace features baguette-cut diamonds
weighing a total of approximately 18.50 carats,
set in platinum. Gross weight 56.80 grams.
Dimensions: 16-1/4 inches x 1/4 inch

Estimate: $20,000-$25,000
Starting Bid: $10,000

55234
Aquamarine, Diamond, Platinum Ring
The ring features an emerald-cut aquamarine
measuring 18.90 x 13.70 x 10.10 mm and weighing
approximately 16.00 carats, accented by baguette-
cut diamonds weighing a total of approximately 0.80
carat, set in platinum. Gross weight 12.40 grams.
Size: 4 (sizeable)

Estimate: $4,000-$6,000
Starting Bid: $2,000

55235
Diamond, Platinum Earrings, Tiffany & Co.
The star earrings feature full-cut diamonds weighing
a total of approximately 2.30 carats, set in platinum,
marked T&Co. Gross weight 12.92 grams.
Dimensions: 2 inches x 1-1/8 inches
Note: earrings are designed for pierced ears

Estimate: $4,000-$6,000
Starting Bid: $2,000

55236

Coral, Colored Diamond, Sapphire, Gold Necklace

The necklace is composed of coral beads ranging in size from 15.60 mm to 18.60 mm, forming a single knotted strand, enhanced by full-cut brown diamonds weighing a total of approximately 6.15 carats, completed by an 18k gold clasp accented by round-cut yellow sapphires weighing a total of approximately 3.00 carats. A GIA report # 5182151685, dated February 14, 2017, stating *Coral, No Indications of Dye*, accompanies the three largest beads. Gross weight 203.90 grams. *Length: 20-1/2 inches*
Note: brown diamonds not tested for origin of color

Estimate: $10,000-$12,000
Starting Bid: $8,000

55237

Colored Diamond, Diamond, Gold Earrings

The earrings feature full-cut colored diamonds and full-cut diamonds weighing a total of 21.63 carats, set in 18k gold. Gross weight 20.60 grams. *Dimensions: 2-3/4 inches x 1-3/8 inches*
Note: earrings are designed for pierced or non-pierced ears, colored diamonds not tested for origin of color

Estimate: $9,000-$11,000
Starting Bid: $7,500

55236

55237

55238

55238

Diamond, White Gold Pendant-Brooch-Bracelet-Necklace, Kwiat
The convertible *Vintage* pendant-brooch-necklace features full and rose-cut diamonds weighing a total of 4.70 carats, set in 18k white gold, marked Kwiat. Gross weight 24.33 grams.
Pendant Dimensions: 2-3/8 inches x 1-7/8 inches
Chain Length: 34 inches

Estimate: $7,000-$9,000
Starting Bid: $6,000

55239

55239

Diamond, Platinum Eternity Band
The eternity ring features cushion-cut diamonds weighing a total of 4.76 carats, set in platinum. Gross weight 6.94 grams.
Size: 5 (not sizeable)

Estimate: $5,000-$7,000
Starting Bid: $3,000

55240

55240

Diamond, Platinum Ring
The ring features a round brilliant-cut diamond measuring 7.63 - 7.68 x 4.59 mm and weighing 1.65 carats, enhanced by round brilliant-cut diamonds weighing a total of approximately 1.00 carat, set in platinum. A GIA report # 11325056, dated July 31, 2017, stating *G color, VS2 clarity*, accompanies the center stone. Gross weight 8.16 grams.
Size: 6 (sizeable)

Estimate: $9,000-$11,000
Starting Bid: $8,000

55241

55241

Jadeite Jade, Diamond, White Gold Bracelet
The bracelet features oval-shaped jadeite jade cabochons, accented by full-cut diamonds weighing a total of approximately 1.90 carats, set in 18k white gold. A Mason-Kay report # 327030, dated July 17, 2017, stating *Natural Jadeite Jade, No Dye or Polymer Detected, 'A' Jade*, accompanies three stones. Gross weight 20.30 grams.
Length: 7-3/4 inches

Estimate: $15,000-$20,000
Starting Bid: $13,000

55242

55242
Kyanite, Diamond, White Gold Necklace
The torsade is composed of kyanite briolette, forming
three graduated knotted strands, completed
by an 18k white gold clasp, accented by full-
cut diamonds weighing a total of approximately
1.40 carats. Gross weight 90.00 grams.
Length: 18 inches

Estimate: $6,000-$8,000
Starting Bid: $5,000

55243
Sapphire, Emerald, Gold Brooch, M. Buccellati
The floral brooch features a carved sapphire
and carved emerald, set in 18k gold, marked
M. Buccellati. Gross weight 28.50 grams.
Dimensions: 2-1/2 inches x 2 inches

Estimate: $6,000-$8,000
Starting Bid: $4,500

55243

55244

55244
South Sea Cultured Pearl, Diamond, White Gold Necklace
The necklace features cultured pearls ranging in size from 11.50 mm to 14.00 mm, accented by full-cut diamonds weighing a total of 5.73 carats, set in 18k white gold. Gross weight 40.40 grams.
Length: 19 inches

Estimate: $7,000-$9,000
Starting Bid: $6,000

55245

55245
Diamond, White Gold Earrings
The earrings feature round brilliant-cut diamonds, one measuring 7.68 - 7.76 x 4.67 mm and weighing 1.69 carats, and one measuring 7.60 - 7.66 x 4.53 mm and weighing 1.57 carats, set in 18k white gold. A GIA report #2185624868, stating *H color, SI2 clarity*, accompanies the 1.69 carat diamond, and report # 5181624866, stating *J color, VS1 clarity*, accompanies the 1.57 carat diamond, both dated July 21, 2017. Gross weight 3.68 grams.
Note: earrings are designed for pierced ears

Estimate: $12,000-$15,000
Starting Bid: $8,000

55246

55246
Lapis Lazuli, Diamond, Enamel, Platinum Ring
The ring features oval-shaped lapis lazuli cabochons ranging in size from 8.40 x 3.30 x 2.80 mm to 20.65 x 11.95 x 5.95 mm, framed by enamel, accented by European, full, and single-cut diamonds weighing a total of approximately 0.80 carat, set in platinum. Gross weight 12.80 grams.
Size: 7 (sizeable)

Estimate: $4,000-$5,000
Starting Bid: $2,000

55247

55247

Turquoise, Diamond, White Gold Necklace

The necklace is composed of turquoise beads ranging in size from 14.60 mm to 21.80 mm, forming a continuous knotted strand, interspersed with 18k white gold rondelles, accented by full-cut diamonds weighing a total of approximately 4.00 carats. A GIA report # 6187151686, dated February 23, 2017, stating *Natural Turquoise, No Indications of Treatment*, accompanies the three largest beads. Gross weight 225.80 grams.
Length: 25 inches

Estimate: $8,000-$10,000
Starting Bid: $5,000

55248

55248

Tanzanite, Diamond, White Gold Ring

The ring features an oval-shaped tanzanite measuring 18.75 x 14.10 x 10.20 mm and weighing 18.22 carats, accented by full-cut diamonds weighing a total of 1.83 carats, set in 18k white gold. Gross weight 11.00 grams.
Size: 6-1/2 (sizeable)

Estimate: $5,000-$7,000
Starting Bid: $4,000

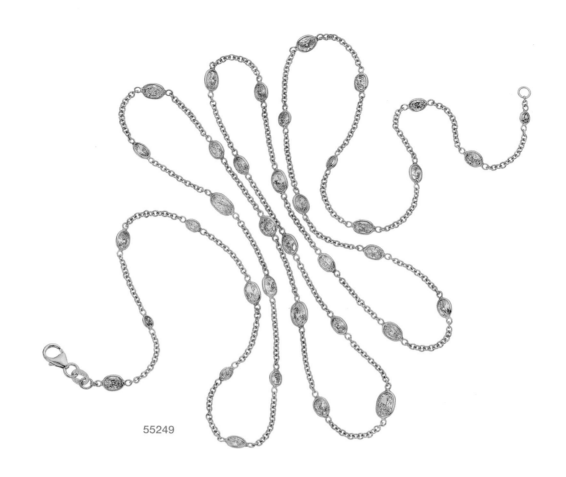

55249

55250

55249
Diamond, White Gold Necklace
The necklace features oval-shaped diamonds
weighing a total of approximately 11.00 carats, set
in 18k white gold. Gross weight 9.70 grams.
Length: 36 inches

Estimate: $9,000-$10,000
Starting Bid: $8,000

55250
Jadeite Jade, Diamond, White Gold Earrings
The earrings feature heart-shaped jadeite jade cabochons
measuring 16.30 x 11.09 x 5.22 mm and weighing 7.56
carats and 15.95 x 11.22 x 5.08 mm and weighing 7.53
carats, enhanced by pear and full-cut diamonds weighing
a total of approximately 0.50 carat, set in 18k white gold. A
GIA report # 1182551775, dated July , 2017, stating *Natural
Jadeite Jade, Natural Color, No Indications of Impregnation*,
accompanies the jade. Gross weight 10.51 grams.
Dimensions: 1-1/8 inches x 1/2 inch
Note: earrings are designed for pierced ears

Estimate: $9,000-$12,000
Starting Bid: $4,500

55251

55251
South Sea Cultured Pearl, Diamond, White Gold Jewelry
The lot includes a necklace composed of South Sea cultured pearls ranging in size from 13.00 mm to 17.00 mm, forming a single knotted strand, completed by an 18k white gold ball clasp accented by full-cut diamonds weighing a total of 2.51 carats; together with a pair of earrings featuring South Sea cultured pearls measuring 13.50 mm. Gross weight 137.54 grams.
Necklace Length: 18 inches
Note: earrings are designed for pierced ears

Property of a Las Vegas, NV Estate

Estimate: $8,000-$10,000
Starting Bid: $4,000

55252

55252
Diamond, White Gold Earrings
The earrings feature full-cut diamonds weighing a total of approximately 6.00 carats, set in 18k white gold. Gross weight 18.77 grams.
Diameter: 11/16 inch
Note: earrings are designed for pierced ears

Estimate: $4,000-$6,000
Starting Bid: $2,000

55253

55253
Diamond, Amber, Gold Necklace
The necklace features oval-shaped amber cabochons, accented by full-cut diamonds weighing a total of 0.70 carat, set in 18k gold. Gross weight 75.00 grams.
Length: 18-7/8 inches

Estimate: $5,000-$7,000
Starting Bid: $4,000

55254
Fancy Colored Diamond, Diamond, White Gold Ring
The ring centers an oval modified brilliant-cut fancy brownish orangy yellow diamond measuring 8.05 x 5.72 x 3.40 mm and weighing 1.24 carats, flanked by full-cut diamonds weighing a total of approximately 1.90 carats, set in 18k white gold. A GIA report # 16275936, dated October 9, 2007 stating *Natural Fancy Brownish Orangy Yellow,* accompanies the center diamond. Gross weight 4.50 grams.
Size: 7 (sizeable)

Estimate: $5,000-$7,000
Starting Bid: $3,000

55255
Colored Diamond, Diamond, Gold Brooch, Sabbadini
The rose brooch features full-cut yellow diamonds weighing a total of approximately 7.50 carats, enhanced by full-cut near-colorless diamonds weighing a total of approximately 0.60 carat, centering a round brilliant-cut diamond weighing approximately 0.30 carat, set in 18k white and yellow gold, marked Sabbadini. Gross weight 40.92 grams.
Dimensions: 2 inches x 1-7/8 inches
Note: colored diamonds not tested for origin of color

Estimate: $14,000-$16,000
Starting Bid: $12,000

55254

55255

55256

55256
Multi-Stone, Gold Necklaces
The six necklaces feature oval-shaped faceted colorless quartz, citrine, amethyst, smoky quartz, blue topaz and rose quartz, three set in 18k rose gold and three in 18k green gold. Gross weight 189.70 grams.
Lengths: 16 inches, 18 inches, 20 inches, 19 inches, 21 inches, 24 inches

Estimate: $4,000-$6,000
Starting Bid: $3,000

55257

55257
Fancy Deep Brownish Yellow Diamond, Colored Diamond, White Gold Ring
The ring features an oval-shaped yellow diamond measuring 14.27 x 9.82 x 7.06 mm and weighing 6.16 carats, enhanced by pear-shaped brownish-pink diamonds weighing a total of approximately 0.30 carat, set in 14k white gold. A GIA report # 2185551390, dated July 11, 2017, stating *Fancy Deep Brownish Yellow color, I1 clarity*, accompanies the center stone. Gross weight 4.03 grams.
Size: 7-1/4 (sizeable)

Estimate: $20,000-$30,000
Starting Bid: $15,000

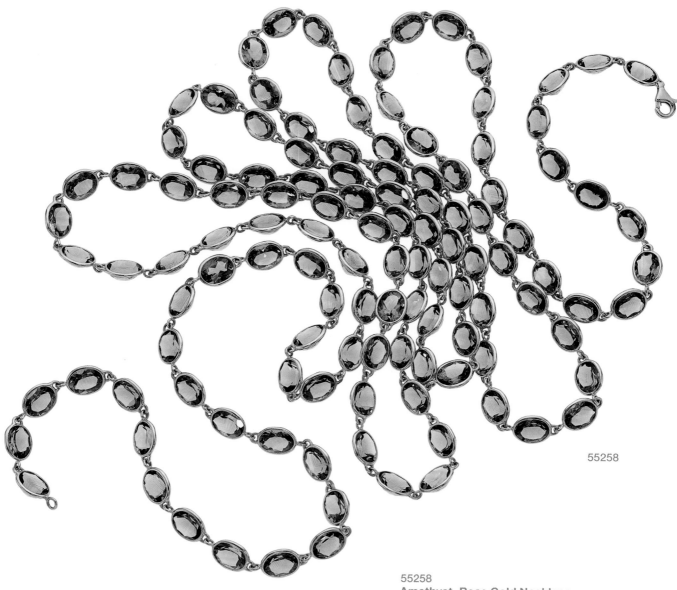

55258

55259

55258
Amethyst, Rose Gold Necklace
The necklace features oval-shaped amethyst
weighing a total of approximately 240.00 carats,
set in 18k rose gold. Gross weight 94.50 grams.
Length: 70 inches

Estimate: $5,000-$7,000
Starting Bid: $3,500

55259
Opal, Diamond, Gold Ring
The oval-shaped opal cabochon measures 20.10
x 11.70 x 4.00 mm and weighs approximately
4.90 carats, enhanced by full-cut diamonds
weighing a total of approximately 1.40 carats,
set in 14k gold. Gross weight 9.70 grams.
Size: 6-1/2 (sizeable)

Property of an Oklahoma Lady

Estimate: $4,000-$6,000
Starting Bid: $3,000

55260

55260

Diamond, Moonstone, Gold Pendant-Necklace
The pendant features moonstone cabochons weighing a total of 35.60 carats, accented by full-cut diamonds weighing a total of 2.70 carats, set in 18k gold. Gross weight 33.60 grams.
Pendant Dimensions: 2-1/4 inches x 2 inches
Chain Length: 16-1/4 inches

Estimate: $4,000-$6,000
Starting Bid: $3,200

55261

Diamond, Gold Earrings
The earrings feature full-cut diamonds weighing a total of approximately 4.80 carats, set in 18k gold. Gross weight 23.10 grams
Dimensions: 1-1/8 inches x 3/16 inch
*Note: earrings are designed for pierced ears

From the Collection of a San Antonio, TX Lady

Estimate: $4,000-$6,000
Starting Bid: $2,000

55261

55262

Diamond, Sapphire, Gold Ring
The ring features a European-cut diamond measuring 8.30 - 8.48 x 5.33 mm and weighing 2.31 carats, enhanced by marquise-shaped sapphires and diamond, set in 14k gold. A GIA report # 2185631956, dated July 31, 2017, stating *L color, VS2 clarity*, accompanies the center stone. Gross weight 7.53 grams.
Size: 7-1/2 (sizeable)

Estimate: $5,000-$7,000
Starting Bid: $2,500

55262

55263

Diamond, Gold Bracelet
The bracelet features full and single-cut diamonds weighing a total of approximately 12.00 carats, set in 18k gold. Gross weight 59.83 grams.
Dimensions: 6-3/4 inches x 3/4 inch

Estimate: $6,000-$8,000
Starting Bid: $5,000

55263

55264

55265

55266

55264
Diamond, White Gold Necklace
The necklace features full-cut diamonds weighing a total of approximately 5.00 carats, set in 18k white gold. Gross weight 17.70 grams.
Length: 32 inches

Estimate: $4,000-$5,000
Starting Bid: $3,000

55265
Sapphire, Diamond, Platinum Earrings, David Webb
The earrings feature oval-shaped sapphire cabochons measuring 13.60 x 11.70 x 9.40 mm and 14.10 x 11.20 x 8.60 mm and weighing a total of approximately 29.60 carats, enhanced by full-cut diamonds weighing a total of approximately 6.40 carats, set in platinum, marked Webb. Gross weight 29.01 grams.
Dimensions: 1 inch x 7/8 inch
Note: earrings are designed for non-pierced ears

Estimate: $10,000-$15,000
Starting Bid: $7,500

55266
Sapphire, Diamond, White Gold Bracelet
The articulated snake bracelet features black and near colorless full-cut diamonds weighing a total of 4.98 carats, enhanced by round-cut sapphires weighing a total of 8.32 carats, set in 18k white gold. Gross weight 41.70 grams.
Dimensions: 7 inches x 2-1/2 inches
Note: colored diamonds not tested for origin of color

Estimate: $8,000-$10,000
Starting Bid: $7,500

55267

55267
South Sea Cultured Pearl, Gold Jewelry Suite
The suite includes a necklace featuring South Sea cultured
pearls ranging in size from 9.25 mm to 11.50 mm; together with
a matching bracelet enhanced by South Sea cultured pearls
ranging in size from 9.80 mm to 10.50 mm; and a pair of earrings
centering South Sea cultured pearls measuring 10.65 - 10.75
mm, all set in 18k gold. Gross weight 130.98 grams.
Necklace Length: 16 inches
Bracelet Length: 6 inches
Earring Dimensions: 3/4 inch x 3/8 inch
*Note: earrings are designed for pierced ears

Estimate: $4,000-$5,000
Starting Bid: $2,000

55268

55268
Pink Tourmaline, Diamond, Gold Ring
The ring features an oval-shaped pink tourmaline measuring
15.15 x 13.77 x 9.46 mm and weighing 12.98 carats, enhanced
by full-cut diamonds weighing a total of 0.24 carat, set in black
rhodium finished 18k gold. Gross weight 8.59 grams.
Size: 6-1/2 (sizeable with caution)

Estimate: $4,000-$5,000
Starting Bid: $2,500

55269
Diamond, Gold Necklace
The rivière necklace features full-cut diamonds weighing a total of approximately 12.85 carats, set in 18k gold. Gross weight 46.93 grams.
Length: 15-3/4 inches

Property of a Collector

Estimate: $8,000-$12,000
Starting Bid: $4,000

55270
Diamond, Ruby, Gold Earrings,
Van Cleef & Arpels, NY
The earrings feature oval-shaped ruby cabochons measuring 10.00 x 6.00 mm, enhanced by pear-shaped ruby cabochons measuring 14.00 x 10.00 mm, framed by full-cut diamonds weighing a total of approximately 6.60 carats, set in 18k gold, marked Van Cleef & Arpels, NY. Gross weight 30.00 grams.
Dimensions: 2 inches x 3/4 inch
*Note: earrings are designed for pierced ears

Property of a Collector

Estimate: $15,000-$25,000
Starting Bid: $7,500

55269

55270

55271

55271
Aquamarine, Diamond, Colored Diamond,
Ruby, Gold Necklace
The necklace features an emerald-cut aquamarine
measuring 29.00 x 22.00 x 14.75 mm and weighing
approximately 64.00 carats, enhanced by full-cut
colorless diamonds and a full-cut blue diamond
weighing a total of approximately 0.55 carat, accented
by round-cut rubies weighing approximately
0.20 carat, set in 18k gold, attributed to Gregory
Saint-Thomas. Gross weight 99.20 grams.
Dimensions: 18 inches x 1-3/4 inches
*Note: blue diamond not tested for origin of color

Estimate: $8,000-$12,000
Starting Bid: $4,000

55272
Diamond, Gold Earrings
The hinged hoops feature full-cut diamonds weighing a
total of approximately 7.00 carats, set in 14k gold. Gross
weight 12.10 grams.
Diameter: 1-1/2 inches
*Note: earrings are designed for pierced ears

55272

Estimate: $5,000-$6,000
Starting Bid: $4,500

55273
Diamond, Gold Bracelet
The bracelet features full-cut diamonds weighing
a total of approximately 7.00 carats, set in
14k gold. Gross weight 21.80 grams.
Dimensions: 7-1/4 inches x 3/16 inch

55273

Estimate: $4,000-$6,000
Starting Bid: $2,000

55274

55274

Diamond, Kunzite, White Gold Pendant-Necklace
The pendant-necklace features a pear-shaped kunzite weighing 6.50 carats, accented by full-cut diamonds weighing a total of 4.98 carats, set in 18k white gold. Gross weight 22.10 grams.
Length: 16 inches
Pendant Length: 3-1/16 inches

Estimate: $4,000-$6,000
Starting Bid: $3,500

55275

55275

Diamond, Multi-Stone, Platinum Brooch
The poodle brooch features full and single-cut diamonds weighing a total of approximately 3.30 carats, accented by square-cut emeralds and round-cut rubies, set in platinum. Gross weight 18.90 grams.
Dimensions: 1-9/16 inches x 1-3/8 inches

Estimate: $4,000-$5,000
Starting Bid: $2,400

55276

55276

Aquamarine, Diamond, White Gold Ring, Eli Frei
The ring features a square-cut aquamarine measuring 11.82 x 11.86 x 8.89 mm and weighing approximately 7.80 carats, enhanced by full-cut diamonds weighing a total of approximately 0.45 carat, set in 18k white gold, marked Frei. Gross weight 11.20 grams.
Size: 6-3/4 (sizeable)

Estimate: $5,000-$7,000
Starting Bid: $3,000

55277

Diamond, Yellow Sapphire, Gold Necklace
The necklace features oval-shaped yellow
sapphires weighing a total of approximately
16.20 carats, enhanced by full-cut diamonds
weighing a total of approximately 1.75 carats,
set in 18k gold. Gross weight 45.20 grams.
Dimensions: 16-1/4 inches x 1/4 inch

Estimate: $6,000-$8,000
Starting Bid: $3,000

55278

Citrine, Diamond, Gold Earrings
The earrings feature faceted round and briolette
citrine, accented by full-cut diamonds, set
in 14k gold. Gross weight 19.67 grams.
Dimensions: 1-5/8 inches x 7/8 inch
Note: earrings are designed for pierced ears

Estimate: $5,000-$7,000
Starting Bid: $3,000

55279

Colored Diamond, Gold Bracelet
The bracelet features radiant-cut yellow diamonds
weighing a total of approximately 13.00 carats,
set in 14k gold. Gross weight 17.90 grams.
Dimensions: 7-1/8 inches x 3/16 inch
Note: diamonds not tested for origin of color

Estimate: $10,000-$15,000
Starting Bid: $7,000

55277

55279

55278

55280

55281

55280
Diamond, Sapphire, White Gold Necklace
The necklace features pear-shaped sapphires weighing a total of approximately 18.00 carats, enhanced by full-cut diamonds weighing a total of approximately 19.00 carats, set in 18k white gold. Gross weight 73.40 grams.
Length: 14 inches

Estimate: $15,000-$20,000
Starting Bid: $12,000

55281
Sapphire, Diamond, White Gold Ring, Zydo
The bypass ring features a marquise-cut purple sapphire measuring 10.70 x 5.40 x 3.63 mm and weighing approximately 1.50 carats, and a marquise-cut blue sapphire measuring 11.00 x 5.60 x 4.73 mm and weighing approximately 2.00 carats, accented by full-cut diamonds weighing a total of approximately 4.65 carats, set in 18k white gold, marked Zydo. Gross weight 13.80 grams.
Size: 9-1/4 (sizeable within reason)

Estimate: $4,000-$6,000
Starting Bid: $2,900

55282
Diamond, White Gold Earrings
The earrings feature full-cut diamonds weighing
a total of approximately 6.20 carats, set in 18k
white gold. Gross weight 38.62 grams.
Dimensions: 2-11/16 inches x 1-3/8 inches
*Note: earrings are designed for pierced ears

Estimate: $4,000-$6,000
Starting Bid: $2,000

55282

55283
Green Tourmaline, Diamond, White Gold Ring, Sarosi
The ring features a cushion-shaped green tourmaline
measuring 15.30 x 11.75 x 7.62 mm and weighing
9.24 carats, enhanced by full-cut diamonds
weighing a total of 0.84 carat, set in 14k white
gold, marked Sarosi. Gross weight 9.94 grams.
Size: 6-3/4 (sizeable)

Estimate: $4,000-$5,000
Starting Bid: $2,000

55283

55284
Diamond, White Gold Bracelet
The bracelet features full-cut diamonds weighing
a total of approximately 10.00 carats, set in 18k
white gold. Gross weight 73.20 grams.
Dimensions: 7 inches x 1-1/8 inches

Estimate: $4,000-$6,000
Starting Bid: $2,000

55284

55285

55285
Diamond, Gold Necklace
The necklace features marquise, square, and full-cut diamonds weighing a total of approximately 8.00 carats, set in 18k gold. Gross weight 95.80 grams. *Dimensions: 15-1/2 inches x 2-1/4 inches*

Estimate: $8,000-$10,000
Starting Bid: $7,000

55286

55286
Diamond, White Gold Ring
The ring features a radiant-cut diamond measuring 6.63 x 5.88 x 4.39 mm and weighing 1.50 carats, accented by full-cut diamonds weighing a total of 1.49 carats, set in 18k white gold. A GIA report # 14048720, dated December 7, 2004, stating *F color, SI1 clarity,* accompanies the center stone. Gross weight 7.00 grams. *Size: 6-1/2 (sizeable)*

Estimate: $9,000-$11,000
Starting Bid: $7,500

55287

55287
Emerald, Diamond, Gold Ring
The ring features a rectangular emerald-cut emerald measuring 9.47 x 8.95 x 6.28 mm, accented by marquise and baguette-cut diamonds weighing a total of approximately 2.95 carats, set in 18k gold. An AGL report # 1084909, dated June 26, 2017, stating *Natural Beryl, Emerald, Origin Colombia, Minor Modern Clarity Enhancement,* accompanies the emerald. Gross weight 10.80 grams. *Size: 4-1/4 (sizeable)*

Estimate: $4,000-$6,000
Starting Bid: $3,000

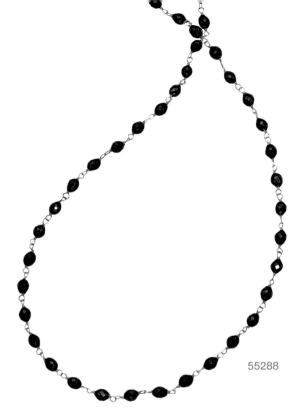

55288
Black Diamond, White Gold Necklace
The necklace features faceted black diamond beads weighing a total of 34.00 carats, set in 18k white gold. Gross weight 8.80 grams.
Length: 36 inches
Note: colored diamonds not tested for origin of color

Estimate: $4,000-$6,000
Starting Bid: $3,000

55288

55289
Colored Diamond, Diamond, Gold Ring
The ring features near-colorless full-cut diamonds weighing a total of 1.36 carats, full-cut black diamonds weighing a total of 1.44 carats, and full-cut yellow diamonds weighing a total of 1.37 carats, set in 18k white, yellow and black rhodium finished gold. Gross weight 15.30 grams.
Size: 6-1/2 (not sizeable)
Note: colored diamonds not tested for origin of color

Estimate: $4,000-$6,000
Starting Bid: $3,000

55289

55290
Diamond, Platinum Bracelet
The bracelet features radiant-cut diamonds weighing a total of approximately 8.00 carats, set in platinum. Gross weight 29.00 grams.
Length: 6-3/4 inches

Property of a Las Vegas, NV Estate

Estimate: $4,000-$6,000
Starting Bid: $2,000

55290

55291

55291
Ruby, Diamond, Platinum Necklace
The necklace features oval-shaped rubies weighing a total of .18.68 carats, enhanced by full and baguette-cut diamonds weighing a total of 11.72 carats, set in platinum. Gross weight 71.59 grams.
Dimensions: 16 inches x 1/4 inch

Property of a Collector
Estimate: $12,000-$16,000
Starting Bid: $7,000

55292

55292
Diamond, Sapphire, Platinum Earrings
The earrings feature full, rectangular and tapered baguette-cut diamonds weighing a total of approximately 8.00 carats, enhanced by oval-shaped sapphires weighing a total of approximately 6.70 carats, set in platinum. Gross weight 31.00 grams.
Dimensions: 2 inches x 3/4 inch
Note: earrings are designed for pierced and non-pierced ears

Estimate: $6,500-$7,500
Starting Bid: $5,500

55293

55293
Diamond, White Gold Ring
The ring features a round brilliant-cut diamond measuring 7.97 - 8.07 x 5.05 mm and weighing 2.04 carats, enhanced by full-cut diamonds weighing a total of approximately 1.20 carats, set in 18k white gold. A GIA report # 2185632318, dated July 25, 2017, stating *I color, VS1 clarity*, accompanies the center stone. Gross weight 5.77 grams.
Size: 3 (sizeable)

Estimate: $8,000-$10,000
Starting Bid: $5,000

55294

Diamond, Gold Jewelry Suite
The suite includes one ring featuring full and baguette-cut diamonds weighing a total of 4.00 carats, set in 18k gold; together with a matching pair of earrings featuring full and baguette-cut diamonds weighing a total of 7.12 carats, set in 18k gold. Gross weight 40.30 grams.
Ring Size: 6-1/2 (sizeable)
Earring Dimensions: 15/16 inch x 13/16 inch
Note: earrings are designed for pierced ears

Estimate: $5,000-$7,000
Starting Bid: $3,500

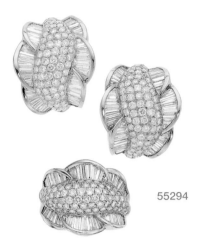

55294

55295

Multi-Stone, Diamond, Enamel, Gold Pendant-Brooches
The fish brooches feature round-cut pink and yellow sapphires weighing a total of approximately 3.70 carats, enhanced by calibré-cut rubies and sapphires, accented by full-cut diamonds weighing a total of approximately 0.20 carat, completed by emerald cabochons and black enamel applied on 18k gold. Gross weight 16.77 grams.
Dimensions: 1 inch x 7/8 inch

Estimate: $4,000-$6,000
Starting Bid: $2,000

55295

55296

Diamond, White Gold Ring
The ring features a round brilliant-cut diamond measuring 7.91 - 8.03 x 4.50 mm and weighing 1.69 carats, set in 14k white gold. Accompanied by GIA report # 5181628811, dated July 31, 2017, stating *I color, SI1 clarity*. Gross weight 3.07 grams.
Size: 6-3/4 (sizeable)

Estimate: $4,000-$6,000
Starting Bid: $2,000

55296

55297

55297
Jadeite Jade, Lapis Lazuli, Gold Pendant-Necklace, David Webb
The enhancer-pendant features pierced and carved jadeite jade plaques, enhanced by lapis lazuli tablets, set in hammered 18k gold, suspended by a green cord capped with gold hook closures, marked Webb. Gross weight 34.60 grams.
Pendant Dimensions: 2-1/2 inches x 1-1/2 inches
Cord Length: 15 inches
*Note: jadeite jade not tested for origin of color or treatment

Estimate: $10,000-$15,000
Starting Bid: $7,000

55298

55298
Emerald, Diamond, Gold Ring
The ring features an oval-shaped emerald cabochon measuring 16.40 x 11.20 x 9.80 mm and weighing 13.85 carats, enhanced by rectangular and full-cut diamonds weighing a total of 3.56 carats, set in 18k gold. Gross weight 16.61 grams.
Size: 7-1/2 (sizeable)

Estimate: $5,000-$7,000
Starting Bid: $3,000

55299

55299
Diamond, Gold Bracelet
The bracelet features full-cut diamonds weighing a total of approximately 6.00 carats, set in 14k gold. Gross weight 16.10 grams.
Length: 7-1/4 inches

Estimate: $4,000-$6,000
Starting Bid: $3,000

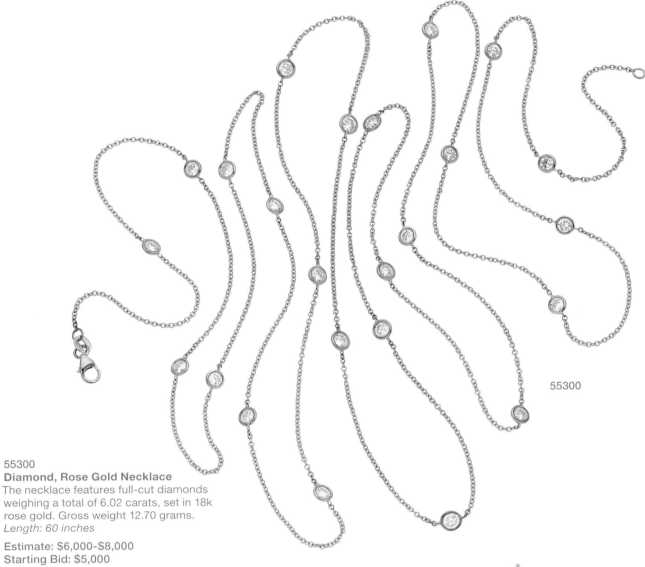

55300

55300
Diamond, Rose Gold Necklace
The necklace features full-cut diamonds
weighing a total of 6.02 carats, set in 18k
rose gold. Gross weight 12.70 grams.
Length: 60 inches

Estimate: $6,000-$8,000
Starting Bid: $5,000

55301

55301
Aquamarine, Diamond, White Gold Pendant-Ring
The ring centers a pear-shaped aquamarine
measuring 22.50 x 11.90 x 8.60 mm and
weighing approximately 11.30 carats, enhanced
by full and baguette-cut diamonds weighing
a total of approximately 1.50 carats, set in 14k
white gold. Gross weight 14.31 grams.
Ring Size: 6 (sizeable)
Pendant Dimensions: 1-1/4 inches x 7/8 inch

Estimate: $4,000-$6,000
Starting Bid: $2,000

55302

55302
Diamond, Rose Gold Bracelet
The bangle features full-cut diamonds with
a total of a 7.03 carats, set in 18k rose
gold. Gross weight 34.82 grams.
Dimensions: 7-1/2 inches x 5/16 inch

Estimate: $5,000-$7,000
Starting Bid: $3,000

55303

55303
Diamond, White Gold Necklace
The rivière necklace features round brilliant and full-cut diamonds weighing a total of 13.13 carats, set in 18k white gold. Gross weight 44.56 grams.
Length: 17 inches

Property of a Collector

Estimate: $7,000-$9,000
Starting Bid: $4,000

55304

55304
Emerald, Diamond, Platinum Ring, Gübelin
The ring features an oval-shaped emerald cabochon measuring 13.00 x 10.20 x 5.70 mm and weighing approximately 5.00 carats, enhanced by full and single-cut diamonds weighing a total of approximately 1.00 carat, set in platinum, maker's mark for Gübelin. Gross weight 9.40 grams.
Size: 7-1/4 (not easily sized)

Estimate: $7,000-$9,000
Starting Bid: $6,000

55305

Diamond, Sapphire, White Gold Bracelet
The bracelet features full-cut diamonds
weighing a total of approximately 2.00 carats,
enhanced by calibré-cut sapphires, set in 18k
white gold. Gross weight 55.80 grams.
Dimensions: 7-3/8 inches x 1/2 inch

Estimate: $5,000-$7,000
Starting Bid: $2,500

55305

55306

**Yellow Sapphire, Diamond, Gold
Earrings, Sabbadini**
The earrings feature oval-shaped yellow sapphires
measuring 16.05 x 14.10 mm and 16.05 x 13.70 mm,
enhanced by full-cut diamonds weighing a total of
approximately 3.50 carats, accented by round-cut
yellow sapphires weighing a total of approximately
9.10 carats, set in 18k gold. Gross weight 27.20 grams.
Dimensions: 1-1/8 inches x 1 inch
*Note: earrings are designed for non-pierced ears

Estimate: $10,000-$15,000
Starting Bid: $8,000

55306

55307

Diamond, Gold Bracelet
The bracelet features full-cut diamonds weighing
a total of approximately 15.65 carats, set
in 14k gold. Gross weight 31.10 grams.
Dimensions: 7 inches x 3/8 inch

Estimate: $7,000-$9,000
Starting Bid: $4,000

55307

55308

55308
Emerald, Diamond, Gold Necklace
The graduated necklace features oval-shaped emeralds weighing a total of approximately 34.00 carats, enhanced by full-cut diamonds weighing a total of approximately 4.40 carats, set in 18k gold. Gross weight 49.49 grams.
Dimensions: 14-1/2 inches x 5/16 inch

Property of a Collector

Estimate: $12,000-$16,000
Starting Bid: $7,000

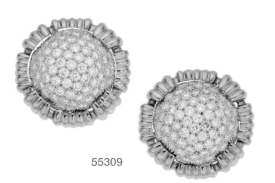

55309

55309
Diamond, Platinum, Gold Earrings, David Webb
The earring feature full-cut diamonds weighing a total of approximately 6.95 carats, set in platinum and 18k gold, marked Webb. Gross weight 45.80 grams.
Diameter: 1-3/16 inches
*Note: earrings are designed for non-pierced ears

Estimate: $10,000-$15,000
Starting Bid: $8,000

55310

55310
Diamond, Gold Ring
The ring features a marquise-shaped diamond measuring 8.00 x 4.65 mm and weighing approximately 0.55 carat, enhanced by full and tapered baguette-cut diamonds weighing a total of approximately 1.90 carats, set in 18k gold. Gross weight 8.35 grams.
Size: 6-3/4 (sizeable)

Estimate: $4,000-$6,000
Starting Bid: $2,000

55311

Diamond, White Gold Earrings
The hoops feature full-cut diamonds weighing
a total of approximately 3.70 carats, set in 14k
white gold. Gross weight 12.60 grams.
Dimensions: 1-3/8 inches x 1/8 inch
Note: earrings are designed for pierced ears

Estimate: $4,000-$6,000
Starting Bid: $3,000

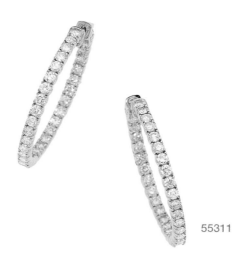

55311

55312

Tanzanite, Diamond, Colored Diamond,
White Gold Ring, Sarosi
The ring features an oval-shaped tanzanite measuring
16.30 x 9.80 x 6.70 mm and weighing 7.11 carats,
enhanced by full-cut diamonds weighing a total of
0.67 carat, accented by irradiated full-cut purple
diamonds weighing a total of 0.38 carat, set in 18k white
gold, marked Sarosi. Gross weight 12.48 grams.
Size: 7 (sizeable)

Estimate: $4,000-$5,000
Starting Bid: $3,000

55312

55313

Colored Diamond, Diamond, White Gold Bracelet
The bracelet features full-cut brown diamonds weighing a
total of approximately 4.65 carats, enhanced by full-cut near-
colorless diamonds weighing a total of approximately 1.90
carats, set in 18k white gold. Gross weight 14.70 grams.
Dimensions: 7 inches x 1/4 inch
Note: brown diamonds not tested for origin of color

55313

Estimate: $5,000-$7,000
Starting Bid: $2,500

55314

Diamond, White Gold Bracelet
The bracelet features full-cut diamonds weighing
a total of approximately 21.00 carats, set in 18k
white gold. Gross weight 52.20 grams.
Dimensions: 7-1/8 inches x 9/16 inch

Estimate: $10,000-$15,000
Starting Bid: $5,000

55314

55315

55315

Colombian Emerald, Diamond, White Gold Earrings, Craig Drake

The earrings feature pear-shaped emeralds, one measuring 10.60 x 6.70 x 4.45 mm and weighing approximately 1.40 carats, and one measuring 10.80 x 6.60 x 4.85 mm and weighing approximately 1.50 carats, enhanced by full-cut diamonds weighing a total of approximately 3.00 carats, set in 18k white gold, maker's mark for Craig Drake. An AGL report # 1085036 A and B, dated July 19, 2017, stating *Natural Beryl, Origin Colombia, Clarity Enhancement Minor, Traditional,* accompanies the emeralds. Gross weight 12.96 grams.
Dimensions: 2-1/4 inches x 1/2 inch
*Note: earrings are designed for pierced ears

Property of a Collector

Estimate: $8,000-$12,000
Starting Bid: $4,000

55316

55316

Topaz, Diamond, Platinum Ring

The ring features an emerald-cut topaz measuring 13.80 x 12.50 x 8.20 mm and weighs 14.33 carats, accented by full-cut diamonds weighing a total of 0.27 carat, set in platinum. Gross weight 12.00 grams.
Size: 6-3/4 (sizeable)

Estimate: $4,000-$5,000
Starting Bid: $2,000

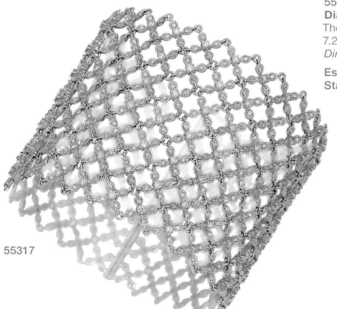

55317

55317

Diamond, White Gold Bracelet

The bracelet features full-cut diamonds weighing a total of 7.28 carats, set in 18k white gold. Gross weight 65.45 grams.
Dimensions: 7-1/2 inches x 2-1/4 inches

Estimate: $5,000-$7,000
Starting Bid: $4,000

55318

55318
Diamond, White Gold Necklace, Bailey Banks & Biddle
The *Dancing Diamond Tiara* necklace features full-cut
diamonds weighing a total of approximately 14.00 carats,
set in 18k white gold. Gross weight 108.68 grams.
Dimensions: 15 inches x 1-7/8 inches

Estimate: $8,000-$10,000
Starting Bid: $6,500

55319
Padparadscha Sapphire, Diamond, White Gold Ring
The ring features a cushion-shaped sapphire measuring 8.83 x
7.18 x 4.98 mm and weighing 2.95 carats, accented by pear and
full-cut diamonds weighing a total of approximately 1.50 carats,
set in 18k white gold. A GRS report, #GRS2010-121129, dated 6th
December 2010, stating, *Natural Orangy-Pink Sapphire "Natural
Padparadscha" 2.95 ct., No Indication of Thermal Treatment,*
accompanies the center stone. Gross weight 5.50 grams.
Size: 6 (sizeable)

55319

Estimate: $4,500-$6,500
Starting Bid: $3,500

55320
Sapphire, Diamond, Platinum Ring
The ring features an oval-shaped sapphire measuring 9.58 x 8.59
x 5.35 mm and weighing approximately 3.15 carats, enhanced
by European-cut diamonds weighing a total of approximately
1.20 carats, set in platinum. An AGL report # 1081476, dated
February 13, 2017, stating *Natural Corundum, Origin Madagascar,
No Gemological Evidence of Heat, Clarity Enhancement
None,* accompanies the sapphire. Gross weight 9.00 grams.
Size: 8-1/2 (sizeable)

55320

Estimate: $5,000-$7,000
Starting Bid: $3,000

55321

55321
Ruby, Diamond, Gold Earrings, Massoni
The earrings feature oval and pear-shaped rubies weighing a total of approximately 15.00 carats, set in 18k yellow gold, enhanced by full-cut diamonds weighing a total of approximately 3.00 carats, set in 18k white gold, marked Massoni. Gross weight 30.78 grams.
Dimensions: 1-3/8 inches x 7/8 inch
Note: earrings are designed for non-pierced ears

Estimate: $6,000-$8,000
Starting Bid: $4,500

55322

55322
Star Ruby, Diamond, White Gold Ring
The ring features an oval-shaped star ruby measuring 11.40 x 9.35 x 6.10 mm and weighing approximately 6.30 carats, enhanced by full-cut diamonds weighing a total of approximately 1.20 carats, set in 18k white gold. Gross weight 6.79 grams.
Size: 6 (sizeable)

Estimate: $9,000-$12,000
Starting Bid: $7,000

55323

55323
Ruby, Diamond, White Gold Bracelet
The bracelet features square-cut rubies weighing a total of 8.48 carats, accented by full-cut diamonds weighing a total of 2.14 carats, set in 18k white gold. Gross weight 19.70 grams.
Length: 7-1/4 inches

Estimate: $8,000-$10,000
Starting Bid: $6,500

55324

55324
Diamond, White Gold Bracelet
The bracelet features radiant-cut diamonds weighing a total of approximately 14.00 carats, set in 18k white gold. Gross weight 39.90 grams.
Dimensions: 7 inches x 1/4 inch

Estimate: $10,000-$15,000
Starting Bid: $5,000

55325
South Sea Cultured Pearl, Diamond, Gold Earrings
The earrings feature golden South Sea cultured pearls measuring 12.85 - 13.60 mm, enhanced by full-cut diamonds weighing a total of 2.74 carats, set in 18k gold. Gross weight 23.88 grams.
Dimensions: 1-1/2 inches x 3/4 inch
Note: earrings are designed for pierced ears

Estimate: $5,000-$7,000
Starting Bid: $3,600

55325

55326
Ceylon Sapphire, Diamond, Platinum Ring
The ring features an oval-shaped sapphire measuring 12.13 x 8.58 x 6.60 mm and weighing approximately 5.45 carats, framed by full-cut diamonds weighing a total of approximately 0.70 carat, set in platinum. An AGL report #1084359, dated May 22, 2017, stating *Natural Corundum, Origin Ceylon (Sri Lanka), No Gemological Evidence of Heat*, accompanies the sapphire. Gross weight 7.20 grams.
Size: 7-1/2 (sizeable)

Estimate: $5,000-$6,000
Starting Bid: $4,000

55326

55327
Diamond, Platinum, Gold Ring
The ring features full-cut and triangle-shaped diamonds weighing a total of approximately 17.00 carats, set in platinum with gold plating. Gross weight 22.79 grams.
Size: 6 (sizeable)

Estimate: $4,000-$6,000
Starting Bid: $2,000

55327

55328
Aquamarine, Diamond, Gold Bracelet, Temple St. Clair
The bracelet features round-cut aquamarine weighing a total of approximately 9.30 carats, accented by full-cut diamonds weighing a total of approximately 0.45 carat, set in 18k gold, maker's mark for Temple St. Clair. Gross weight 22.70 grams.
Length: 6-7/8 inches

Estimate: $4,000-$6,000
Starting Bid: $3,000

55328

55329

55329
Diamond, Ruby, White Gold Earrings, Assil
The earrings feature full and baguette-cut diamonds weighing a total of 1.50 carats, accented by baguette-cut rubies weighing a total of 2.79 carats, set in 18k white gold, marked Assil. Gross weight 16.30 grams.
Dimensions: 11/16 inch x 5/8 inch
*Note: earrings are designed for pierced ears

Estimate: $6,000-$8,000
Starting Bid: $4,500

55330

55330
Aquamarine, Diamond, White Gold Ring
The ring features a cushion modified brilliant-cut aquamarine measuring 20.48 x 13.22 x 9.05 mm and weighing 18.20 carats, accented by full-cut diamonds weighing a total of approximately 0.85 carat, set in 14k white gold. A GIA report # 62127555014, dated February 17, 2016, stating *Natural Beryl, Aquamarine,* accompanies aquamarine. Gross weight 11.80 grams.
Size: 6-3/4 (sizeable)

Estimate: $4,000-$6,000
Starting Bid: $2,000

55331

55331
Diamond, Platinum Ring
The ring features a rectangular-cut diamond measuring 7.28 x 5.93 x 3.62 mm and weighing 1.27 carats, enhanced by full-cut diamonds weighing a total of 0.71 carat, set in platinum. A GIA report # 14191146, dated February 4, 2008, stating *G color, VS2 clarity,* accompanies the stone. Gross weight 8.10 grams.
Size: 5-1/2 (sizeable)

Estimate: $3,000-$5,000
Starting Bid: $2,500

55332

55332
Diamond, White Gold Bracelet
The hinged bangle features square-cut diamonds weighing a total of 7.73 carats, set in 18k white gold. Gross weight 19.85 grams.
Dimensions: 6-3/4 inches

Estimate: $6,000-$8,000
Starting Bid: $4,000

55333

55333
Ruby, Diamond, White Gold Pendant
The pedant features a pear-shaped ruby cabochon
measuring 17.18 x 9.80 x 5.45 mm and weighing 8.91 carats,
accented by full-cut diamonds weighing a total of 5.69
carats, set in 18k white gold. Gross weight 37.20 grams.
Dimensions: 4-7/8 inches x 2-1/8 inches

Estimate: $9,000-$12,000
Starting Bid: $6,000

55334
Ruby, Diamond, White Gold Earrings
The earrings feature pear-shape ruby cabochons measuring
13.00 x 7.65 x 4.10 mm and 13.30 x 8.00 x 4.70 mm, weighing
a total of 8.06 carats, enhanced by full-cut diamonds weighing
3.13 carats, set in 18k white gold. Gross weight 28.50 grams.
Dimensions: 2-3/4 inches x 3/4 inch
*Note: earrings are designed for pierced ears

Estimate: $7,000-$9,000
Starting Bid: $5,000

55334

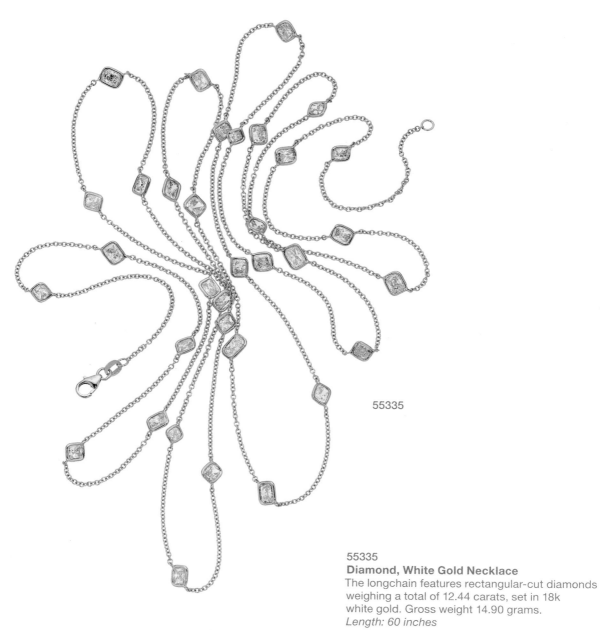

55335

55336

55335
Diamond, White Gold Necklace
The longchain features rectangular-cut diamonds weighing a total of 12.44 carats, set in 18k white gold. Gross weight 14.90 grams.
Length: 60 inches

Estimate: $7,000-$9,000
Starting Bid: $6,000

55336
Tanzanite, Diamond, White Gold Ring
The ring features an oval-shaped tanzanite measuring 13.25 x 11.63 x 9.15 mm and weighing 6.02 carats, enhanced by tapered baguette-cut diamonds weighing a total of 0.64 carat, set in 18k white gold. Gross weight 8.04 grams.
Size: 7-1/4 (sizeable)

Estimate: $4,000-$6,000
Starting Bid: $2,000

55337

55337
South Sea Cultured Pearl, Diamond, White Gold Necklace
The necklace features full-cut diamonds weighing a total of approximately 14.50 carats, set in 18k white gold, suspending South Sea pearls ranging in size from 11.80 x 12.14 mm to 14.80 x 11.90 mm. Gross weight 99.80 grams.
Dimensions: 16 inches x 2 inches

Estimate: $5,000-$7,000
Starting Bid: $3,500

55338
Ceylon Sapphire, Diamond, White Gold Ring
The ring features an octagonal-shaped sapphire measuring 10.31 x 8.15 x 4.98 mm and weighing 4.32 carats, framed by square and full-cut diamonds weighing a total of approximately a total of approximately 1.45 carats, set in 18k white gold. A GIA report # 6177893780, dated October 6, 2016, stating *Natural Corundum, Origin Sri Lanka, No Indications of Heating*, accompanies the sapphire. Gross weight 8.97 grams.
Size: 6-1/2 (sizeable)

Estimate: $6,000-$8,000
Starting Bid: $4,000

55338

55339

55340

55339
Diamond, Gold Necklace
The necklace features full, baguette, square and triangle-cut diamonds weighing a total of approximately 23.00 carats, set in 18k gold. Gross weight 99.98 grams.
Length: 17 inches

Estimate: $15,000-$20,000
Starting Bid: $9,000

55340
Sapphire, Diamond, Gold Earrings, Aletto Bros.
The earrings feature oval-shaped sapphires weighing a total of 16.00 carats, enhanced by full-cut diamonds weighing a total of 1.60 carats, set in platinum and 18k gold, marked Aletto Bros. Gross weight 40.14 grams.
Diameter: 1 inch
Note: earrings are designed for non-pierced ears

Estimate: $10,000-$12,000
Starting Bid: $8,000

55341
Diamond, White Gold Necklace
The necklace features full-cut diamonds weighing
a total of approximately 10.00 carats, set in
18k white gold. Gross weight 33.20 grams.
Dimensions: 16 inches x 1/4 inch

Estimate: $4,000-$6,000
Starting Bid: $3,500

55341

55342
Turquoise, Diamond, White Gold Jewelry Suite
The lot includes a floral brooch and earrings
inset with carved turquoise panels, accented
by full-cut diamonds weighing a total of
approximately 4.90 carats, set in 18k white
gold. Gross weight 67.90 grams.
Brooch Dimensions: 2-1/8 inches x 2-1/8 inches
Earring Dimensions: 1-1/4 inches x 1-1/8 inches
*Note: earrings are designed for
pierced and non-pierced ears*

Estimate: $4,000-$6,000
Starting Bid: $2,000

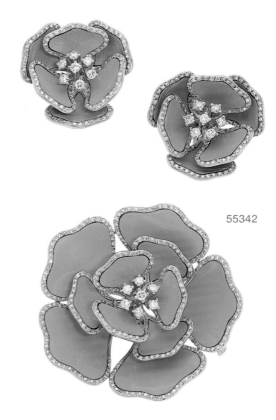

55342

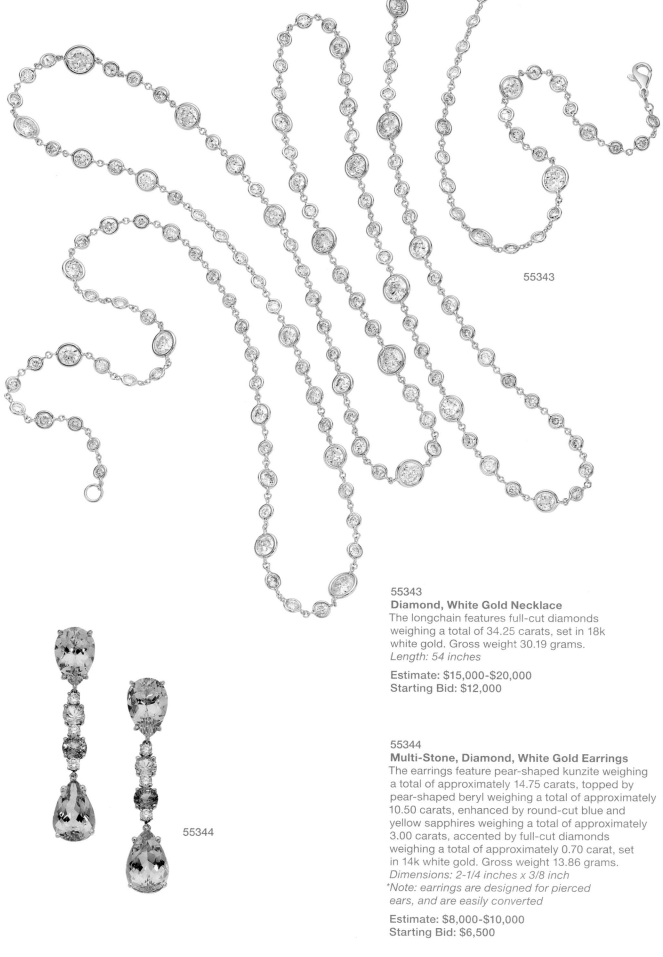

55343

55343
Diamond, White Gold Necklace
The longchain features full-cut diamonds weighing a total of 34.25 carats, set in 18k white gold. Gross weight 30.19 grams.
Length: 54 inches

Estimate: $15,000-$20,000
Starting Bid: $12,000

55344

55344
Multi-Stone, Diamond, White Gold Earrings
The earrings feature pear-shaped kunzite weighing a total of approximately 14.75 carats, topped by pear-shaped beryl weighing a total of approximately 10.50 carats, enhanced by round-cut blue and yellow sapphires weighing a total of approximately 3.00 carats, accented by full-cut diamonds weighing a total of approximately 0.70 carat, set in 14k white gold. Gross weight 13.86 grams.
Dimensions: 2-1/4 inches x 3/8 inch
Note: earrings are designed for pierced ears, and are easily converted

Estimate: $8,000-$10,000
Starting Bid: $6,500

55345

Colored Diamond, Gold Necklace
The necklace features round brilliant-cut brown diamonds weighing a total of approximately 33.00 carats, set in 18k gold. Gross weight 40.44 grams.
Length: 15-1/2 inches
Note: diamonds have not been tested for origin of color

Property of a Collector

Estimate: $12,000-$15,000
Starting Bid: $8,000

55345

55346

Colored Diamond, Diamond, Gold Earrings, Cartier
The *Sauvage* earrings feature full-cut pink, brown, yellow and near-colorless diamonds weighing a total of approximately 4.00 carats, set in 18k gold, marked Cartier. Gross weight 12.90 grams.
Dimensions: 3/4 inch x 7/16 inch
Note: earrings are designed for pierced ears, colored diamonds not tested for origin of color

Estimate: $6,000-$8,000
Starting Bid: $4,500

55346

55347

Colored Diamond, Diamond, Gold Ring, Cartier
The *Sauvage* ring features pink, brown, yellow and near-colorless full-cut diamonds weighing a total of approximately 3.20 carats, set in 18k gold, marked Cartier. Gross weight 11.63 grams.
Size: 6-1/4 (sizeable)
Note: colored diamonds not tested for origin of color

Estimate: $4,000-$5,000
Starting Bid: $2,400

55347

55348
Multi-Colored Diamond, Platinum Necklace
The graduated rivière necklace features round brilliant-cut colored diamonds weighing a total of approximately 29.15 carats, set in platinum. A GIA report # 2181613684, dated July 31. 2017, stating *Natural Color, Pink, Greenish Yellow, and Orange-Yellow*, accompanies three of the diamonds. Gross weight 43.30 grams.
Length: 18-1/4 inches
*Note: only three diamonds tested for origin of color

Property of a Collector

Estimate: $12,000-$15,000
Starting Bid: $8,000

55348

55349
Multi-Colored Diamond, Platinum Bracelet
The bracelet features multi-colored round brilliant-cut diamonds weighing a total of approximately 11.90 carats, set in platinum. A GIA report # 2185505999, dated June 16, 2017 stating: *One Orangy Yellow Round Brilliant measuring approximately 4.54 - 4.56 x 3.03 mm, One Greenish Yellow Round Brilliant measuring approximately 4.77 - 4.81 x 3.10 mm and One Pink Round Brilliant measuring 4.54 - 4.56 x 2.47 mm of Natural Color.* Gross weight 31.00 grams.
Length: 7 inches

Estimate: $15,000-$20,000
Starting Bid: $8,000

55349

55350
Multi-Colored Diamond, Platinum Bracelet
The bracelet features multi-colored round brilliant-cut diamonds weighing a total of approximately 7.20 carats, set in platinum. A GIA report # 5182505973, dated June 16, 2017 stating: *One Brownish Orange Round Brilliant measuring approximately 3.62 - 3.63 x 2.16 mm, One Yellow Round Brilliant measuring approximately 3.58 - 3.61 x 2.32 mm and One Pink Round Brilliant measuring approximately 3.56 - 3.57 x 2.13 mm, as Natural Color.* Gross weight 20.30 grams.
Length: 7 inches

Estimate: $8,000-$12,000
Starting Bid: $5,000

55350

55351

Colombian Emerald, Diamond, Gold Pendant
The pendant features an emerald-cut emerald measuring 19.73 x 17.66 x 12.63 mm and weighing 30.78 carats, enhance by full-cut diamonds weighing a total of approximately 0.45 carat, set in 14k gold. An AGL report # 1085187, dated July 11, 2017, stating *Natural Beryl, Origin Colombia, Minor Modern Clarity Enhancement*, accompanies the emerald. Gross weight 17.65 grams.
Dimensions: 1-5/8 inches x 1 inch

Estimate: $8,000-$12,000
Starting Bid: $4,000

55351

55352

Diamond, Gold Ring
The ring features a round brilliant-cut diamond measuring 9.65 - 9.81 x 5.70 mm and weighing 3.23 carats, set in 18k gold. A GIA report # 6157653523, dated September 25, 2013, *stating I color, VVS2 clarity*, accompanies the diamond. Gross weight 19.70 grams.
Size: 8 (sizeable)

From the Collection of a San Antonio, TX Lady

Estimate: $30,000-$50,000
Starting Bid: $20,000

55352

55353

Colored Diamond, Diamond, White Gold Bracelet
The bracelet features alternating marquise and pear-shaped light yellow diamonds weighing a total of approximately 8.35 carats, surrounded by full-cut diamonds weighing a total of approximately 3.40 carats, set in 18k white gold. Gross weight 13.80 grams.
Dimensions: 7-1/4 inches x 1/4 inch
*Note: yellow diamonds not tested for origin of color

Estimate: $15,000-$20,000
Starting Bid: $12,500

55353

55354

Diamond, White Gold Bracelet
The bracelet features full-cut diamonds weighing a total of 6.01 carats, set in 18k white gold. Gross weight 25.80 grams.
Length: 7 inches

Estimate: $6,000-$8,000
Starting Bid: $4,500

55354

55355

Tanzanite, Diamond, Gold Ring
The ring features a triangular brilliant-cut tanzanite weighing approximately 5.25 carats, accented by full and radiant-cut diamonds weighing a total of approximately 0.70 carat, completed by round-cut tanzanite, set in 18k gold. Gross weight 19.90 grams.
Size: 6-1/2 (sizeable)

Estimate: $4,000-$5,000
Starting Bid: $2,500

55355

55356

55356

Ruby, Diamond, Gold Earrings
The hoop earrings feature oval-shaped rubies
weighing a total of approximately 20.00 carats,
bordered by full-cut diamonds weighing a total
of approximately 2.50 carats, set in 18k gold with
rhodium accents. Gross weight 35.20 grams.
Dimensions: 1-1/2 inches x 3/4 inch
*Note: earrings are designed for pierced ears

Estimate: $5,000-$6,000
Starting Bid: $4,000

55357

55357

**Burma Ruby, Diamond, Platinum, Gold
Ring, David Webb**
The ring features an oval-shaped ruby cabochon
measuring 18.56 x 14.30 x 9.78 mm and weighing
approximately 25.00 carats, accented by marquise-
cut diamonds weighing a total of approximately
1.10 carats, set in platinum with 18k gold accents,
marked Webb. An AGL report # 1083091, dated April
12, 2017, stating *Natural Corundum, Origin Burma
(Myanmar), No Evidence of Heat Enhancement,*
accompanies the ruby. Gross weight 14.00 grams.
Size: 6-3/4 (sizeable)

Estimate: $20,000-$30,000
Starting Bid: $10,000

55358

55358

Emerald, Diamond, Ruby, Gold Ring
The ring centers a square emerald-cut emerald
measuring 17.60 x 16.80 x 6.50 mm and weighing
approximately 10.80 carats, enhanced by baguette-
cut diamonds weighing a total of approximately
3.00 carats, accented by rectangle and trapezoid-
shaped rubies weighing a total of approximately 2.00
carats, set in 18k gold. Gross weight 20.10 grams.
Size: 6-1/2 (sizeable)

Estimate: $7,000-$9,000
Starting Bid: $3,500

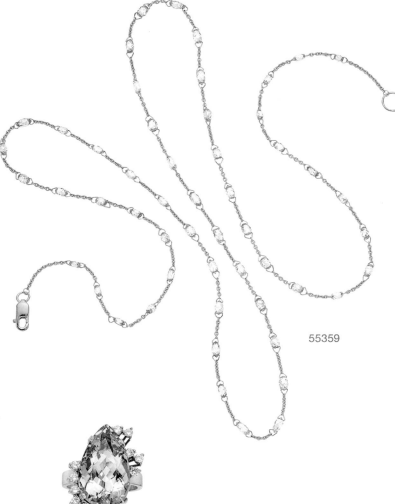

55359

Diamond, White Gold Necklace
The necklace features diamond briolette weighing a total of 7.12 carats, set in 18k white gold. Gross weight 3.70 grams.
Length: 24 inches

Estimate: $5,000-$7,000
Starting Bid: $4,200

55359

55360

Aquamarine, Diamond, White Gold Ring
The ring features a pear-shaped aquamarine measuring 20.90 x 12.20 x 9.90 mm and weighing approximately 11.20 carats, accented by full-cut diamonds weighing a total of approximately 0.40 carat, set in 18k white gold. Gross weight 8.80 grams.
Size: 6-1/2 (sizeable)

Estimate: $4,000-$5,000
Starting Bid: $2,000

55360

55361

Fancy Intense Yellow Diamond, Diamond, White Gold Ring
The ring features a round brilliant-cut yellow diamond measuring 6.49 - 6.51 x 3.75 mm and weighing 0.94 carat, enhanced by full-cut diamonds weighing a total of approximately 0.95 carat, set in 18k white gold. A GIA report # 2183265068, dated April 5, 2017, stating *Natural, Fancy Intense Yellow color, I2 clarity, Inscription: GIA 2183265068*, accompanies the center stone. Gross weight 5.17 grams.
Size: 6 (sizeable)

Estimate: $4,000-$6,000
Starting Bid: $3,000

55361

55362

55362
Diamond, Platinum Necklace
The necklace features a square modified brilliant-cut diamond measuring 12.26 x 11.86 x 8.77 mm and weighing 10.13 carats, enhanced by full-cut diamonds weighing a total of 7.00 carats, set in platinum. A GIA report # 2185551114, dated June 23, 2017, stating *K color, I1 clarity*, accompanies the square brilliant-cut diamond. Gross weight 36.69 grams.
Length: 16-1/2 inches
Centerpiece Dimensions: 5/8 inch x 5/8 inch

Estimate: $40,000-$70,000
Starting Bid: $30,000

55363

55363
Emerald, Diamond, White Gold Ring
The ring features an emerald-cut emerald measuring 12.35 x 12.00 x 6.49 mm and weighing approximately 6.50 carats, enhanced by triangle-shaped diamonds weighing a total of approximately 1.00 carat, set in 14k white gold. An AGL report # 1085035, dated July 19, 2017, stating *Natural Beryl, Origin Brazil, Clarity Enhancement Minor, Traditional*, accompanies the emerald. Gross weight 8.02 grams.
Size: 6 (sizeable)

Property of a Collector

Estimate: $15,000-$18,000
Starting Bid: $7,500

55364

55364
Diamond, White Gold Bracelet
The bracelet features radiant-cut diamonds weighing a total of approximately 8.50 carats, set in 18k white gold. Gross weight 11.77 grams.
Dimensions: 6-7/8 inches x 3/16 inch

Estimate: $12,000-$15,000
Starting Bid: $8,000

55365
Diamond, White Gold Earrings
The hoops feature full-cut diamonds weighing
a total of approximately 10.50 carats, set in 18k
white gold. Gross weight 17.60 grams.
Dimensions: 1-1/2 inches x 3/16 inch
Note: earrings are designed for pierced ears

Estimate: $4,000-$6,000
Starting Bid: $3,000

55365

55366
Diamond, Platinum Ring
The ring centers a pear-shaped diamond
measuring 15.55 x 9.93 x 6.03 mm and weighing
5.15 carats, accented by kite-shaped diamonds,
set in platinum. Gross weight 7.10 grams.
Size: 5-1/4 (sizeable)

Estimate: $30,000-$40,000
Starting Bid: $20,000

55366

55367
Diamond, White Gold Earrings
The earrings feature round brilliant-cut diamonds
measuring 6.42 x 6.42 x 4.20 mm and 6.40 x 6.40 x
4.00 mm and weighing a total of 2.13 carats, enhanced
by full-cut diamonds weighing a total of 0.83 carat,
set in 14k white gold. Gross weight 3.80 grams.
Dimensions: 1 inch x 7/16 inch
Note: earrings are designed for pierced ears

Estimate: $4,000-$6,000
Starting Bid: $3,000

55367

55368
Ruby, Diamond, White Gold Bracelet
The bracelet features oval-shaped rubies
weighing a total of 3.03 carats, accented by full-
cut diamonds weighing a total of 1.18 carats, set
in 18k white gold. Gross weight 14.20 grams.
Length: 7-1/2 inches

Estimate: $4,000-$6,000
Starting Bid: $2,500

55368

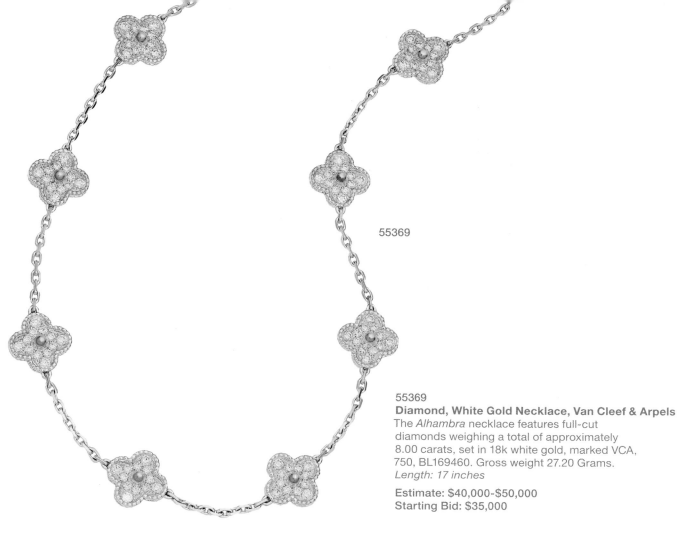

55369

55369
Diamond, White Gold Necklace, Van Cleef & Arpels
The *Alhambra* necklace features full-cut diamonds weighing a total of approximately 8.00 carats, set in 18k white gold, marked VCA, 750, BL169460. Gross weight 27.20 Grams.
Length: 17 inches

Estimate: $40,000-$50,000
Starting Bid: $35,000

55370

55370
Diamond, White Gold Earrings, Van Cleef & Arpels, French
The *Alhambra* earrings feature full-cut diamonds weighing a total of approximately 0.90 carat, set in 18k white gold, marked VCA, with French marks. Gross weight 8.30 grams.
Diameter: 9/16 inch
Note: earrings are designed for pierced ears

Estimate: $11,000-$13,000
Starting Bid: $9,000

55371

55371
Burma Ruby, Diamond, White Gold Ring, French
The ring features an oval-shaped ruby measuring 10.17 x 8.46 x 4.34 mm and weighing 3.29 carats, flanked by oval-shaped diamonds weighing a total of 0.84 carat, accented by full-cut diamonds weighing a total of 0.93 carat, set in 18k white gold, with French assay marks. An SSEF report dated October 2, 2012 stating *Natural Corundum, Burma Origin, Indications of Heating, Moderate Residue in Healed Fissures*, accompanies the ruby. Gross weight 7.80 grams.
Size: 7-3/4 (sizeable)

Estimate: $25,000-$30,000
Starting Bid: $18,000

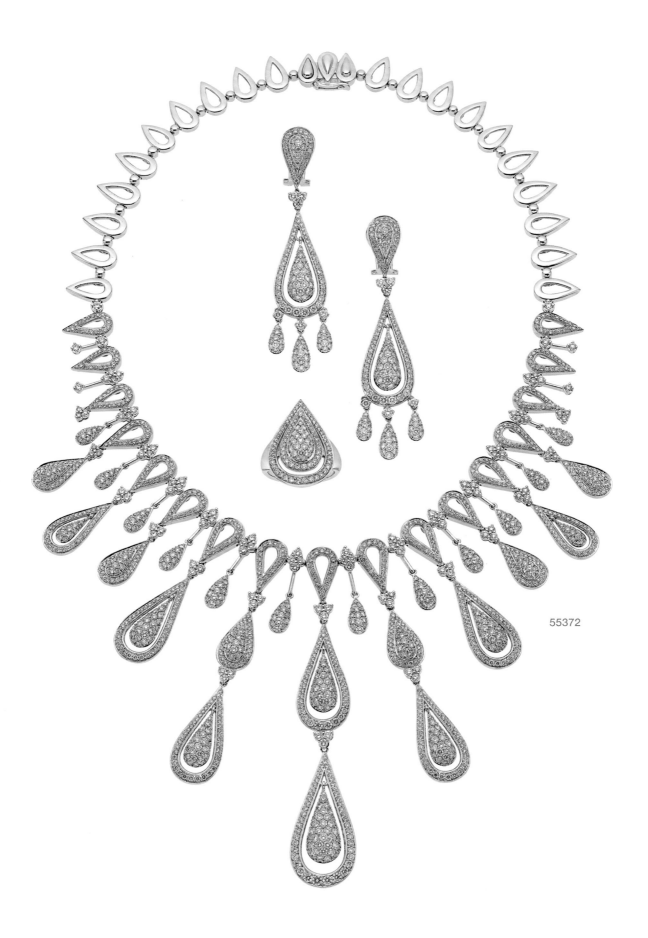

55372

55372

Diamond, White Gold Jewelry Suite, Montega by Elie Chatila
The suite includes a necklace featuring full-cut diamonds weighing a total of approximately 17.00 carats; a bracelet featuring full-cut diamonds weighing a total of approximately 8.50 carats; earrings featuring full-cut diamonds weighing a total of approximately 4.00 carats; and a ring featuring full-cut diamonds weighing a total of approximately 1.30 carats; all set in 18k white gold, all marked Montega. Total diamond weight is approximately 30.80 carats. Gross weight 159.60 grams.
Necklace Dimensions: 15-1/2 inches x 3-1/2 inches
Bracelet Dimensions: 6-1/8 inches x 1-3/4 inches
Ring Size: 5-1/2 (sizeable)
Earring Dimensions: 2-1/2 inches x 1/2 inch
*Note: earrings are designed for pierced and non-pierced ears

Property of a Private Texas Collector

Estimate: $50,000-$70,000
Starting Bid: $35,000

55372

55373

55373

Diamond, Gold Necklace
The necklace features triangle-shaped diamonds
weighing a total of approximately 4.60 carats, enhanced
by full-cut diamonds weighing a total of approximately
30.40 carats, set in 18k gold. Gross weight 68.96 grams.
Dimensions: 15-1/2 inches x 1/2 inch

Estimate: $20,000-$30,000
Starting Bid: $12,000

55374

Diamond, Platinum Eternity Band
The ring features a pear-shaped diamond measuring
15.25 x 9.90 x 5.78 mm and weighing 5.08 carats,
enhanced by pear-shaped diamonds weighing a total
of approximately 1.60 carats, enhanced by full-cut
diamonds weighing a total of approximately 1.60 carats,
set in platinum. A GIA report # 2183614044, dated
July 20, 2017, stating *K color, SI1 clarity*, accompanies
the center diamond. Gross weight 17.62 grams.
Size: 7 (not sizeable)

Property of a Las Vegas, NV Estate

Estimate: $30,000-$50,000
Starting Bid: $15,000

55374

55375

55375

Burma Sapphire, Diamond, Platinum Ring, Bvlgari

The ring centers an oval-shaped sapphire measuring 10.42 x 8.56 x 5.70 mm and weighing approximately 4.66 carats, framed by marquise and pear-shaped diamonds weighing a total of approximately 2.60 carats, set in platinum, marked Bvlgari. An AGL report # 1082347, dated March 16, 2017, stating *Natural Corundum, Sapphire, Burma Origin, No Gemological Evidence of Heat,* accompanies the sapphire. Gross weight 6.37 grams.
Size: 5-1/2 (sizeable)

Estimate: $50,000-$70,000
Starting Bid: $46,000

55376

55376

Fancy Light Yellow Diamond, Diamond, Platinum, Gold Ring

The ring features a radiant-cut diamond measuring 9.06 x 8.32 x 4.57 mm and weighing 3.04 carats, enhanced by triangle-shaped diamonds weighing a total of approximately 0.60 carats, set it platinum and 18k gold. A GIA report # 2185551289, dated July 11, 2017, stating *Natural, Fancy Light Yellow color, SI2 clarity,* accompanies the center stone. Gross weight 6.94 grams.
Size: 7-1/2 (sizeable)

Estimate: $10,000-$12,000
Starting Bid: $6,000

55377

55377

Sapphire, Diamond, White Gold Bracelet

The bracelet features blue, pink, yellow, orange, and green emerald-cut sapphires weighing a total of approximately 23.00 carats, enhanced by baguette-cut diamonds weighing a total of approximately 1.20 carats, set in 18k white gold. Gross weight 27.53 grams.
Dimensions: 7 inches x 1/4 inch

Estimate: $25,000-$30,000
Starting Bid: $22,000

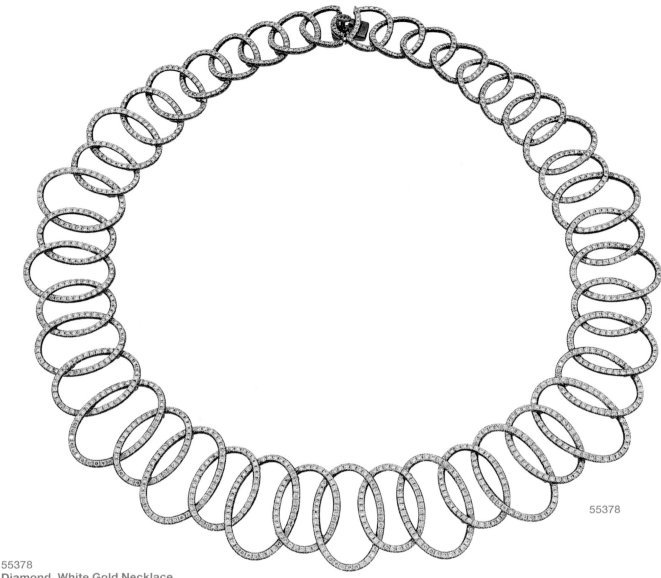

55378

55378
Diamond, White Gold Necklace
The necklace features full-cut diamonds weighing
a total of 14.22 carats, set in 18k white gold with
black rhodium accents. Gross weight 67.20 grams.
Dimensions: 16 inches x 3/4 inch
to 1-1/8 inches (tapered)

Estimate: $18,000-$24,000
Starting Bid: $16,000

55379

55379
Colombian Emerald, Diamond, Platinum Ring
The ring features a sugarloaf-shaped emerald
cabochon measuring 14.00 x 12.20 x 7.53 mm and
weighing approximately 8.50 carats, enhanced by
full and single-cut diamonds weighing a total of
approximately 3.15 carats, accented by baguette-
cut diamonds weighing a total of approximately 0.90
carat, set in platinum. An AGL report # 1085186,
dated July 11, 2017, stating *Natural Beryl, Origin
Colombia, Traditional Insignificant Clarity Enhancement,*
accompanies the emerald. Gross weight 15.12 grams.
Size: 6-1/2 (sizeable)

Estimate: $10,000-$12,000
Starting Bid: $6,000

55380

55380
Padparadscha Sapphire, Diamond, White Gold Ring
The ring features an oval-shaped orangey-pink sapphire measuring 11.02 x 9.58 x 5.72 mm and weighing 5.235 carats, enhanced by full-cut diamonds weighing a total of approximately 1.65 carats, set in 18k white gold. An SSEF report # 67497, dated April 8, 2013, stating *Natural Corundum, Padparadscha, No Indications of Heating, Origin Madagascar*, and a GRS report # GRS2012-013268L, dated January 16, 2012, stating *Natural Padparadscha, No Indication of Thermal Treatment*, accompany the sapphire. Gross weight 9.11 grams. *Size: 6-1/2 (sizeable)*

Estimate: $25,000-$35,000
Starting Bid: $20,000

55381

55381
Diamond, Gold Bracelet,
Diane von Furstenberg by H. Stern
The *Sutra* bracelet features full-cut diamonds weighing a total 46.88 carats, set in 18k gold, maker's mark for H. Stern. Gross weight 106.69 grams. *Dimensions: 7-1/2 inches x 7/8 inch*

Estimate: $45,000-$55,000
Starting Bid: $40,000

The Diane von Furstenberg by H. Stern collaboration is inspired by the story of the famed Belgian-American fashion legacy herself. H. Stern draws on the personal style of von Furstenberg, feminine, iconic, and powerful, to inspire this collection. The Sutra bracelet uses bold gold links set with diamond pave and finished with a love knot to create this modern take on a classic accessory.

55382
Colored Diamond, Gold Necklace
The riviére necklace features round brilliant-cut yellow diamonds weighing a total of approximately 45.00 carats, set in 18k gold. Gross weight 44.50 grams.
Dimensions: 20-3/4 inches x 1/4 inch
Note: diamonds not tested for origin of color

Estimate: $30,000-$40,000
Starting Bid: $20,000

55382

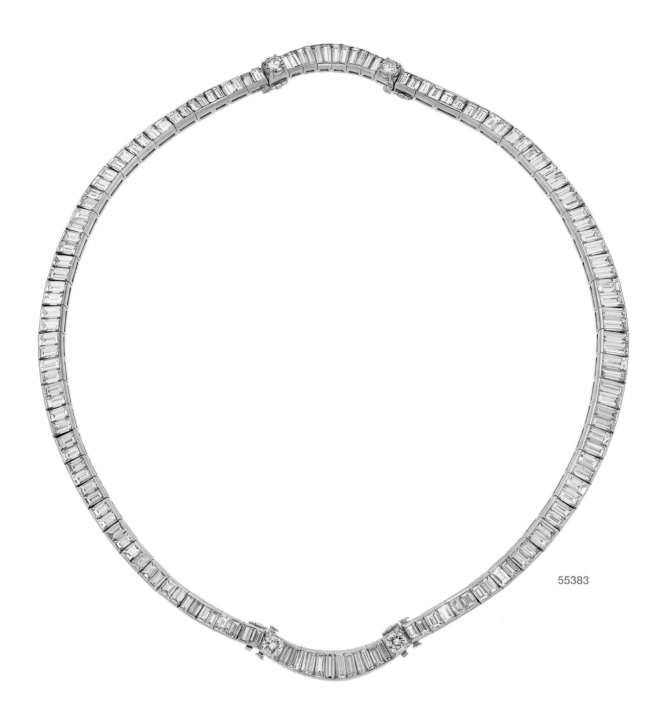

55383

55383
Diamond, Platinum Necklace
The convertible necklace features baguette and full-cut diamonds weighing a total of approximately 52.00 carats, set in platinum. Gross weight 75.30 grams.
Necklace Dimensions: 18 inches x 1/4 inch
Bracelet Lengths: 7-1/2 inches

Estimate: $50,000-$70,000
Starting Bid: $30,000

55384
Fancy Yellow Diamond, Diamond, White Gold Earrings
The earrings feature radiant-cut fancy yellow diamonds, one
measuring 8.42 x 8.26 x 5.34 mm and weighing 3.59 carats,
and one measuring 8.86 x 8.19 x 4.84 mm and weighing 3.06
carats, enhanced by triangle and marquise-cut diamonds
weighing a total of approximately 2.00 carats, set in 14k
white gold. GIA reports # 2181507817 and 1182507792, dated
June 14, 2017, stating *Natural, Fancy Yellow color, Even*,
accompanies the center stones. Gross weight 8.93 grams.
Dimensions: 11/16 inch x 5/8 inch
*Note: earrings are designed for pierced
ears, and are easily converted*

Property of a Collector

Estimate: $25,000-$35,000
Starting Bid: $12,500

55384

55385
Diamond, Platinum Ring
The ring features an emerald-cut diamond measuring
8.36 x 5.99 x 4.42 mm and weighing 2.09 carats, flanked
by an emerald-cut diamond measuring 7.22 x 4.68 x 3.25
mm and weighing 1.01 carats, and one measuring 7.25 x
4.80 x 3.24 mm and weighing 1.01 carats, enhanced by
radiant-cut diamonds weighing a total of approximately
2.40 carats, set in platinum. Total diamond weight is
approximately 6.51 carats. Gross weight 26.30 grams.
Size: 4-1/2 (not sizeable)

*Three GIA reports, dated June 12, 2017, accompany
the featured diamonds:
report # 5182497725, stating I color, VS1 clarity, 2.09 carats
report # 2181495836, stating J color, VS1 clarity, 1.01 carats
report # 6187497734, stating I color, VVS2 clarity, 1.01 carats*

Estimate: $20,000-$30,000
Starting Bid: $10,000

55385

55386
Diamond, Platinum Ring
The ring features a pear-shaped diamond measuring 16.47
x 10.84 x 6.88 mm and weighing 7.20 carats, enhanced by
round brilliant-cut diamonds weighing a total of approximately
1.30 carats, set in platinum and 14k white gold. A GIA report
11659362, dated July 20, 2017, stating *L color, VS2 clarity*,
accompanies the center stone. Gross weight 11.91 grams.
Size: 4 (not easily sized)

Estimate: $40,000-$50,000
Starting Bid: $30,000

55386

55387

Shown with Jacket

55387
Diamond, Platinum Ring
The ring features a radiant-cut diamond measuring 12.46 x 8.41 x 5.81 mm and weighing 5.01 carats, enhanced by triangle-cut diamonds weighing a total of approximately 0.80 carat, together with a ring jacket accented by triangle, radiant and full-cut diamonds weighing a total of approximately 1.90 carats, all set in platinum. A GIA report # 2185614012, dated July 19, 2017, stating *D color, SI2 clarity,* accompanies the central diamond. Gross weight 28.06 grams.
Size: 7 (sizeable)

Property of a Las Vegas, NV Lady

Estimate: $30,000-$50,000
Starting Bid: $15,000

55388

55388
Fancy Yellow Diamond, Diamond, Platinum, Gold Ring
The ring features an oval modified brilliant-cut fancy yellow diamond measuring 16.26 x 10.06 x 7.37 mm and weighing 10.45 carats, set in 18k gold, enhanced by triangle-shaped diamonds weighing a total of approximately 1.00 carat, set in platinum. A GIA report # 2183505448, dated June 16, 2017, stating *Natural, Fancy Yellow color, Even,* accompanies the center stone. Gross weight 9.20 grams.
Size: 6 (sizeable)

Property of a Collector

Estimate: $40,000-$70,000
Starting Bid: $25,000

55389

55389
Burma Ruby, Diamond, Platinum Ring
The ring features an oval-shaped ruby measuring 11.44 x 8.15 x 5.24 mm and weighing 4.48 carats, enhanced by triangle-shaped diamonds weighing a total of approximately 0.80 carat, set in platinum. An AGL report # 1085188, dated July 11, 2017, stating *Natural Corundum, Origin Burma, Enhancement: Heat, Minor Heating Residues, Color Stability Excellent,* accompanies the ruby. Gross weight 7.02 grams.
Size: 4-1/2 (sizeable)

Estimate: $12,000-$15,000
Starting Bid: $7,000

55390

55390
Diamond, Platinum Ring
The ring features an emerald-cut diamond measuring
10.91 x 9.05 x 6.08 mm and weighing 5.50 carats,
accented by tapered baguette-cut diamonds, set
in platinum. A GIA report # 2181605594, dated July
17, 2017, stating *D color, VS1 clarity,* accompanies
the diamond. Gross weight 9.20 grams.
Size: 7 (sizeable)

Property of an Oklahoma Lady

Estimate: $200,000-$250,000
Starting Bid: $175,000

55391
Fancy Intense Yellow Diamond, White Gold Ring
The ring features a cut-cornered rectangular-cut fancy
intense yellow diamond measuring 11.72 x 10.16 x 6.58
mm and weighing 7.48 carats, set in 18k white gold. A
GIA report # 6187505390, dated June 16, 2017, stating
Natural, Fancy Intense Yellow color, accompanies
the center stone. Gross weight 9.31 grams.
Size: 5-3/4 (sizeable)

Property of a Collector

Estimate: $40,000-$70,000
Starting Bid: $25,000

55391

55392

55392
Fancy Intense Purplish-Pink Diamond, Diamond, Platinum Ring
The ring features a cushion-shaped fancy intense purplish-pink diamond measuring 9.88 x 9.15 x 6.35 mm and weighing 5.04 carats, enhanced by bullet-shaped diamonds weighing a total of approximately 0.35 carat, set in platinum. A GIA report # 1182505402, dated June 14, 2017, stating *Natural, Fancy Intense Purplish-Pink color*, accompanies the center stone. Gross weight 6.81 grams.
Size: 6 (sizeable)

Property of a Collector

Estimate: $100,000-$150,000
Starting Bid: $60,000

55393

55393
Fancy Blue Diamond, Diamond, Platinum Ring
The ring features a cushion-shaped blue diamond measuring 8.11 x 7.98 x 5.38 mm and weighing 3.23 carats, enhanced by round brilliant-cut diamonds weighing a total of approximately 1.00 carat, set in platinum. A GIA report # 2185595637, dated July 21, 2017, stating *Natural, Fancy Blue color, SI2 clarity*, accompanies the center stone. Gross weight 8.10 grams.
Size: 6 (sizeable)

Property of a Collector

Estimate: $900,000-$1,200,000
Starting Bid: $600,000

End of Session One

SESSION TWO

Property from the Collection of
Lupita Tovar
Lots 55394 – 55423

55394
Ruby, Gold, Sterling Silver Compact

Estimate: $1,000-$1,500
Starting Bid: $500

55396
Sapphire, Diamond, Gold Bracelet

Estimate: $1,000-$1,500
Starting Bid: $500

55398
Ruby, Gold Brooch

Estimate: $1,500-$2,500
Starting Bid: $800

55395
Gold Bracelet

Estimate: $4,000-$6,000
Starting Bid: $2,000

55397
**Ruby, Diamond, Sapphire,
Gold Pendant-Brooch**

Estimate: $1,500-$2,000
Starting Bid: $800

55399
Cultured Pearl, Ruby, Gold Brooch

Estimate: $1,000-$1,500
Starting Bid: $500

55400
Diamond, Platinum Brooch and Diamond, Platinum-Topped Gold Stickpin

Estimate: $1,000-$1,500
Starting Bid: $500

55401
Cultured Pearl, Sapphire, Gold Brooch

Estimate: $1,000-$1,500
Starting Bid: $500

55402
Diamond, Gold Earrings, Tiffany & Co.

Estimate: $1,000-$1,500
Starting Bid: $500

55403
Black Onyx, Diamond, Gold Earrings, Tiffany & Co.

Estimate: $1,500-$2,000
Starting Bid: $800

55404
Sapphire, Diamond, Gold Earrings

Estimate: $2,000-$3,000
Starting Bid: $1,000

55405
Ruby, Gold Earrings

Estimate: $1,000-$1,500
Starting Bid: $500

55406
Aquamarine, Diamond, White Gold Earrings

Estimate: $4,000-$5,000
Starting Bid: $2,000

55407
Citrine, Gold Earrings

Estimate: $1,000-$1,500
Starting Bid: $500

55408
Diamond, Sapphire, White Gold Necklace

Estimate: $3,000-$4,000
Starting Bid: $1,500

55409
Ruby, Diamond, Gold Necklace

Estimate: $1,500-$2,500
Starting Bid: $800

55410
Diamond, Platinum Pendant-Necklace, Tiffany & Co.

Estimate: $1,000-$1,500
Starting Bid: $500

55411
Pink Tourmaline, Diamond, Gold Ring

Estimate: $2,000-$3,000
Starting Bid: $1,000

55412
Star Sapphire, Diamond, Gold Ring

Estimate: $1,500-$2,000
Starting Bid: $800

55413
Sapphire, Diamond, White Gold Ring

Estimate: $3,000-$5,000
Starting Bid: $2,000

55414
Diamond, Gold Ring

Estimate: $2,000-$3,000
Starting Bid: $1,000

55415
Blue Topaz, Diamond, Gold Ring

Estimate: $1,000-$1,500
Starting Bid: $500

55416
Antique Diamond, Silver-Topped Gold Ring

Estimate: $3,000-$5,000
Starting Bid: $1,500

55417
Coral, Gold Ring

Estimate: $1,000-$1,500
Starting Bid: $500

55418
Diamond, Mabe Pearl, Gold Rings

Estimate: $1,000-$1,500
Starting Bid: $500

55419
Diamond, Multi-Stone, Seed Pearl, Platinum-Topped Gold, Gold Rings

Estimate: $2,000-$3,000
Starting Bid: $1,000

55420
Mabé Pearl, Gold Jewelry

Estimate: $1,000-$1,500
Starting Bid: $500

55421
Jadeite Jade, Diamond, White Gold Jewelry

Estimate: $3,000-$4,000
Starting Bid: $1,500

55422
Chopard Lady's Diamond, Integral Bracelet Gold Watch

Estimate: $4,000-$5,000
Starting Bid: $2,000

55423
Art Deco Swiss Lady's Diamond, Platinum, Gold Watch

Estimate: $1,000-$1,500
Starting Bid: $500

Heritage Auctions is proud to present pieces from the collection of entertainer Fina Rox (1910-1989). Ms. Rox sang in nine languages and performed as a stage, cabaret and radio artist.

Rox, a British subject of Russian birth, avoided internment by the Japanese while performing in Manila during the three-year occupation. Offered are some of the pieces that were not lost during this time.

Property from the Collection of Fina Rox
Lots 55424 – 55429

55424
Diamond, Gold Stickpin

Estimate: $1,500-$2,000
Starting Bid: $750

55426
Retro Diamond, Gold Earrings

Estimate: $1,500-$2,000
Starting Bid: $750

55428
Antique Star Sapphire, Diamond, Platinum, Gold Ring

Estimate: $3,000-$4,000
Starting Bid: $1,500

55425
Ruby, Diamond, White Gold Earrings

Estimate: $1,000-$1,500
Starting Bid: $500

55427
Star Ruby, Diamond, Platinum Ring

Estimate: $2,500-$3,500
Starting Bid: $1,250

55429
Art Deco Sapphire, Diamond, Platinum Ring

Estimate: $3,000-$4,000
Starting Bid: $1,500

55430
Silver Niello Snuff Box, Russian

Est.: $1,500-$2,000
Starting Bid: $1,000

55431
Gold Box

Est.: $2,000-$2,500
Starting Bid: $1,600

55432
Sapphire, Sterling Silver Limited Edition "Princess Marcella Borghese" Compact, Bvlgari

Est.: $1,000-$2,000
Starting Bid: $500

55433
Gold Bracelet, Michael Good

Est.: $3,000-$4,000
Starting Bid: $1,800

55434
Diamond, White Gold Bracelet

Est.: $1,500-$2,000
Starting Bid: $1,000

55435
Colored Diamond, Diamond, White Gold Bracelet

Est.: $2,000-$3,000
Starting Bid: $1,000

55436
Diamond, White Gold Bracelet

Est.: $4,000-$6,000
Starting Bid: $3,400

55437
Diamond, White Gold Bracelet

Est.: $1,200-$1,600
Starting Bid: $800

55438
Diamond, Enamel, Gold Bracelet, Franck Muller

Est.: $3,000-$4,000
Starting Bid: $1,900

55439
Diamond, Gold Bracelet, Chopard

Est.: $2,000-$3,000
Starting Bid: $1,500

55440
Diamond, Gold, Silver-Topped Gold, Brooch-Bracelet

Est.: $3,000-$4,000
Starting Bid: $2,400

55441
Diamond, Gold Bracelet, Henry Dunay

Est.: $2,000-$3,000
Starting Bid: $1,600

55442
Art Nouveau Diamond, Synthetic Ruby, Gold Bracelet

Est.: $3,000-$4,000
Starting Bid: $2,000

55443
Multi-Stone, Glass, Gold Charm Bracelet

Est.: $2,000-$3,000
Starting Bid: $1,000

55444
Tourmaline, Diamond, White Gold Bracelet

Est.: $3,000-$4,000
Starting Bid: $1,500

55445
Gold Bracelet, Cartier

Est.: $2,000-$3,000
Starting Bid: $1,000

55446
Gold Bracelet, Van Cleef & Arpels

Est.: $2,000-$3,000
Starting Bid: $1,200

55447
Pink Star Sapphire, Ruby, Diamond, Cultured Pearl, Platinum Bracelet

Est.: $3,000-$5,000
Starting Bid: $1,500

55448
Gold Bracelet

Est.: $1,000-$2,000
Starting Bid: $500

55449
Diamond, Gold Bracelet

Est.: $1,000-$1,500
Starting Bid: $500

55450
Coral, Diamond, Gold Bracelet

Est.: $1,000-$1,500
Starting Bid: $500

55451
Coral, Black Onyx, Diamond, Gold Bracelet

Est.: $2,000-$3,000
Starting Bid: $1,000

55452
Diamond, Platinum Bracelet

Est.: $2,000-$3,000
Starting Bid: $1,250

55453
Diamond, Enamel, Gold Bracelet

Est.: $1,000-$1,500
Starting Bid: $500

55454
Diamond, Rose Gold Bracelet

Est.: $2,500-$4,500
Starting Bid: $1,700

55455
Diamond, White Gold Bracelet

Est.: $1,500-$2,500
Starting Bid: $800

55456
Diamond, Gold Bracelet

Est.: $2,000-$3,000
Starting Bid: $1,000

55457
Victorian Seed Pearl, Enamel, Gold Bracelet

Est.: $1,500-$2,500
Starting Bid: $1,000

55458
Coral, Gold Bracelet

Est.: $1,000-$2,000
Starting Bid: $500

55459
Turquoise, Diamond, White Gold Bracelet

Est.: $1,500-$2,500
Starting Bid: $1,000

55460
Victorian Enamel, Gold Bracelet

Est.: $1,000-$1,500
Starting Bid: $500

55461
Gold Bracelet

Est.: $1,500-$2,500
Starting Bid: $1,200

55462
Victorian Gold Bracelet

Est.: $1,000-$1,500
Starting Bid: $500

55463
Multi-Stone, Cultured Pearl, Gold Bracelet

Est.: $1,500-$2,000
Starting Bid: $750

55464
Diamond, Gold Bracelet

Est.: $1,000-$1,500
Starting Bid: $500

55465
Sapphire, Diamond, Gold Bracelet

Est.: $1,000-$1,500
Starting Bid: $500

55466
Retro Diamond, Multi-Stone, Platinum-Topped Gold, Gold Bracelet

Est.: $2,000-$3,000
Starting Bid: $1,000

55467
Gold Coin, Gold Bracelet

Est.: $2,500-$4,500
Starting Bid: $1,500

55468
Diamond, Gold Bracelet

Est.: $1,200-$1,800
Starting Bid: $800

55469
Diamond, White Gold Bracelet

Est.: $2,000-$3,000
Starting Bid: $1,200

55470
Diamond, White Gold Bracelet

Est.: $2,000-$3,000
Starting Bid: $1,200

55471
Sapphire, Gold Bracelet, Chopard

Est.: $1,000-$2,000
Starting Bid: $500

55472
Gold Bracelet

Est.: $1,000-$2,000
Starting Bid: $500

55473
Gold Coin, Gold Bracelet

Est.: $3,000-$4,000
Starting Bid: $1,500

55474
Citrine, Diamond, Gold Bracelet

Est.: $2,000-$3,000
Starting Bid: $1,000

55475
Diamond, Painted Portrait, Enamel, Gold Bracelet

Est.: $2,000-$3,000
Starting Bid: $1,000

55476
Gold Bracelet

Est.: $2,000-$3,000
Starting Bid: $1,000

55477
Multi-Stone, Gold Bracelet

Est.: $2,000-$3,000
Starting Bid: $1,200

55478
Multi-Stone, Gold Bracelet

Est.: $3,000-$4,000
Starting Bid: $2,000

55479
Gold Bracelet, CB Stark

Est.: $2,000-$3,000
Starting Bid: $1,000

55480
Gold Coin, Gold Bracelet

Est.: $2,000-$3,000
Starting Bid: $1,500

55481
Diamond, White Gold Bracelet

Est.: $2,000-$3,000
Starting Bid: $1,000

55482
Multi-Stone, Gold Bracelet

Est.: $4,000-$6,000
Starting Bid: $3,000

55483
Diamond, Gold Bracelet, Carrera y Carrera

Est.: $2,000-$3,000
Starting Bid: $1,500

55484
Diamond, Sapphire, White Gold Bracelet

Est.: $1,000-$2,000
Starting Bid: $500

55485
Pink Sapphire, Diamond, Cultured Pearl, White Gold Bracelet

Est.: $1,000-$2,000
Starting Bid: $500

55486
Multi-Stone, Diamond, Seed Pearl, Gold Bracelet

Est.: $3,000-$4,000
Starting Bid: $2,000

55487
South Sea Cultured Pearl, Diamond, White Gold Bracelet

Est.: $2,000-$3,000
Starting Bid: $1,000

55488
Multi-Stone, Diamond, Gold Bracelet

Est.: $3,000-$4,000
Starting Bid: $1,500

55489
Multi-Stone, Gold Bracelet

Est.: $2,000-$3,000
Starting Bid: $1,000

55490
Diamond, Ancient Coin, Gold Bracelet

Est.: $2,000-$3,000
Starting Bid: $1,200

55491
Ruby, Gold Bracelet

Est.: $3,000-$4,000
Starting Bid: $2,000

55492
**South Sea Cultured Pearl,
Diamond, White Gold Bracelet**

Est.: $2,000-$3,000
Starting Bid: $1,500

55493
Victorian Micromosaic, Gold Bracelet

Est.: $2,000-$3,000
Starting Bid: $1,000

55494
**Multi-Stone, Diamond,
White Gold Bracelet**

Est.: $2,000-$3,000
Starting Bid: $1,500

55495
Diamond, Gold Bracelet

Est.: $1,000-$2,000
Starting Bid: $500

55496
Diamond, Multi-Stone, Gold Bracelet

Est.: $2,000-$3,000
Starting Bid: $1,000

55497
**Pink Tourmaline, Pink Sapphire,
Diamond, Rose Gold Bracelet**

Est.: $2,000-$3,000
Starting Bid: $1,000

55498
Gold Bracelet

Est.: $1,000-$2,000
Starting Bid: $750

55499
Garnet, Gold Bracelet

Est.: $3,000-$4,000
Starting Bid: $2,000

55500
Gold Bracelet

Est.: $2,000-$3,000
Starting Bid: $1,000

55501
Shell Cameo, Ruby, White Gold Bracelet

Est.: $1,000-$2,000
Starting Bid: $500

55502
Diamond, Enamel, Gold Bracelet

Est.: $2,000-$3,000
Starting Bid: $1,200

55503
**Multi-Stone, Diamond,
White Gold Bracelet**

Est.: $2,000-$3,000
Starting Bid: $1,000

55504
Pink Opal, Colored Diamond, Diamond, White Gold Bracelet

Est.: $2,000-$3,000
Starting Bid: $1,000

55505
Diamond, Cultured Pearl, Gold Bracelet

Est.: $1,000-$2,000
Starting Bid: $750

55506
South Sea Cultured Pearl, Diamond, White Gold Bracelet

Est.: $2,000-$3,000
Starting Bid: $1,000

55507
Multi-Stone, Gold Bracelet

Est.: $1,000-$2,000
Starting Bid: $500

55508
Ruby, Gold Bracelet

Est.: $2,000-$3,000
Starting Bid: $1,500

55509
South Sea Cultured Pearl, Diamond, White Gold Bracelet

Est.: $2,000-$3,000
Starting Bid: $1,000

55510
South Sea Cultured Pearl, Diamond, White Gold Bracelet

Est.: $2,000-$3,000
Starting Bid: $1,000

55511
Gold Bracelet

Est.: $2,000-$3,000
Starting Bid: $1,500

55512
Multi-Stone, Gold Bracelet

Est.: $1,000-$2,000
Starting Bid: $750

55513
Multi-Stone, Diamond, Gold Bracelet

Est.: $1,000-$2,000
Starting Bid: $750

55514
Gold Bracelet, Marco Bicego

Est.: $1,000-$1,500
Starting Bid: $500

55515
Diamond, White Gold Bracelet, Pasquale Bruni

Est.: $1,000-$1,500
Starting Bid: $500

55516
Gold Coin, Gold Bracelet

Est.: $5,000-$7,000
Starting Bid: $4,000

55517
Diamond, Gold Bracelet

Est.: $1,000-$2,000
Starting Bid: $500

55518
Victorian Aquamarine, Diamond, Seed Pearl, Gold Bracelet

Est.: $2,000-$3,000
Starting Bid: $1,200

55519
Multi-Stone, Gold Bracelet

Est.: $1,000-$1,500
Starting Bid: $500

55520
Diamond, White Gold Bracelet

Est.: $1,000-$1,500
Starting Bid: $800

55521
Diamond, Ruby, White Gold Bracelet

Est.: $3,000-$5,000
Starting Bid: $1,500

55522
Multi-Stone, Gold Bracelet

Est.: $1,500-$2,000
Starting Bid: $750

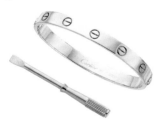

55523
White Gold Bracelet, Cartier

Est.: $3,000-$4,000
Starting Bid: $1,500

55524
Retro Gold Bracelet

Est.: $1,000-$1,500
Starting Bid: $500

55525
Gold Bracelet

Est.: $1,000-$1,500
Starting Bid: $500

55526
Gold Bracelet

Est.: $1,000-$1,500
Starting Bid: $500

55527
Garnet, Amethyst, Gold Bracelet, Andrew Sarosi

Est.: $1,000-$2,000
Starting Bid: $500

55528
Garnet, Citrine, Gold Bracelet, Andrew Sarosi

Est.: $1,000-$2,000
Starting Bid: $500

55529
Turquoise, Amethyst, Gold Bracelet, Andrew Sarosi

Est.: $1,000-$2,000
Starting Bid: $500

55530
Diamond, White Gold Bracelet

Est.: $1,200-$2,000
Starting Bid: $800

55531
Diamond, Gold Bracelet

Est.: $2,500-$3,500
Starting Bid: $1,500

55532
Diamond, White Gold Bracelet

Est.: $2,500-$3,500
Starting Bid: $1,500

55533
Diamond, Gold Bracelet

Est.: $1,500-$2,000
Starting Bid: $750

55534
Diamond, Gold Bracelet

Est.: $2,500-$3,500
Starting Bid: $1,250

55535
Diamond, Gold Bracelet, Chimento

Est.: $2,500-$3,500
Starting Bid: $1,500

55536
South Sea Cultured Pearl, Gold Bracelet

Est.: $1,000-$1,500
Starting Bid: $500

55537
Diamond, White Gold Bracelet

Est.: $2,500-$3,500
Starting Bid: $1,800

55538
Multi-Stone, Diamond, Enamel, Gold Bracelet

Est.: $1,500-$2,000
Starting Bid: $1,000

55539
Jadeite Jade Bracelet

Est.: $2,000-$3,000
Starting Bid: $1,200

55540
Jadeite Jade Bracelet

Est.: $2,000-$3,000
Starting Bid: $1,000

55541
Diamond, Ruby, Gold, Silver Bracelet

Est.: $2,000-$4,000
Starting Bid: $1,500

55542
Peridot, Diamond, Silver-Topped Gold Bracelet

Est.: $1,000-$1,500
Starting Bid: $500

55543
Art Nouveau Opal, Gold Bracelet

Est.: $1,500-$2,000
Starting Bid: $800

55544
Diamond, Platinum Bracelet, Sophia D.

Est.: $2,000-$4,000
Starting Bid: $1,000

55545
Gold Coin, Gold Bracelet

Est.: $2,000-$3,000
Starting Bid: $1,000

55546
Agate Bracelet, Frank Gehry for Tiffany & Co.

Est.: $2,000-$3,000
Starting Bid: $1,000

55547
Gold Bracelet, French

Est.: $1,500-$2,000
Starting Bid: $750

55548
Cultured Pearl, Gold Bracelet

Est.: $1,000-$2,000
Starting Bid: $500

55549
Diamond, Gold Bracelet

Est.: $1,500-$2,000
Starting Bid: $750

55550
Diamond, White Gold Bracelet, Aaron Basha

Est.: $2,000-$3,000
Starting Bid: $1,000

55551
Diamond, Gold Bracelet, Kieselstein-Cord

Est.: $2,500-$3,500
Starting Bid: $1,250

55552
Diamond, Gold Bracelet, Kieselstein-Cord

Est.: $2,500-$3,500
Starting Bid: $1,250

55553
Diamond, Pyrite, Gold, Sterling Silver Bracelet, Frederica Rettore

Est.: $1,500-$2,000
Starting Bid: $750

55554
Jadeite Jade, Green Tourmaline, Yellow Metal Bracelet

Est.: $1,000-$2,000
Starting Bid: $500

55555
Turquoise, Diamond, Gold Bracelet

Est.: $1,000-$1,500
Starting Bid: $500

55556
Mother-of-Pearl, Diamond, Gold Bracelet

Est.: $1,200-$1,600
Starting Bid: $750

55557
Tiger's-Eye Quartz, Diamond, Gold Bracelet

Est.: $1,000-$1,500
Starting Bid: $600

55558
Tiger's-Eye Quartz, Gold Bracelet

Est.: $2,000-$3,000
Starting Bid: $1,200

55559
Diamond, Black Onyx, Gold Bracelet

Est.: $3,000-$4,000
Starting Bid: $1,800

55560
Chalcedony, Wood, Gold Bracelet

Est.: $2,000-$3,000
Starting Bid: $1,500

55561
Sapphire, Diamond, Gold Bracelet

Est.: $2,500-$3,000
Starting Bid: $1,250

55562
Diamond, Platinum Bracelet

Est.: $5,000-$7,000
Starting Bid: $2,500

55563
Cultured Pearl, Diamond, Ruby, Platinum-Topped Gold Bracelet

Est.: $2,000-$2,500
Starting Bid: $1,200

55564
Diamond, White Gold Bracelet

Est.: $1,000-$1,500
Starting Bid: $500

55565
Emerald, Diamond, Cultured Pearl, Gold Bracelet

Est.: $4,000-$6,000
Starting Bid: $3,200

55566
Diamond, Sapphire, Platinum, Gold Bracelet

Est.: $3,000-$4,000
Starting Bid: $1,500

55567
Diamond, Glass, Gold, Sterling Silver Bracelet, Pandora

Est.: $1,000-$2,000
Starting Bid: $500

55568
Diamond, Gold Bracelet

Est.: $1,000-$2,000
Starting Bid: $500

55569
Diamond, Sapphire, Platinum-Topped Gold Bracelet

Est.: $1,500-$2,000
Starting Bid: $750

55570
Diamond, White Gold Bracelet

Est.: $3,500-$4,500
Starting Bid: $2,700

55571
Ruby, Diamond, Gold Bracelet

Est.: $3,500-$4,500
Starting Bid: $2,500

55572
Diamond, Gold Bracelet

Est.: $1,200-$2,200
Starting Bid: $1,000

55573
Diamond, White Gold Bracelet

Est.: $2,000-$3,000
Starting Bid: $1,000

55574
Diamond, Gold Bracelet, Hammerman Bros.

Est.: $3,000-$4,000
Starting Bid: $1,500

55575
Sapphire, Sterling Silver Bracelet

Est.: $3,000-$5,000
Starting Bid: $1,500

55576
Gold Bracelets
Est.: $1,500-$2,000
Starting Bid: $1,200

55577
Victorian Gold Bracelets
Est.: $2,000-$3,000
Starting Bid: $1,000

55578
Colored Diamond, White Gold Bracelets
Est.: $3,000-$4,000
Starting Bid: $2,600

55579
Multi-Stone, Gold Bracelets
Est.: $2,000-$3,000
Starting Bid: $1,000

55580
Gold Bracelets
Est.: $2,000-$3,000
Starting Bid: $1,500

55581
Tourmaline, Diamond, Gold Bracelets
Est.: $3,000-$5,000
Starting Bid: $2,000

55582
Diamond, Coral, Chalcedony, Gold Brooch
Est.: $1,500-$2,000
Starting Bid: $1,000

55583
Tsavorite Garnet, Diamond, White Gold Brooch
Est.: $2,000-$3,000
Starting Bid: $1,500

55584
Emerald, Diamond, Cultured Pearl, Gold Clip-Brooch, French
Est.: $2,500-$3,500
Starting Bid: $1,800

55585
Pink Sapphire, Diamond, Gold Brooch
Est.: $2,000-$3,000
Starting Bid: $1,500

55586
Victorian Diamond, Gold, Silver-Topped Gold Brooch, French
Est.: $3,000-$4,000
Starting Bid: $2,000

55587
Irradiated Diamond, Diamond, Gold Brooch
Est.: $1,500-$2,000
Starting Bid: $750

55588
Diamond, Gold Brooch
Est.: $1,000-$1,500
Starting Bid: $500

55589
Diamond, Gold Brooch, Piaget
Est.: $1,000-$1,500
Starting Bid: $500

55590
Pink Tourmaline, Gold Brooch, Burle Marx
Est.: $3,000-$5,000
Starting Bid: $1,500

55591
Diamond, Gold Pendant-Brooch
Est.: $1,000-$1,500
Starting Bid: $500

55592
Emerald, Cultured Pearl, Diamond, Silver-Topped Gold Brooch
Est.: $1,000-$1,500
Starting Bid: $500

55593
Jadeite Jade, Diamond, White Gold Pendant-Brooch
Est.: $1,200-$1,500
Starting Bid: $800

55594
Citrine, Gold Pendant-Brooch
Est.: $1,500-$2,000
Starting Bid: $750

55595
Coral, Multi-Stone, Gold Brooch
Est.: $2,000-$3,000
Starting Bid: $1,000

55596
Diamond, Ruby, Sapphire, Gold Brooch, Laykin et Cie
Est.: $2,000-$3,000
Starting Bid: $1,000

55597
Antique Smoky Quartz, Colored Diamond, Silver-Topped Gold Brooch
Est.: $1,200-$1,800
Starting Bid: $600

55598
Diamond, Ruby, Silver-Topped Gold Brooch
Est.: $2,000-$3,000
Starting Bid: $1,000

55599
Diamond, Coral, Enamel, Gold Brooch, La Triomphe
Est.: $2,000-$3,000
Starting Bid: $1,000

55600
Diamond, Cultured Pearl, Multi-Stone, White Gold Brooch

Est.: $2,000-$3,000
Starting Bid: $1,000

55601
Cultured Pearl, Gold Brooch

Est.: $1,000-$1,500
Starting Bid: $500

55602
Retro Aquamarine, Gold Brooch, Cartier

Est.: $1,000-$1,500
Starting Bid: $500

55603
Emerald, Diamond, Gold Brooch

Est.: $1,000-$1,500
Starting Bid: $500

55604
Diamond, Gold Brooch

Est.: $1,000-$1,500
Starting Bid: $500

55605
Diamond, Synthetic Sapphire, Platinum-Topped Gold Brooch, French

Est.: $1,000-$2,000
Starting Bid: $500

55606
Art Nouveau Diamond, Cultured Pearl, Gold Brooch

Est.: $1,000-$1,500
Starting Bid: $500

55607
Multi-Stone, Diamond, Gold Brooch

Est.: $1,500-$2,000
Starting Bid: $750

55608
Freshwater Cultured Pearl, Diamond, Sapphire, Platinum, Gold Brooch, Ruser

Est.: $1,000-$2,000
Starting Bid: $500

55609
Multi-Stone, Diamond, Gold Brooch

Est.: $2,000-$3,000
Starting Bid: $1,200

55610
Multi-Stone, Diamond, Gold Brooch, English

Est.: $1,000-$2,000
Starting Bid: $500

55611
Sapphire, Gold Brooch, Tiffany & Co.

Est.: $1,000-$2,000
Starting Bid: $500

55612
Multi-Stone, Diamond, Gold Brooch

Est.: $2,000-$3,000
Starting Bid: $1,000

55613
Diamond, Ruby, Enamel,
Gold Clip-Brooch

Est.: $2,000-$3,000
Starting Bid: $1,000

55614
Diamond, Sapphire, Enamel,
Gold Pendant-Brooch

Est.: $2,000-$3,000
Starting Bid: $1,500

55615
Turquoise, Ruby, Gold Brooch

Est.: $1,000-$2,000
Starting Bid: $500

55616
Diamond, Gold Brooch

Est.: $2,000-$3,000
Starting Bid: $1,500

55617
Diamond, Ruby, Gold Brooch

Est.: $1,000-$2,000
Starting Bid: $500

55618
Diamond, Ruby, Cultured
Pearl, Enamel, Gold Brooch

Est.: $1,000-$2,000
Starting Bid: $500

55619
Diamond, Multi-Stone, Cultured
Pearl, Gold Brooch

Est.: $1,000-$2,000
Starting Bid: $500

55620
Diamond, Colored Diamond, Frosted
Rock Crystal Quartz, Gold Brooch

Est.: $2,000-$3,000
Starting Bid: $1,000

55621
Chalcedony, Diamond,
Cultured Pearl, Gold Brooch

Est.: $1,000-$2,000
Starting Bid: $500

55622
Ruby, Diamond, Platinum, Gold Brooch

Est.: $2,000-$3,000
Starting Bid: $1,000

55623
Diamond, Multi-Stone, Gold Brooch

Est.: $3,000-$4,000
Starting Bid: $1,500

55624
Ruby, Cultured Pearl, Gold
Brooch, Cartier, Paris

Est.: $1,500-$2,500
Starting Bid: $1,000

55625
**Diamond, Multi-Stone, White
Gold Pendant-Brooch**

Est.: $2,000-$3,000
Starting Bid: $1,000

55626
Diamond, Multi-Stone, Gold Brooch

Est.: $2,000-$3,000
Starting Bid: $1,500

55627
Sapphire, Emerald, Gold Brooch

Est.: $1,000-$2,000
Starting Bid: $500

55628
**Diamond, Multi-Stone, Gold
Brooch, circa 1940**

Est.: $4,000-$6,000
Starting Bid: $3,000

55629
**Colored Diamond, Diamond, Freshwater
Cultured Pearl, Ruby, Gold Brooch**

Est.: $2,000-$3,000
Starting Bid: $1,000

55630
**Freshwater Cultured Pearl,
Diamond, Gold Brooch**

Est.: $2,000-$3,000
Starting Bid: $1,500

55631
**Amethyst, Green Tourmaline,
Diamond, Gold Brooch**

Est.: $1,000-$2,000
Starting Bid: $500

55632
**Diamond, Nephrite Jade,
Chalcedony, Gold Brooch**

Est.: $2,000-$3,000
Starting Bid: $1,000

55633
**Multi-Stone, Diamond, Enamel,
Platinum, Gold Brooch, Valentin Magro**

Est.: $3,000-$5,000
Starting Bid: $2,000

55634
Tourmaline, Diamond, Gold Brooch

Est.: $2,000-$3,000
Starting Bid: $1,000

55635
**Diamond, Multi-Stone, Cultured
Pearl, Gold Brooch**

Est.: $1,000-$1,500
Starting Bid: $500

55636
Multi-Stone, Diamond, Gold Brooch

Est.: $1,000-$2,000
Starting Bid: $750

55637
Diamond, Gold, Sterling Silver Brooch

Est.: $2,000-$3,000
Starting Bid: $1,500

55638
Freshwater Pearl, Ruby,
Gold Brooch, Ruser

Est.: $3,000-$5,000
Starting Bid: $2,500

55639
Diamond, Multi-Stone, Gold Brooch

Est.: $1,000-$2,000
Starting Bid: $750

55640
Ruby, Diamond, White Gold Brooch

Est.: $3,000-$4,000
Starting Bid: $2,000

55641
Victorian Diamond, Silver-Topped
Gold Brooch

Est.: $1,000-$2,000
Starting Bid: $750

55642
Diamond, Freshwater Cultured
Pearl, Platinum Brooch

Est.: $2,500-$3,500
Starting Bid: $1,250

55643
Diamond, White Gold Brooch

Est.: $1,000-$2,000
Starting Bid: $500

55644
Art Deco Diamond, Platinum Brooch

Est.: $1,000-$2,000
Starting Bid: $500

55645
Victorian Diamond, Multi-Stone,
Enamel, Gold Brooch

Est.: $1,000-$2,000
Starting Bid: $500

55646
Diamond, Lapis Lazuli, Gold
Brooch, French

Est.: $1,000-$2,000
Starting Bid: $500

55647
Diamond, Pearl, Gold Pendant-Brooch

Est.: $1,000-$1,500
Starting Bid: $500

55648
Diamond, Cultured Pearl, Platinum-
Topped Gold Brooch

Est.: $1,000-$1,500
Starting Bid: $500

55649
Retro Ruby, Cultured Pearl, Gold Brooch

Est.: $1,000-$2,000
Starting Bid: $500

55650
Retro Diamond, Garnet, Platinum, Rose Gold Brooch

Est.: $3,000-$4,000
Starting Bid: $2,000

55651
Diamond, Multi-Stone, White Gold Brooch, Andrew Sarosi

Est.: $1,000-$2,000
Starting Bid: $500

55652
Gold Brooch, Henry Dunay

Est.: $2,000-$3,000
Starting Bid: $1,500

55653
Emerald, White Gold Brooch, Cartier

Est.: $3,000-$4,000
Starting Bid: $1,800

55654
Diamond, Multi-Stone, Platinum Brooch

Est.: $2,000-$3,000
Starting Bid: $1,500

55655
Art Deco Diamond, Platinum Brooch

Est.: $3,000-$4,000
Starting Bid: $1,900

55656
Retro Ruby, Diamond, Cultured Pearl, Gold Brooch

Est.: $1,200-$1,600
Starting Bid: $900

55657
Edwardian Diamond, Platinum Brooch

Est.: $3,000-$4,000
Starting Bid: $2,000

55658
Diamond, Ruby, Gold Brooch

Est.: $1,200-$1,600
Starting Bid: $900

55659
Diamond, Multi-Stone, Gold Brooch, Ralston

Est.: $1,800-$2,400
Starting Bid: $1,200

55660
Gold Brooch, Tiffany & Co.

Est.: $1,200-$1,800
Starting Bid: $800

55661
Victorian Coral, Gold Brooch

Est.: $1,000-$1,500
Starting Bid: $500

55662
Art Deco Diamond, Synthetic Sapphire, Platinum Brooch

Est.: $1,000-$1,500
Starting Bid: $500

55663
Jadeite Jade, Diamond, Gold Brooch

Est.: $1,000-$2,000
Starting Bid: $600

55664
Labradorite, Emerald,
Enamel, Gold Stickpin

Est.: $2,000-$3,000
Starting Bid: $1,200

55665
Diamond, Platinum Brooch,
Oscar Heyman Bros.

Est.: $1,000-$2,000
Starting Bid: $500

55666
Moonstone, Diamond, Gold Brooch

Est.: $1,000-$1,500
Starting Bid: $500

55667
Diamond, Emerald, Enamel,
Gold Brooch, Van Cleef & Arpels

Est.: $1,500-$2,000
Starting Bid: $750

55668
Tsavorite Garnet, Diamond,
White Gold Brooch

Est.: $2,000-$3,000
Starting Bid: $1,000

55669
South Sea Cultured Pearl, Diamond,
Gold Pendant-Brooch

Est.: $1,200-$1,600
Starting Bid: $750

55670
Emerald, Diamond, Gold
Pendant-Brooch

Est.: $2,500-$3,500
Starting Bid: $1,700

55671
Diamond, Emerald, South Sea
Cultured Pearl, Gold Brooch

Est.: $2,000-$3,000
Starting Bid: $1,000

55672
Diamond, Multi-Stone, Gold Brooch

Est.: $5,000-$7,000
Starting Bid: $2,500

55673
Opal, Diamond, Gold Brooch

Est.: $2,000-$3,000
Starting Bid: $1,000

55674
Diamond, Sapphire, Ruby,
Platinum-Topped Gold Brooch

Est.: $2,000-$3,000
Starting Bid: $1,000

55675
Diamond, Ruby, Gold Brooches,
Rosenthal

Est.: $3,000-$4,000
Starting Bid: $1,500

55676
Diamond, Ruby, White Gold Brooch

Est.: $2,500-$3,000
Starting Bid: $1,250

55677
Diamond, Turquoise, Lapis Lazuli, Gold Brooch

Est.: $2,000-$3,000
Starting Bid: $1,000

55678
Multi-Stone, Gold Brooches

Est.: $1,000-$1,500
Starting Bid: $500

55679
Victorian Gold Nugget, Gold Brooches

Est.: $1,000-$1,500
Starting Bid: $500

55680
Diamond, Multi-Stone, Enamel, Gold Brooches, Hammerman Bros.

Est.: $1,500-$2,500
Starting Bid: $750

55681
Diamond, Multi-Stone, Gold Brooches

Est.: $1,200-$1,500
Starting Bid: $600

55682
Ruby, Sapphire, Diamond, Gold Brooches, Van Cleef & Arpels

Est.: $2,000-$3,000
Starting Bid: $1,000

55683
Gold Cuff Links

Est.: $1,500-$2,000
Starting Bid: $1,000

55684
Black Onyx, Diamond, White Gold Cuff Links, Eli Frei

Est.: $2,200-$2,800
Starting Bid: $1,900

55685
Black Onyx, Diamond, White Gold Cuff Links, Eli Frei

Est.: $2,000-$3,000
Starting Bid: $1,400

55686
Diamond, Enamel, Gold Cuff Links, Peter Lindeman

Est.: $1,000-$1,500
Starting Bid: $500

55687
Diamond, Gold Cuff Links

Est.: $1,000-$2,000
Starting Bid: $500

55688
Opal, Diamond, Gold Cuff Links

Est.: $1,000-$1,500
Starting Bid: $600

55689
Gold Coin, Gold Cuff Links

Est.: $1,000-$1,500
Starting Bid: $600

55690
Diamond, Enamel, Gold Cuff Links

Est.: $1,000-$1,500
Starting Bid: $600

55691
**Lapis Lazuli, Gold Cuff Links,
Angela Cummings**

Est.: $1,500-$2,500
Starting Bid: $750

55692
Gold Cuff Links

Est.: $1,000-$1,500
Starting Bid: $500

55693
Diamond, Gold Cuff Links

Est.: $1,000-$1,500
Starting Bid: $600

55694
**Sapphire, Diamond, White
Gold Cuff Links, Assil**

Est.: $3,000-$4,000
Starting Bid: $2,000

55695
**Lapis Lazuli, Diamond, Gold
Cuff Links, Assil**

Est.: $1,800-$2,400
Starting Bid: $1,200

55696
Ruby, Diamond, Gold Cuff Links

Est.: $1,200-$1,600
Starting Bid: $800

55697
**Gentleman's Diamond, Black Onyx, Gold
Cuff Links and Tie Tac Set, Bvlgari**

Est.: $3,000-$4,000
Starting Bid: $2,400

55698
**Diamond, Gold, Steel Cuff Links,
Carrera y Carrera**

Est.: $1,000-$1,500
Starting Bid: $500

55699
**Diamond, Moonstone, Gold
Earrings, Temple St. Clair**

Est.: $1,500-$2,000
Starting Bid: $1,000

55700
Carnelian, Gold Earrings

Est.: $1,500-$2,000
Starting Bid: $1,200

55701
**Colored Diamond, Diamond, Turquoise,
Mabe Pearl, Gold Earrings**

Est.: $4,000-$6,000
Starting Bid: $3,000

55702
**Coral, Colored Diamond, White
Gold Earrings, Eli Frei**

Est.: $2,000-$3,000
Starting Bid: $1,000

55703
Diamond, Enamel, White Gold Earrings

Est.: $2,000-$3,000
Starting Bid: $1,300

55704
Enamel, Gold Earrings, Yanes

Est.: $1,000-$1,500
Starting Bid: $750

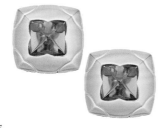

55705
Blue Topaz, White Gold Earrings, Bvlgari

Est.: $2,000-$3,000
Starting Bid: $1,500

55706
Gold Earrings, Cartier, French

Est.: $1,500-$2,000
Starting Bid: $1,200

55707
Colored Diamond, Diamond, White Gold Earrings

Est.: $1,500-$2,000
Starting Bid: $1,100

55708
Yellow Sapphire, Diamond, Gold Earrings

Est.: $2,000-$3,000
Starting Bid: $1,000

55709
Diamond, Coral, Platinum Earrings

Est.: $3,000-$4,000
Starting Bid: $2,200

55710
Peridot, Diamond, Gold Earrings

Est.: $2,500-$3,500
Starting Bid: $2,000

55711
Emerald, Diamond, Gold Earrings

Est.: $2,000-$3,000
Starting Bid: $1,800

55712
Diamond, Gold Earrings, Schlumberger for Tiffany & Co.

Est.: $1,000-$1,500
Starting Bid: $700

55713
Sapphire, Gold Earrings

Est.: $2,000-$3,000
Starting Bid: $1,800

55714
Colored Diamond, Diamond, White Gold Earrings

Est.: $2,400-$3,000
Starting Bid: $2,200

55715
Aquamarine, Diamond, Colored Diamond, White Gold Earrings, French

Est.: $2,500-$3,500
Starting Bid: $2,000

55716
Diamond, White Gold Earrings

Est.: $3,000-$4,000
Starting Bid: $1,500

55717
Gold Earrings, Cynthia Bach

Est.: $1,000-$1,500
Starting Bid: $500

55718
Diamond, Tanzanite, Emerald, White Gold Earrings

Est.: $4,000-$6,000
Starting Bid: $2,500

55719
Peridot, Diamond, White Gold Earrings

Est.: $2,500-$3,500
Starting Bid: $1,500

55720
Amethyst, Diamond, Gold Earrings

Est.: $1,400-$1,800
Starting Bid: $700

55721
Aquamarine, Pink Tourmaline, Diamond, Gold Earrings

Est.: $2,200-$2,800
Starting Bid: $1,600

55722
Coral, Diamond, Gold Earrings

Est.: $2,000-$3,000
Starting Bid: $1,000

55723
Coral, Diamond, Gold Earrings

Est.: $2,000-$3,000
Starting Bid: $1,000

55724
Shell, Sapphire, Gold Earrings, Seaman Schepps

Est.: $2,000-$3,000
Starting Bid: $1,000

55725
Lapis Lazuli, Gold Earrings, David Webb

Est.: $3,000-$4,000
Starting Bid: $1,500

55726
Lapis Lazuli, Diamond, Gold Earrings

Est.: $1,000-$1,500
Starting Bid: $500

55727
Gold Earrings, David Webb

Est.: $3,000-$4,000
Starting Bid: $1,500

55728
Gold Earrings, David Webb

Est.: $3,000-$4,000
Starting Bid: $1,500

55729
Aquamarine, Gold Earrings, Katy Briscoe

Est.: $2,000-$3,000
Starting Bid: $1,000

55730
Peridot, Gold Earrings, Elizabeth Locke

Est.: $1,000-$1,500
Starting Bid: $500

55731
Peridot, Gold Earrings, Katy Briscoe

Est.: $2,000-$3,000
Starting Bid: $1,000

55732
Pink Tourmaline, Gold Earrings, Katy Briscoe

Est.: $2,000-$3,000
Starting Bid: $1,000

55733
Amber, Gold Earrings, Gurhan

Est.: $1,500-$2,000
Starting Bid: $750

55734
Diamond, Gold Earrings

Est.: $3,000-$4,000
Starting Bid: $1,500

55735
Citrine, Gold Earrings, Katy Briscoe

Est.: $2,000-$3,000
Starting Bid: $1,000

55736
Diamond, Gold Earrings

Est.: $1,000-$1,500
Starting Bid: $500

55737
Diamond, White Gold Earrings

Est.: $2,500-$3,500
Starting Bid: $1,400

55738
Ruby, Sapphire, Diamond, Gold Earrings

Est.: $2,000-$3,000
Starting Bid: $1,000

55739
**Garnet, Tanzanite, Gold
Earrings, SeidanGang**

Est.: $1,500-$2,000
Starting Bid: $800

55740
**Sapphire, Diamond, Platinum-Topped
Gold Earrings, French,
early 20th Century**

Est.: $2,000-$3,000
Starting Bid: $1,000

55741
**Sapphire, Diamond, Enamel,
White Gold Earrings**

Est.: $4,500-$6,500
Starting Bid: $3,250

55742
Diamond, Rose Gold Earrings

Est.: $4,000-$6,000
Starting Bid: $3,000

55743
Diamond, Rose Gold Earrings

Est.: $3,000-$4,000
Starting Bid: $1,900

55744
Diamond, Rose Gold Earrings

Est.: $2,500-$3,500
Starting Bid: $1,700

55745
Diamond, White Gold Earrings

Est.: $3,500-$5,500
Starting Bid: $2,300

55746
**Turquoise, Diamond, White
Gold Earrings, Pejmani**

Est.: $2,500-$3,500
Starting Bid: $1,700

55747
Diamond, White Gold Earrings

Est.: $4,500-$6,500
Starting Bid: $3,000

55748
Diamond, White Gold Earrings

Est.: $2,500-$4,500
Starting Bid: $1,800

55749
Diamond, Rose Gold Earrings

Est.: $2,000-$3,000
Starting Bid: $1,200

55750
Turquoise, Diamond, Gold Earrings

Est.: $2,000-$3,000
Starting Bid: $1,000

55751
Diamond, White Gold Earrings

Est.: $1,000-$1,500
Starting Bid: $500

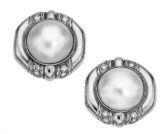

55752
Cultured Pearl, Diamond, Gold Earrings

Est.: $1,000-$1,500
Starting Bid: $500

55753
Diamond, White Gold Earrings

Est.: $2,000-$3,000
Starting Bid: $1,000

55754
Diamond, White Gold Earrings

Est.: $1,000-$1,500
Starting Bid: $500

55755
Diamond, Sapphire, Black Onyx, White Gold Earrings

Est.: $3,000-$5,000
Starting Bid: $1,500

55756
Diamond, White Gold Earrings

Est.: $2,000-$3,000
Starting Bid: $1,000

55757
South Sea Cultured Pearl, Zircon, Gold Earrings

Est.: $4,000-$6,000
Starting Bid: $3,000

55758
Citrine, Diamond, Gold Earrings

Est.: $1,000-$2,000
Starting Bid: $800

55759
Emerald, Gold Earrings

Est.: $1,000-$2,000
Starting Bid: $800

55760
Multi-Stone, Diamond, Gold Earrings

Est.: $1,000-$2,000
Starting Bid: $500

55761
Diamond, Multi-Stone, Gold Earrings

Est.: $2,000-$3,000
Starting Bid: $1,500

55762
Chalcedony, Pink Sapphire, Gold Earrings, Paolo Costagli

Est.: $2,000-$3,000
Starting Bid: $1,000

55763
Amethyst, Diamond, White Gold Earrings

Est.: $1,000-$2,000
Starting Bid: $500

55764
**Diamond, Mother-of-Pearl,
Gold Earrings**

Est.: $2,000-$3,000
Starting Bid: $1,000

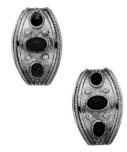

55765
Multi-Stone, Diamond, Gold Earrings

Est.: $1,000-$2,000
Starting Bid: $500

55766
Peridot, Diamond, Gold Earrings

Est.: $2,000-$3,000
Starting Bid: $1,000

55767
**Diamond, Gold Earrings,
Orlando Orlandini**

Est.: $1,000-$2,000
Starting Bid: $500

55768
Sapphire, Diamond, Gold Earrings

Est.: $2,000-$3,000
Starting Bid: $1,000

55769
Gold Earrings, Kieselstein-Cord

Est.: $1,000-$2,000
Starting Bid: $500

55770
Lapis Lazuli, Diamond, Gold Earrings

Est.: $2,000-$3,000
Starting Bid: $1,000

55771
**Lapis Lazuli, Gold Earrings,
Angela Cummings**

Est.: $2,000-$3,000
Starting Bid: $1,000

55772
Diamond, White Gold Earrings

Est.: $2,000-$3,000
Starting Bid: $1,000

55773
Diamond, White Gold Earrings

Est.: $3,000-$4,000
Starting Bid: $1,500

55774
**Amethyst, Ruby, Gold Earrings,
SeidenGang**

Est.: $1,500-$2,000
Starting Bid: $800

55775
Diamond, White Gold Earrings

Est.: $3,000-$4,000
Starting Bid: $2,000

55776
Aquamarine, Diamond, White Gold Earrings

Est.: $3,600-$4,600
Starting Bid: $2,600

55777
Chalcedony, Diamond, White Gold Earrings

Est.: $2,500-$3,500
Starting Bid: $1,500

55778
Ruby, Diamond, White Gold Earrings

Est.: $3,000-$4,000
Starting Bid: $2,000

55779
Diamond, Gold Earrings

Est.: $1,000-$2,000
Starting Bid: $500

55780
Yellow Sapphire, Diamond, Gold Earrings, Andrew Sarosi

Est.: $1,000-$2,000
Starting Bid: $500

55781
Diamond, Gold Earrings

Est.: $2,500-$3,500
Starting Bid: $1,250

55782
Colored Diamond, Diamond, White Gold Earrings

Est.: $3,000-$4,000
Starting Bid: $1,500

55783
Rose Gold, Titanium Earrings, JAR, French

Est.: $2,000-$3,000
Starting Bid: $1,500

55784
Pink Sapphire, Silver Earrings

Est.: $1,200-$1,600
Starting Bid: $750

55785
Turquoise, Gold Earrings

Est.: $1,800-$2,400
Starting Bid: $1,300

55786
Gold Earrings, Pomellato

Est.: $1,200-$1,600
Starting Bid: $800

55787
Diamond, Rose Gold Earrings

Est.: $2,000-$3,000
Starting Bid: $1,600

55788
Multi-Stone, Diamond, Freshwater Cultured Pearl, Gold Earrings

Est.: $4,000-$5,000
Starting Bid: $3,000

55789
Colored Diamond, Gold Earrings

Est.: $3,000-$4,000
Starting Bid: $1,900

55790
Diamond, White Gold Earrings

Est.: $2,200-$2,800
Starting Bid: $1,800

55791
Diamond, Turquoise, Gold Earrings

Est.: $1,000-$1,500
Starting Bid: $500

55792
Diamond, White Gold Earrings, Hearts on Fire®

Est.: $1,000-$1,500
Starting Bid: $700

55793
Mother-of-Pearl, Gold Earrings

Est.: $1,000-$2,000
Starting Bid: $700

55794
Diamond, South Sea Cultured Pearl, Gold Earrings

Est.: $3,000-$4,000
Starting Bid: $1,500

55795
Diamond, Gold Earrings

Est.: $1,000-$2,000
Starting Bid: $500

55796
Diamond, Gold Earrings, Kieselstein-Cord

Est.: $2,000-$3,000
Starting Bid: $1,000

55797
Diamond, Gold Earrings, Kieselstein-Cord

Est.: $1,200-$1,600
Starting Bid: $600

55798
Multi-Stone, Diamond, White Gold Earrings, Chanel, French

Est.: $3,000-$5,000
Starting Bid: $1,500

55799
Diamond, Gold Earrings, Kieselstein-Cord

Est.: $1,000-$2,000
Starting Bid: $700

55800
Diamond, White Gold Earrings, Chanel, French

Est.: $2,500-$3,500
Starting Bid: $1,500

55801
Sapphire, Diamond, Gold Earrings, Chanel, French

Est.: $2,500-$3,500
Starting Bid: $1,500

55802
Colored Diamond, Cultured Pearl, Gold Earrings, Damiani

Est.: $1,200-$1,600
Starting Bid: $700

55803
Turquoise, Diamond, Gold Earrings

Est.: $1,000-$1,500
Starting Bid: $500

55804
Sapphire, Gold Earrings

Est.: $2,000-$3,000
Starting Bid: $1,560

55805
Coral, Opal, Gold Earrings

Est.: $1,000-$1,500
Starting Bid: $700

55806
Amethyst, Diamond, Gold Earrings

Est.: $1,000-$1,500
Starting Bid: $500

55807
Cultured Pearl, Diamond, Gold Earrings

Est.: $1,000-$1,500
Starting Bid: $500

55808
South Sea Cultured Pearl, Diamond, Gold Earrings

Est.: $1,000-$1,500
Starting Bid: $500

55809
Mabe Pearl, Diamond, Gold Earrings

Est.: $1,000-$1,500
Starting Bid: $500

55810
South Sea Cultured Pearl, Diamond, Gold Earrings

Est.: $1,500-$2,500
Starting Bid: $800

55811
Morganite, Diamond, White Gold Earrings, Assil
Est.: $3,000-$4,000
Starting Bid: $2,500

55812
Lapis Lazuli, Diamond, Gold Earrings
Est.: $2,400-$2,800
Starting Bid: $1,800

55813
Turquoise, Diamond, White Gold Earrings
Est.: $1,800-$2,400
Starting Bid: $1,400

55814
Coral, Diamond, Sapphire, Gold Earrings
Est.: $2,000-$3,000
Starting Bid: $1,400

55815
Moonstone, Diamond, White Gold Earrings
Est.: $2,400-$2,800
Starting Bid: $1,800

55816
Diamond, Rose Gold Earrings
Est.: $2,000-$3,000
Starting Bid: $1,500

55817
Multi-Stone, Diamond, Gold Earrings
Est.: $1,500-$2,000
Starting Bid: $1,000

55818
Diamond, White Gold Earrings
Est.: $3,000-$4,000
Starting Bid: $2,000

55819
Amethyst, Colored Diamond, Gold Earrings
Est.: $1,000-$2,000
Starting Bid: $750

55820
Multi-Stone, Diamond, Gold Earrings
Est.: $1,500-$2,000
Starting Bid: $800

55821
Diamond, Enamel, White Gold Earrings
Est.: $1,500-$2,500
Starting Bid: $750

55822
Diamond, Emerald, White Gold Earrings
Est.: $2,000-$3,000
Starting Bid: $1,000

55823
Diamond, Pink Sapphire, Gold Earrings

Est.: $2,000-$3,000
Starting Bid: $1,000

55824
Diamond, White Gold Earrings

Est.: $2,000-$2,500
Starting Bid: $1,000

55825
Diamond, Gold Earrings, Wempe

Est.: $1,500-$2,000
Starting Bid: $750

55826
Diamond, White Gold Earrings

Est.: $3,000-$5,000
Starting Bid: $2,000

55827
Tanzanite, Diamond, Gold Earrings

Est.: $1,000-$1,500
Starting Bid: $500

55828
Diamond, Gold Earrings

Est.: $1,500-$2,000
Starting Bid: $750

55829
Diamond, Gold Earrings, Neiman Marcus

Est.: $2,500-$3,500
Starting Bid: $1,250

55830
Diamond, Rose Gold Earrings

Est.: $3,000-$5,000
Starting Bid: $1,500

55831
Citrine, Diamond, Gold Earrings

Est.: $2,500-$4,500
Starting Bid: $1,500

55832
Diamond, White Gold Earrings

Est.: $2,000-$3,000
Starting Bid: $1,100

55833
Pink Tourmaline, Pink Sapphire, Diamond, Gold Earrings

Est.: $2,000-$3,000
Starting Bid: $1,000

55834
Diamond, Gold Earrings

Est.: $2,000-$3,000
Starting Bid: $1,000

55835
Coral, Diamond, Gold Earrings

Est.: $2,000-$3,000
Starting Bid: $1,000

55836
Diamond, Gold Earrings

Est.: $1,000-$2,000
Starting Bid: $500

55837
Diamond, Gold Earrings

Est.: $2,000-$3,000
Starting Bid: $1,000

55838
Multi-Stone, Diamond, Gold Earrings

Est.: $1,000-$2,000
Starting Bid: $500

55839
Gold Earrings, Henry Dunay

Est.: $1,000-$2,000
Starting Bid: $500

55840
Enamel, Gold Earrings

Est.: $3,000-$4,000
Starting Bid: $2,000

55841
Multi-Stone, Colored Diamond, Gold Earrings

Est.: $1,000-$2,000
Starting Bid: $500

55842
Multi-Stone, Diamond, Gold Earrings

Est.: $1,000-$2,000
Starting Bid: $750

55843
Diamond, Rose Gold Earrings

Est.: $1,000-$2,000
Starting Bid: $500

55844
Diamond, Rose Gold Earrings

Est.: $1,000-$1,500
Starting Bid: $500

55845
South Sea Cultured Pearl, Diamond, Gold Ear Pendants

Est.: $1,000-$1,500
Starting Bid: $750

55846
Multi-Stone, Diamond, Gold Earrings

Est.: $2,000-$3,000
Starting Bid: $1,000

55847
Diamond, Platinum Earrings

Est.: $3,000-$4,000
Starting Bid: $1,500

55848
Diamond, White Gold Earrings

Est.: $3,000-$4,000
Starting Bid: $1,500

55849
Gold Necklace, Cartier

Est.: $3,000-$4,000
Starting Bid: $2,000

55850
**Jadeite Jade, Quartz,
Gold Necklace**

Est.: $1,000-$1,500
Starting Bid: $500

55851
Jadeite Jade, Gold Necklace

Est.: $1,000-$1,500
Starting Bid: $500

55852
**Lapis Lazuli, Diamond,
White Gold Necklace**

Est.: $1,500-$2,000
Starting Bid: $1,000

55853
**Citrine, Diamond, Gold
Pendant-Necklace**

Est.: $1,500-$2,000
Starting Bid: $800

55854
Gold Necklace, Tiffany & Co.

Est.: $3,000-$4,000
Starting Bid: $2,500

55855
**Colored Diamond, Diamond,
Rose Gold Necklace**

Est.: $4,000-$6,000
Starting Bid: $2,600

55856
**Pink Sapphire, Cultured Pearl,
White Gold Necklace**

Est.: $1,000-$1,500
Starting Bid: $700

55857
**Colored Diamond, Diamond,
White Gold Necklace**

Est.: $1,500-$2,000
Starting Bid: $1,200

55858
Gold Necklace, Pomellato

Est.: $1,200-$1,600
Starting Bid: $900

55859
Diamond, White Gold Necklace

Est.: $4,000-$5,000
Starting Bid: $2,000

55860
Emerald, Diamond, Gold Necklace, Elsa Peretti for Tiffany & Co.

Est.: $1,200-$1,500
Starting Bid: $800

55864
Coral, Diamond, White Gold Necklace

Est.: $1,500-$2,500
Starting Bid: $1,000

55868
Coral Necklace

Est.: $1,000-$2,000
Starting Bid: $700

55861
Gold Necklace, Cartier, French

Est.: $2,000-$3,000
Starting Bid: $1,600

55865
Cultured Pearl, Diamond, Platinum Necklace

Est.: $2,000-$3,000
Starting Bid: $1,000

55869
Amethyst, Diamond, Gold Necklace

Est.: $1,000-$1,500
Starting Bid: $500

55862
Art Nouveau Coral, Diamond, Gold Necklace

Est.: $3,000-$4,000
Starting Bid: $2,200

55866
Gold Necklace

Est.: $2,000-$3,000
Starting Bid: $1,500

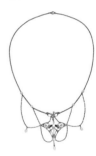

55870
Art Nouveau Diamond, Enamel, Freshwater Cultured Pearl, Gold Necklace

Est.: $1,000-$1,500
Starting Bid: $500

55863
Conch Pearl, Diamond, White Gold Necklace

Est.: $2,500-$3,500
Starting Bid: $1,800

55867
Amethyst, Gold Necklace

Est.: $3,000-$5,000
Starting Bid: $1,500

55871
Cultured Pearl, Gold Necklace

Est.: $1,000-$1,500
Starting Bid: $500

55872
Coral, Gold Necklace
Est.: $1,000-$1,500
Starting Bid: $500

55876
Diamond, Gold Necklace
Est.: $1,500-$2,500
Starting Bid: $900

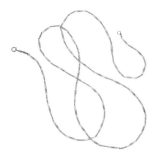

55880
Gold Necklace
Est.: $1,000-$1,500
Starting Bid: $500

55873
**Coral, Diamond, Lapis Lazuli,
Gold Necklace**
Est.: $3,000-$5,000
Starting Bid: $1,500

55877
Diamond, Rose Gold Necklace
Est.: $2,500-$4,500
Starting Bid: $1,600

55881
Diamond, White Gold Necklace
Est.: $3,000-$5,000
Starting Bid: $1,500

55874
Gold Necklace
Est.: $1,500-$2,000
Starting Bid: $750

55878
Sapphire, White Gold Necklace
Est.: $1,000-$1,500
Starting Bid: $600

55882
Enamel, Gold Necklace
Est.: $1,000-$1,500
Starting Bid: $500

55875
**Colored Diamond, Coral,
Peridot, Gold Necklace**
Est.: $3,000-$4,000
Starting Bid: $1,500

55879
**Edwardian Peridot, Freshwater
Cultured Pearl, Gold Necklace**
Est.: $2,000-$3,000
Starting Bid: $1,000

55883
Diamond, White Gold Necklace
Est.: $1,000-$1,500
Starting Bid: $500

55884
Gold Necklace

Est.: $2,000-$3,000
Starting Bid: $1,000

55885
Antique Diamond, Cultured Pearl, Silver Brooch-Necklace

Est.: $1,000-$1,500
Starting Bid: $500

55886
Cultured Pearl Necklace

Est.: $1,000-$1,500
Starting Bid: $500

55887
Multi-Stone, Gold Necklace

Est.: $1,000-$1,500
Starting Bid: $500

55888
Diamond, Gold Necklace

Est.: $1,500-$2,000
Starting Bid: $750

55889
Sapphire, Diamond, Gold Necklace

Est.: $3,000-$5,000
Starting Bid: $2,000

55890
Sapphire, Diamond, White Gold Necklace

Est.: $1,000-$1,500
Starting Bid: $800

55891
Yellow Sapphire, Colored Diamond, Gold Necklace, de Grisogono

Est.: $2,000-$3,000
Starting Bid: $1,000

55892
Gold Coin, Gold Necklace

Est.: $4,000-$6,000
Starting Bid: $2,000

55893
Multi-Stone, Vermeil Necklace, Frank Ancona

Est.: $3,000-$5,000
Starting Bid: $2,400

55894
Turquoise, Diamond, Rock Crystal Quartz, White Gold Necklace

Est.: $2,000-$3,000
Starting Bid: $1,000

55895
Amethyst, Gold Necklace

Est.: $2,000-$3,000
Starting Bid: $1,000

55896
Multi-Stone, Gold Necklace
Est.: $3,000-$4,000
Starting Bid: $1,500

55900
Diamond, Gold Necklace
Est.: $2,000-$3,000
Starting Bid: $1,500

55904
Rose Quartz, Gold Necklace
Est.: $3,000-$4,000
Starting Bid: $2,000

55897
Turquoise, Gold Necklace, David Yurman
Est.: $1,000-$2,000
Starting Bid: $500

55901
Chrysoprase, Gold Necklace
Est.: $2,000-$3,000
Starting Bid: $1,000

55905
Multi-Stone, Gold Necklace
Est.: $2,000-$3,000
Starting Bid: $1,500

55898
Quartz, Gold Necklace
Est.: $1,000-$2,000
Starting Bid: $800

55902
Multi-Stone, Gold Necklace
Est.: $4,000-$6,000
Starting Bid: $3,500

55906
Multi-Stone, Diamond, Gold Necklace
Est.: $2,000-$3,000
Starting Bid: $1,000

55899
**Amethyst, Diamond, Gold
Pendant-Necklace**
Est.: $3,000-$4,000
Starting Bid: $2,000

55903
Moonstone, Gold Necklace
Est.: $3,000-$4,000
Starting Bid: $2,000

55907
**Pink Tourmaline, Diamond,
Gold Necklace**
Est.: $2,000-$3,000
Starting Bid: $1,000

55908
**Diamond, Gold Necklace,
Van Cleef & Arpels**

Est.: $2,000-$3,000
Starting Bid: $1,000

55909
Malachite, Gold Necklace

Est.: $1,000-$2,000
Starting Bid: $750

55910
Turquoise, Gold Necklace

Est.: $2,000-$3,000
Starting Bid: $1,000

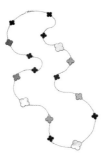

55911
Multi-Stone, Gold Necklace

Est.: $2,000-$3,000
Starting Bid: $1,000

55912
Enamel, Gold Necklace

Est.: $3,000-$5,000
Starting Bid: $2,500

55913
Carnelian, Gold Necklace

Est.: $2,000-$3,000
Starting Bid: $1,000

55914
Diamond, Cultured Pearl, Gold Necklace

Est.: $1,000-$1,500
Starting Bid: $500

55915
Diamond, Gold Necklace

Est.: $2,000-$3,000
Starting Bid: $1,000

55916
Diamond, Gold Pendant-Necklace

Est.: $1,000-$2,000
Starting Bid: $500

55917
**Gold Coin, Peridot, Gold
Pendant-Necklace**

Est.: $1,000-$2,000
Starting Bid: $500

55918
Victorian Amethyst, Gold Necklace

Est.: $2,000-$3,000
Starting Bid: $1,000

55919
**Cultured Pearl, Emerald, Diamond,
Gold, Silver Necklace**

Est.: $1,500-$2,000
Starting Bid: $1,000

55920
Blue Topaz, White Gold Necklace

Est.: $1,000-$1,500
Starting Bid: $700

55921
Gold Necklace

Est.: $2,500-$3,500
Starting Bid: $1,250

55922
Hessonite Garnet, Gold Necklace, Andrew Sarosi

Est.: $1,000-$2,000
Starting Bid: $500

55923
Smoky Quartz, Diamond, Gold, Silver Pendant-Necklace, Andrew Sarosi

Est.: $1,000-$2,000
Starting Bid: $500

55924
Diamond, White Gold Necklace

Est.: $3,000-$4,000
Starting Bid: $2,000

55925
Coral, Gold Necklace, Seaman Schepps

Est.: $3,000-$4,000
Starting Bid: $2,000

55926
Coral, Gold Necklace, Seaman Schepps

Est.: $2,500-$3,500
Starting Bid: $1,500

55927
Gold Necklace

Est.: $1,000-$1,500
Starting Bid: $600

55928
Colored Diamond, Gold Necklace

Est.: $3,000-$4,000
Starting Bid: $2,400

55929
Diamond, Rose Gold Necklace

Est.: $1,500-$2,000
Starting Bid: $1,000

55930
Diamond, White Gold Necklace

Est.: $1,800-$2,400
Starting Bid: $1,500

55931
Jadeite Jade, White Metal Necklace

Est.: $1,000-$1,500
Starting Bid: $500

55932
South Sea Cultured Pearl, Diamond, Gold Necklace

Est.: $1,500-$2,000
Starting Bid: $750

55933
Mother-of-Pearl, Gold Necklace

Est.: $1,500-$2,500
Starting Bid: $900

55934
Cultured Pearl, White Gold Necklace, Mikimoto

Est.: $1,000-$1,500
Starting Bid: $500

55935
Emerald, Diamond, White Gold Necklace

Est.: $5,000-$7,000
Starting Bid: $3,000

55936
Pink Topaz, Diamond, Gold Pendant-Necklace, Judith Ripka

Est.: $1,500-$2,500
Starting Bid: $750

55937
Diamond, Multi-Stone, Cultured Pearl, Silver Necklace, LA Stein

Est.: $1,000-$1,500
Starting Bid: $500

55938
Diamond, Cultured Pearl, White Gold Necklace, Devon Page McCleary

Est.: $1,500-$2,500
Starting Bid: $750

55939
Diamond, Gold Necklace

Est.: $3,000-$4,000
Starting Bid: $2,000

55940
Emerald, Diamond, White Gold Necklace

Est.: $3,000-$4,000
Starting Bid: $2,500

55941
Opal, Diamond, White Gold Necklace

Est.: $3,000-$4,000
Starting Bid: $1,800

55942
Coral, Gold Necklace

Est.: $2,000-$3,000
Starting Bid: $1,000

55943
Blue Topaz, Diamond, Gold Necklace

Est.: $4,000-$6,000
Starting Bid: $2,000

55944
Diamond, White Gold Necklace

Est.: $3,000-$4,000
Starting Bid: $1,500

55948
Ruby, Freshwater Cultured Pearl, Gold Necklace, Gurhan

Est.: $1,000-$1,500
Starting Bid: $500

55952
Coral, Gold Necklaces

Est.: $1,000-$1,500
Starting Bid: $500

55945
Opal, Diamond, Gold Necklace

Est.: $1,200-$1,800
Starting Bid: $800

55949
Emerald, Diamond, Gold Necklace

Est.: $3,000-$4,000
Starting Bid: $2,000

55953
Coral, Gold Necklace

Est.: $1,500-$2,500
Starting Bid: $800

55946
Opal, Diamond, Gold Pendant-Necklace

Est.: $2,500-$3,000
Starting Bid: $1,250

55950
Diamond, Platinum, White Gold Necklace

Est.: $4,000-$6,000
Starting Bid: $2,000

55954
Diamond, Gold Lighter, Cartier

Est.: $1,000-$2,000
Starting Bid: $500

55947
Diamond, White Gold Necklace

Est.: $4,000-$6,000
Starting Bid: $2,800

55951
Diamond, White Gold Pendant-Necklace, Chopard

Est.: $2,500-$3,500
Starting Bid: $1,850

55955
Diamond, Ruby, Gold Coin, Gold Money Clip

Est.: $3,000-$5,000
Starting Bid: $1,500

55956
Multi-Stone, Gold Pendant,
Temple St. Clair

Est.: $1,800-$2,400
Starting Bid: $1,100

55957
Diamond, Ruby, Platinum Charm

Est.: $1,500-$2,000
Starting Bid: $1,000

55958
Diamond, White Gold Pendant

Est.: $1,200-$1,600
Starting Bid: $800

55959
Aquamarine, Diamond, White Gold
Pendant-Necklace, H. Stern

Est.: $3,000-$4,000
Starting Bid: $1,900

55960
Diamond, White Gold Pendant-Necklace

Est.: $2,000-$3,000
Starting Bid: $1,400

55961
Diamond, Gold Pendant-
Necklace, Chopard

Est.: $1,000-$1,500
Starting Bid: $650

55962
Sapphire, Diamond, White Gold
Pendant-Necklace

Est.: $2,000-$3,000
Starting Bid: $1,500

55963
Peridot, Diamond, Silver-Topped
Gold Pendant

Est.: $2,000-$3,000
Starting Bid: $1,500

55964
Diamond, Synthetic Sapphire,
Platinum, White Gold Pendant

Est.: $1,500-$2,500
Starting Bid: $750

55965
South Sea Cultured Pearl,
Diamond, White Gold Pendant

Est.: $3,000-$4,000
Starting Bid: $1,500

55966
Lapis Lazuli, Gold Pendant-Necklace

Est.: $3,000-$4,000
Starting Bid: $1,500

55967
Pink Tourmaline, Peridot,
Diamond, White Gold Pendant

Est.: $3,400-$3,800
Starting Bid: $2,400

55968
Peridot, Diamond, White Gold Pendant

Est.: $3,400-$3,800
Starting Bid: $2,400

55972
Jadeite Jade, Gold Pendant

Est.: $1,000-$1,500
Starting Bid: $500

55976
Diamond, Ruby, Cultured Pearl, White Gold Pendant-Brooch-Necklace

Est.: $1,200-$1,600
Starting Bid: $600

55969
Black Opal, Diamond, Enamel, Gold Pendant

Est.: $3,500-$4,500
Starting Bid: $2,500

55973
Multi-Stone, Diamond, Gold Pendant

Est.: $1,500-$2,500
Starting Bid: $750

55977
Diamond, White Gold Pendant-Necklace

Est.: $1,000-$1,500
Starting Bid: $500

55970
Jade, Gold Pendant, Van Cleef & Arpels, French

Est.: $1,000-$2,000
Starting Bid: $500

55974
Multi-Stone, Gold Pendant

Est.: $1,000-$1,500
Starting Bid: $500

55978
Diamond, Gold Coin, Gold Pendant

Est.: $1,000-$2,000
Starting Bid: $500

55971
Opal, Gold Pendant

Est.: $1,000-$1,500
Starting Bid: $1,000

55975
Diamond, Ruby, Gold Pendant

Est.: $1,000-$1,500
Starting Bid: $500

55979
Gold Pendant, Kieselstein-Cord

Est.: $1,000-$2,000
Starting Bid: $500

55980
Citrine, Diamond, Gold Pendant-Necklace
Est.: $1,000-$2,000
Starting Bid: $500

55984
Diamond, White Gold Pendant-Necklace, Stephen Webster
Est.: $1,000-$1,500
Starting Bid: $500

55988
Multi-Stone, Diamond, Rose Gold Pendant-Necklace
Est.: $1,000-$2,000
Starting Bid: $500

55981
Diamond, Ruby, Gold Enhancer
Est.: $2,000-$3,000
Starting Bid: $1,000

55985
Ruby, Diamond, Gold Pendant
Est.: $2,000-$3,000
Starting Bid: $1,000

55989
Multi-Stone, Gold Enhancer-Pendant, Andrew Sarosi
Est.: $1,000-$2,000
Starting Bid: $500

55982
Gold Coin, Gold Pendant
Est.: $1,500-$2,000
Starting Bid: $1,000

55986
Diamond, Ruby, Gold Pendant-Brooch
Est.: $3,000-$4,000
Starting Bid: $2,000

55990
Jadeite Jade Pendant
Est.: $2,000-$3,000
Starting Bid: $1,000

55983
Opal, Diamond, Emerald, Gold Pendant
Est.: $2,000-$3,000
Starting Bid: $1,000

55987
Diamond, Ruby, Gold Pendant-Necklace
Est.: $1,500-$2,000
Starting Bid: $1,000

55991
Jadeite Jade Pendant
Est.: $2,000-$3,000
Starting Bid: $1,200

55992
Jadeite Jade Pendant

Est.: $1,000-$1,500
Starting Bid: $500

55993
Victorian Hardstone Cameo,
Half-Pearl, Diamond, Gold Pendant

Est.: $1,000-$1,500
Starting Bid: $500

55994
Ruby, Diamond, Enamel,
Gold Pendant-Brooch

Est.: $1,000-$1,500
Starting Bid: $500

55995
Diamond, Gold Pendant-Necklace

Est.: $1,000-$2,000
Starting Bid: $800

55996
Mother-of-Pearl, Gold Pendant-
Necklace, Bvlgari

Est.: $2,500-$3,500
Starting Bid: $2,000

55997
Diamond, White Gold Pendant-
Necklace, Devon Page McCleary

Est.: $1,000-$1,500
Starting Bid: $500

55998
Colored Diamond, Diamond, Gold
Jewelry, Devon Page McCleary

Est.: $2,000-$3,000
Starting Bid: $1,000

55999
Tourmaline, Diamond, Gold,
Stainless Steel Pendant-Necklace

Est.: $1,500-$2,500
Starting Bid: $1,200

56000
Colored Diamond, Gold
Pendant-Brooch-Necklace

Est.: $2,000-$3,000
Starting Bid: $1,500

56001
South Sea Cultured Pearl, Diamond,
Gold Enhancer-Pendant

Est.: $1,500-$2,000
Starting Bid: $900

56002
South Sea Cultured Pearl, Diamond,
Gold Enhancer-Pendant

Est.: $1,200-$1,600
Starting Bid: $700

56003
Diamond, White Gold Pendant

Est.: $1,000-$1,500
Starting Bid: $500

56004
Ceylon Sapphire, Gold Pendant

Est.: $3,000-$4,000
Starting Bid: $1,500

56005
Diamond, Synthetic Sapphire, Platinum, White Gold Pendant-Necklace

Est.: $1,500-$2,000
Starting Bid: $750

56006
Aquamarine, Diamond, Gold Pendant

Est.: $1,500-$2,000
Starting Bid: $750

56007
Multi-Stone, Gold Charms

Est.: $1,200-$1,500
Starting Bid: $800

56008
Gold Ring, Pomellato

Est.: $3,000-$4,000
Starting Bid: $1,800

56009
South Sea Cultured Pearl, Diamond, Gold Ring

Est.: $3,000-$4,000
Starting Bid: $2,000

56010
Ruby, Gold Ring

Est.: $1,200-$1,600
Starting Bid: $800

56011
Diamond, Turquoise, Gold Ring

Est.: $1,500-$2,000
Starting Bid: $1,000

56012
Aquamarine, Diamond, Gold Ring

Est.: $1,200-$1,600
Starting Bid: $1,000

56013
Sapphire, Diamond, Gold Ring

Est.: $3,000-$4,000
Starting Bid: $1,900

56014
Aquamarine, White Gold Ring

Est.: $3,000-$4,000
Starting Bid: $1,900

56015
Colored Diamond, Gold Ring

Est.: $2,000-$3,000
Starting Bid: $1,000

56016
Multi-Stone, Diamond, Gold Ring

Est.: $1,000-$1,500
Starting Bid: $500

56017
Aquamarine, Diamond, Gold Ring

Est.: $2,000-$3,000
Starting Bid: $1,300

56018
Diamond, Black Onyx, Gold Ring

Est.: $1,500-$2,000
Starting Bid: $800

56019
Diamond, Enamel, Gold Ring, French

Est.: $1,200-$1,600
Starting Bid: $800

56020
Blue Topaz, Gold Ring, Bvlgari

Est.: $1,200-$1,600
Starting Bid: $900

56021
Gentleman's Black Onyx, White Gold Ring, Cartier

Est.: $1,500-$2,000
Starting Bid: $1,200

56022
Diamond, Gold Ring, Cartier

Est.: $1,000-$1,500
Starting Bid: $800

56023
Diamond, White Gold Ring, Bvlgari

Est.: $2,000-$3,000
Starting Bid: $1,400

56024
Tanzanite, Colored Diamond, Diamond, White Gold Ring

Est.: $2,000-$3,000
Starting Bid: $1,700

56025
Tanzanite, Diamond, White Gold Ring

Est.: $1,500-$2,000
Starting Bid: $1,100

56026
Moonstone, Diamond, White Gold Ring, Fred

Est.: $1,000-$1,500
Starting Bid: $600

56027
Diamond, White Gold Ring, Boucheron

Est.: $3,000-$4,000
Starting Bid: $2,200

56028
Diamond, Platinum, Gold Ring, Schlumberger for Tiffany & Co.

Est.: $2,000-$3,000
Starting Bid: $1,400

56029
Diamond, White Gold Ring, Picchiotti

Est.: $1,000-$1,500
Starting Bid: $700

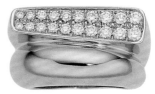

56030
Diamond, Gold Ring, Fred

Est.: $1,000-$1,500
Starting Bid: $750

56031
Colored Diamond, Gold Eternity Band

Est.: $1,000-$1,500
Starting Bid: $600

56032
Diamond, White Gold Ring

Est.: $2,000-$3,000
Starting Bid: $1,000

56033
Peridot, Diamond, Silver-Topped Gold Ring

Est.: $1,500-$2,500
Starting Bid: $1,000

56034
Coral, Gold Ring

Est.: $2,000-$3,000
Starting Bid: $1,500

56036
Victorian Emerald, Diamond, Gold Ring

Est.: $1,500-$2,000
Starting Bid: $900

56037
Diamond, Gold Ring, Bvlgari

Est.: $1,500-$2,000
Starting Bid: $1,000

56038
Diamond, Gold Ring, Bvlgari

Est.: $2,000-$3,000
Starting Bid: $1,000

56039
Diamond, White Gold Ring

Est.: $1,500-$2,500
Starting Bid: $1,000

56040
Diamond, Platinum Ring, Bvlgari

Est.: $2,500-$3,500
Starting Bid: $1,500

56041
Sapphire, Diamond, Rose Gold Ring

Est.: $3,000-$4,000
Starting Bid: $2,000

56042
Cat's-Eye Moonstone, Diamond, Sapphire, White Gold Ring

Est.: $1,500-$2,500
Starting Bid: $1,000

56043
Amethyst, Diamond, Platinum Ring

Est.: $1,500-$2,500
Starting Bid: $1,000

56044
Diamond, Platinum Eternity Band

Est.: $2,000-$3,000
Starting Bid: $1,300

56045
Peridot, Diamond, Platinum Ring

Est.: $3,000-$4,000
Starting Bid: $2,000

56035
Ruby, Diamond, Gold Ring

Est.: $3,000-$4,000
Starting Bid: $2,000

56046
Aquamarine, Sapphire, Diamond, Platinum Ring

Est.: $4,500-$5,500
Starting Bid: $3,500

56047
Yellow Sapphire, Ruby, Diamond, Platinum, Gold Ring

Est.: $4,200-$5,000
Starting Bid: $3,800

56048
Aquamarine, Diamond, Platinum Ring

Est.: $2,500-$3,500
Starting Bid: $1,500

56049
Gentleman's Star Sapphire, Diamond, White Gold Ring

Est.: $1,500-$2,000
Starting Bid: $750

56050
Gentleman's Diamond, Gold Ring

Est.: $2,000-$3,000
Starting Bid: $1,000

56051
Diamond, Gold Ring

Est.: $3,000-$5,000
Starting Bid: $1,500

56052
Diamond, White Gold Eternity Band

Est.: $3,000-$5,000
Starting Bid: $1,500

56053
Diamond, White Gold Ring

Est.: $1,500-$2,000
Starting Bid: $750

56054
Colored Diamond, Diamond, White Gold Ring

Est.: $1,500-$2,500
Starting Bid: $800

56055
Colored Diamond, Diamond, Platinum Ring

Est.: $4,000-$5,000
Starting Bid: $2,000

56056
Gentleman's Emerald, Gold Ring

Est.: $2,000-$3,000
Starting Bid: $1,000

56057
Gentleman's Diamond, Gold Ring, Chopard

Est.: $2,000-$3,000
Starting Bid: $1,000

56058
Gentleman's White Gold Ring, Bvlgari

Est.: $1,000-$1,500
Starting Bid: $500

56059
Diamond, White Gold Ring, Chopard

Est.: $2,000-$3,000
Starting Bid: $1,000

56060
Ruby, Diamond, Gold Ring

Est.: $4,000-$5,000
Starting Bid: $2,000

56061
Ruby, Sapphire, Gold Ring, Cartier

Est.: $1,000-$1,500
Starting Bid: $500

56062
Diamond, Platinum, Gold Ring, Henry Dunay

Est.: $2,000-$3,000
Starting Bid: $1,000

56063
Emerald, Colored Diamond, White Gold Ring

Est.: $1,000-$1,500
Starting Bid: $500

56064
Citrine, Diamond, Gold Ring

Est.: $1,500-$2,000
Starting Bid: $750

56065
Coral, Gold Ring

Est.: $1,500-$2,000
Starting Bid: $750

56066
Coral, Diamond, Gold Ring

Est.: $2,000-$3,000
Starting Bid: $1,000

56067
Aquamarine, Gold Ring, Katy Briscoe

Est.: $2,000-$3,000
Starting Bid: $1,000

56068
Peridot, Gold Ring, Katy Briscoe

Est.: $2,000-$3,000
Starting Bid: $1,000

56069
Pink Tourmaline, Gold Ring, Katy Briscoe

Est.: $2,000-$3,000
Starting Bid: $1,000

56070
Retro Multi-Stone, Diamond, Gold Ring

Est.: $1,500-$2,000
Starting Bid: $750

56071
Coral, Gold Ring

Est.: $1,500-$2,000
Starting Bid: $750

56072
Cachalong, Gold Ring, Pomellato

Est.: $2,500-$3,500
Starting Bid: $1,250

56073
Amethyst, Gold Ring, Pianegonda

Est.: $1,500-$2,000
Starting Bid: $750

56074
Citrine, Gold Ring, Katy Briscoe

Est.: $2,000-$3,000
Starting Bid: $1,000

56075
Jadeite Jade, Rose Gold Ring

Est.: $1,000-$1,500
Starting Bid: $500

56076
Irradiated Diamond, Diamond, White Gold Ring

Est.: $1,200-$1,800
Starting Bid: $600

56077
Diamond, White Gold Eternity Band

Est.: $1,000-$1,500
Starting Bid: $600

56078
Diamond, White Gold Eternity Band

Est.: $4,500-$6,500
Starting Bid: $3,500

56079
Diamond, White Gold Ring

Est.: $1,000-$1,200
Starting Bid: $500

56080
Diamond, Platinum, Gold Ring

Est.: $1,500-$2,500
Starting Bid: $800

56081
Emerald, Diamond, Gold Ring

Est.: $3,000-$5,000
Starting Bid: $1,500

56082
Emerald, Diamond, Rose Gold Ring

Est.: $2,000-$3,000
Starting Bid: $1,100

56083
Sapphire, Diamond, Platinum, Gold Ring

Est.: $2,000-$4,000
Starting Bid: $1,200

56084
Ruby, Diamond, Gold Ring

Est.: $3,000-$5,000
Starting Bid: $2,000

56085
Ruby, Sapphire, Diamond, Gold Ring

Est.: $1,200-$1,800
Starting Bid: $700

56086
Pink Sapphire, Diamond, Gold Ring

Est.: $3,000-$5,000
Starting Bid: $1,500

56087
Colored Diamond, Diamond, Ruby, White Gold Ring

Est.: $1,500-$2,000
Starting Bid: $900

56088
Sapphire, Diamond, White Gold Ring

Est.: $3,000-$5,000
Starting Bid: $2,200

56089
Turquoise, Sapphire, Diamond, White Gold Ring

Est.: $1,500-$2,500
Starting Bid: $900

56090
Sapphire, Diamond, Ruby, Gold Ring

Est.: $2,000-$4,000
Starting Bid: $1,200

56091
Colored Diamond, Diamond, Emerald, White Gold Ring

Est.: $4,000-$6,000
Starting Bid: $2,000

56092
Colombian Emerald, Diamond, Gold Ring

Est.: $9,000-$12,000
Starting Bid: $7,000

56093
Sapphire, Diamond, White Gold Ring

Est.: $2,000-$3,000
Starting Bid: $1,000

56094
Diamond, Gold Ring

Est.: $1,000-$1,500
Starting Bid: $500

56095
Diamond, Gold Ring

Est.: $2,000-$3,000
Starting Bid: $1,000

56096
Emerald, Diamond, Gold Ring

Est.: $2,000-$3,000
Starting Bid: $1,000

56097
Diamond, Rose Gold Ring

Est.: $2,500-$3,500
Starting Bid: $1,900

56098
Diamond, White Gold Ring

Est.: $2,500-$3,500
Starting Bid: $1,500

56099
Turquoise, Diamond, Gold Ring

Est.: $1,000-$1,500
Starting Bid: $500

56100
Sapphire, Diamond, Platinum Ring

Est.: $2,000-$3,000
Starting Bid: $1,000

56101
Colored Diamond, Diamond,
White Gold Ring

Est.: $1,000-$1,500
Starting Bid: $500

56102
Carved Rock Crystal Quartz,
Diamond, White Gold Ring

Est.: $3,000-$5,000
Starting Bid: $1,500

56103
Cultured Pearl, Diamond, Gold Ring

Est.: $1,000-$1,500
Starting Bid: $500

56104
Diamond, Platinum Ring

Est.: $2,000-$3,000
Starting Bid: $1,000

56105
Emerald, Diamond, Gold Ring

Est.: $2,000-$3,000
Starting Bid: $1,000

56106
Sapphire, Diamond, Enamel, Gold Ring

Est.: $2,000-$3,000
Starting Bid: $1,000

56107
Gentleman's Tiger's-Eye
Quartz, Gold Ring, Cartier

Est.: $2,000-$3,000
Starting Bid: $1,000

56108
Multi-Stone, Diamond,
Gold Ring, Cartier

Est.: $2,000-$3,000
Starting Bid: $1,000

56109
Gold Ring, Schlumberger, Tiffany & Co.

Est.: $1,000-$2,000
Starting Bid: $500

56110
Gentleman's Black Onyx, Gold
Ring, Tiffany & Co.

Est.: $1,000-$2,000
Starting Bid: $500

56111
Diamond, Gold Ring, Van Cleef & Arpels

Est.: $2,500-$3,500
Starting Bid: $1,500

56112
Diamond, Ruby, Gold Ring, Lalaounis

Est.: $2,000-$3,000
Starting Bid: $1,000

56113
Colored Diamond, Diamond, Gold Ring

Est.: $1,000-$1,500
Starting Bid: $800

56114
Carnelian, Diamond, Gold, Silver-Topped Gold Ring

Est.: $1,500-$2,500
Starting Bid: $750

56115
Pink Tourmaline, Diamond, White Gold Ring

Est.: $1,500-$2,500
Starting Bid: $750

56116
Diamond Gold Ring

Est.: $1,000-$2,000
Starting Bid: $500

56117
Diamond, Gold Ring, Chopard

Est.: $2,000-$3,000
Starting Bid: $1,000

56118
Diamond, Gold Ring

Est.: $2,000-$3,000
Starting Bid: $1,000

56119
Diamond, Gold Ring

Est.: $2,000-$3,000
Starting Bid: $1,000

56120
Opal, Diamond, White Gold Ring

Est.: $2,000-$3,000
Starting Bid: $1,000

56121
Multi-Stone, Diamond, White Gold Ring

Est.: $1,000-$2,000
Starting Bid: $800

56122
Multi-Stone, Diamond, White Gold Ring

Est.: $1,000-$2,000
Starting Bid: $800

56123
Diamond, Sapphire, Ruby, White Gold Ring

Est.: $2,000-$3,000
Starting Bid: $1,000

56124
Amethyst, Diamond, White Gold Ring

Est.: $1,000-$2,000
Starting Bid: $500

56125
Opal, Diamond, Emerald, White Gold Ring

Est.: $1,000-$2,000
Starting Bid: $500

56126
Colored Diamond, Diamond, White Gold Ring

Est.: $1,000-$2,000
Starting Bid: $500

56127
Diamond, Jadeite Jade, Gold Ring

Est.: $2,000-$3,000
Starting Bid: $1,000

56128
Sapphire, Diamond, Emerald, Gold Ring

Est.: $4,000-$6,000
Starting Bid: $3,000

56129
Amethyst, Gold Ring

Est.: $2,000-$3,000
Starting Bid: $1,000

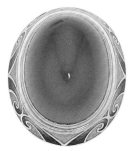

56130
Chalcedony, Enamel, Gold Ring

Est.: $1,000-$2,000
Starting Bid: $500

56131
Diamond, Multi-Stone, White Gold Ring, Kimora Lee Simmons

Est.: $1,000-$2,000
Starting Bid: $500

56132
Diamond, White Gold Ring, Damaso

Est.: $1,000-$2,000
Starting Bid: $500

56133
Pink Tourmaline, Diamond, Gold Ring

Est.: $1,000-$2,000
Starting Bid: $750

56134
Diamond, Pink Sapphire, White Gold Ring

Est.: $2,000-$3,000
Starting Bid: $1,500

56135
Diamond, Multi-Stone, White Gold Ring

Est.: $1,000-$2,000
Starting Bid: $750

56136
Enamel, Diamond, Gold Ring

Est.: $1,000-$2,000
Starting Bid: $500

56137
Gold Ring, Kieselstein-Cord

Est.: $1,000-$2,000
Starting Bid: $500

56138
Pink Tourmaline, Gold, Stainless Steel Ring, Bvlgari

Est.: $1,000-$2,000
Starting Bid: $500

56139
Multi-Stone, Diamond, White Gold Ring

Est.: $2,000-$3,000
Starting Bid: $1,000

56140
Multi-Stone, Colored Diamond, White Gold Ring

Est.: $2,000-$3,000
Starting Bid: $1,000

56141
Ruby, Diamond, Gold Ring

Est.: $2,000-$3,000
Starting Bid: $1,500

56142
Diamond, Gold Ring, Costis

Est.: $1,000-$1,500
Starting Bid: $500

56143
Yellow Sapphire, Diamond, Gold Ring

Est.: $2,000-$3,000
Starting Bid: $1,000

56144
Moonstone, Diamond, White Gold Ring

Est.: $1,000-$2,000
Starting Bid: $500

56145
Diamond, Black Onyx, White Gold Ring

Est.: $1,000-$1,500
Starting Bid: $500

56146
Diamond, White Gold Eternity Band

Est.: $1,000-$2,000
Starting Bid: $500

56147
Peridot, Diamond, Gold Ring, Kieselstein-Cord

Est.: $1,500-$2,000
Starting Bid: $750

56148
Multi-Stone, Diamond, Gold Ring

Est.: $1,000-$1,500
Starting Bid: $500

56149
Diamond, Sapphire, Platinum Ring

Est.: $1,200-$1,500
Starting Bid: $600

56150
Diamond, Gold Ring

Est.: $1,000-$2,000
Starting Bid: $500

56151
Diamond, White Gold Ring

Est.: $2,000-$3,000
Starting Bid: $1,000

56152
Green Tourmaline, Diamond, Platinum Ring

Est.: $1,500-$2,500
Starting Bid: $800

56153
Gentleman's Garnet, Diamond, Gold Ring

Est.: $1,000-$1,500
Starting Bid: $500

56154
Gentleman's Emerald, Gold Ring

Est.: $2,000-$3,000
Starting Bid: $1,000

56155
Goshenite, Diamond, White Gold Ring

Est.: $2,000-$3,000
Starting Bid: $1,000

56156
Multi-Stone, Colored Diamond, Diamond, Gold Ring, LeVian

Est.: $2,000-$3,000
Starting Bid: $1,000

56157
Gentleman's Coin, Gold Ring

Est.: $1,000-$1,500
Starting Bid: $500

56158
Ceylon Sapphire, Diamond, Gold Ring

Est.: $3,000-$5,000
Starting Bid: $2,000

56159
Blue Topaz, Diamond, White Gold Ring

Est.: $1,000-$1,500
Starting Bid: $500

56160
Diamond, Platinum, Gold Ring

Est.: $1,000-$2,000
Starting Bid: $500

56161
Diamond, White Gold Ring

Est.: $1,000-$2,000
Starting Bid: $500

56162
Art Deco Diamond, Platinum Eternity Band, Tiffany & Co.

Est.: $1,000-$2,000
Starting Bid: $500

56163
Pink Tourmaline, Diamond, Gold Ring

Est.: $2,500-$3,500
Starting Bid: $1,500

56164
Aquamarine, Diamond, Gold Ring

Est.: $2,500-$3,500
Starting Bid: $1,500

56165
Gold Ring, Henry Dunay

Est.: $1,500-$2,000
Starting Bid: $1,000

56166
Diamond, Platinum Eternity Band, Tiffany & Co.

Est.: $900-$1,200
Starting Bid: $750

56167
Diamond, Platinum Eternity Band, Tiffany & Co.

Est.: $1,200-$1,500
Starting Bid: $1,000

56168
Diamond, Rock Crystal Quartz, Gold Ring, Mauboussin

Est.: $1,000-$2,000
Starting Bid: $500

56169
Emerald, Diamond, Platinum Ring

Est.: $3,000-$5,000
Starting Bid: $1,500

56170
Colored Diamond, Diamond, Platinum Ring

Est.: $1,000-$3,000
Starting Bid: $500

56171
Gentleman's Diamond, Multi-Stone, Gold Ring

Est.: $1,000-$2,000
Starting Bid: $500

56172
Gentleman's Diamond, Synthetic Sapphire, White Gold Ring

Est.: $1,500-$2,500
Starting Bid: $750

56173
Diamond, Gold Ring Set

Est.: $1,200-$1,600
Starting Bid: $600

56174
Colombian Emerald, Diamond, White Gold Ring

Est.: $3,000-$4,000
Starting Bid: $2,000

56175
Ruby, Diamond, Gold Ring

Est.: $1,000-$2,000
Starting Bid: $500

56176
Garnet, Diamond, Gold Ring

Est.: $1,000-$1,500
Starting Bid: $500

56177
Multi-Stone, Gold Ring, Andrew Sarosi

Est.: $1,000-$2,000
Starting Bid: $500

56178
Diamond, White Gold Ring

Est.: $2,500-$3,500
Starting Bid: $1,250

56179
Diamond, White Gold Ring

Est.: $1,000-$1,500
Starting Bid: $500

56180
Diamond, Gold Ring

Est.: $1,500-$2,000
Starting Bid: $750

56181
South Sea Cultured Pearl, Diamond, White Gold Ring, Robert Wan

Est.: $2,000-$3,000
Starting Bid: $1,000

56182
Diamond, Gold Ring

Est.: $1,500-$2,000
Starting Bid: $750

56183
Pink Sapphire, Gold Ring

Est.: $1,000-$1,500
Starting Bid: $500

56184
Multi-Stone, Diamond, White Gold Ring

Est.: $2,000-$3,000
Starting Bid: $1,000

56185
Blue Topaz, Diamond, Gold Ring

Est.: $1,000-$1,500
Starting Bid: $500

56186
Aquamarine, Gold Ring

Est.: $1,500-$2,000
Starting Bid: $750

56187
Aquamarine, Diamond, Gold Ring

Est.: $1,500-$2,000
Starting Bid: $750

56188
Amethyst, Diamond, Gold Ring

Est.: $2,500-$3,000
Starting Bid: $1,250

56189
South Sea Cultured Pearl, Gold Ring

Est.: $1,500-$2,000
Starting Bid: $750

56190
Gold Ring, Cartier, French

Est.: $1,500-$2,000
Starting Bid: $1,000

56191
Diamond, Gold Ring, Yossi Harari

Est.: $2,000-$3,000
Starting Bid: $1,300

56192
Diamond, Emerald, Gold Ring

Est.: $1,000-$1,500
Starting Bid: $500

56193
Garnet, Gold Ring

Est.: $1,000-$1,500
Starting Bid: $500

56194
Tanzanite, Diamond, Platinum Ring

Est.: $3,000-$4,000
Starting Bid: $1,500

56195
**South Sea Cultured Pearl,
Multi-Stone, White Gold Ring**

Est.: $1,500-$2,000
Starting Bid: $800

56196
Diamond, Gold Ring, Tiffany & Co.

Est.: $1,000-$1,500
Starting Bid: $500

56197
Tanzanite, Diamond, White Gold Ring

Est.: $1,000-$1,500
Starting Bid: $600

56198
Sapphire, Diamond, White Gold Ring

Est.: $1,500-$2,000
Starting Bid: $1,000

56199
Diamond, White Gold Ring

Est.: $1,500-$2,000
Starting Bid: $1,200

56200
Diamond, Ruby, Gold Ring

Est.: $1,500-$2,000
Starting Bid: $800

56201
Tanzanite, Diamond, Gold Ring

Est.: $1,000-$2,000
Starting Bid: $500

56202
Diamond, White Gold Ring

Est.: $1,500-$2,000
Starting Bid: $800

56203
Diamond, White Gold Ring

Est.: $2,000-$3,000
Starting Bid: $1,000

56204
Diamond, Platinum Ring

Est.: $1,500-$2,000
Starting Bid: $800

56205
Diamond, Sapphire, White Gold Ring

Est.: $2,000-$3,000
Starting Bid: $1,200

56206
Sapphire, Diamond, White Gold Ring

Est.: $1,000-$2,000
Starting Bid: $500

56207
Diamond, Ruby, Gold Ring

Est.: $1,000-$1,500
Starting Bid: $700

56208
Amethyst, Gold Ring

Est.: $1,000-$1,200
Starting Bid: $500

56209
Diamond, Sapphire, Gold Ring

Est.: $1,000-$2,000
Starting Bid: $700

56210
Cultured Pearl, Gold Ring, Cartier

Est.: $1,000-$2,000
Starting Bid: $800

56211
Citrine, Diamond, Gold Ring

Est.: $1,500-$2,000
Starting Bid: $750

56212
Diamond, White Gold
Ring, Hearts on Fire®

Est.: $2,000-$3,000
Starting Bid: $1,000

56213
Diamond, White Gold Ring, Neil Joseph

Est.: $1,000-$1,500
Starting Bid: $500

56214
Diamond, White Gold Ring

Est.: $1,000-$1,500
Starting Bid: $500

56215
Diamond, Gold Ring, Kieselstein-Cord

Est.: $1,000-$2,000
Starting Bid: $500

56216
Citrine, Diamond, Gold
Ring, Kieselstein-Cord

Est.: $1,200-$1,600
Starting Bid: $600

56217
Pink Quartz, Diamond, Gold
Ring, Judith Ripka

Est.: $1,000-$2,000
Starting Bid: $500

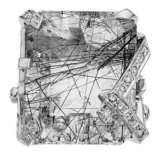

56218
Rutilated Quartz, Diamond, White
Gold Ring, Chanel, French

Est.: $3,000-$4,000
Starting Bid: $1,500

56219
Brown Sapphire, Gold Ring, Gurhan

Est.: $1,000-$1,500
Starting Bid: $500

56220
Gold Ring, Vhernier

Est.: $2,000-$3,000
Starting Bid: $1,000

56221
**Colored Diamond, Diamond,
White Gold Ring**

Est.: $3,000-$4,000
Starting Bid: $2,000

56222
**Colored Diamond, Diamond,
White Gold Ring**

Est.: $2,000-$3,000
Starting Bid: $1,000

56223
Sapphire, Diamond, White Gold Ring

Est.: $2,000-$3,000
Starting Bid: $1,000

56224
**Colored Diamond, Diamond,
White Gold Ring**

Est.: $2,000-$3,000
Starting Bid: $1,000

56225
Diamond, White Gold Ring

Est.: $1,000-$2,000
Starting Bid: $500

56226
Kunzite, Colored Diamond, Gold Ring

Est.: $1,000-$2,000
Starting Bid: $500

56227
Kunzite, Diamond, White Gold Ring

Est.: $1,000-$2,000
Starting Bid: $500

56228
**Citrine, Colored Diamond,
White Gold Ring**

Est.: $1,000-$2,000
Starting Bid: $500

56229
Citrine, Blue Topaz, White Gold Ring

Est.: $1,000-$2,000
Starting Bid: $500

56230
Prasiolite, Diamond, Gold Ring

Est.: $1,000-$2,000
Starting Bid: $500

56231
Citrine, Diamond, Gold Ring, Sarosi

Est.: $2,000-$3,000
Starting Bid: $1,500

56232
Diamond, Gold Ring

Est.: $1,000-$1,500
Starting Bid: $500

56233
Sapphire, Diamond, White Gold Ring

Est.: $4,000-$6,000
Starting Bid: $2,000

56234
Garnet, Diamond, White Gold Ring

Est.: $3,000-$4,000
Starting Bid: $1,500

56235
Sphene, Tourmaline, Gold Ring, Sarosi

Est.: $2,000-$3,000
Starting Bid: $1,500

56236
Pink Tourmaline, Diamond, White Gold Ring, Sarosi

Est.: $3,000-$4,000
Starting Bid: $1,500

56237
Zircon, Ruby, Diamond, Gold Ring, Sarosi

Est.: $3,000-$4,000
Starting Bid: $1,500

56238
Diamond, Gold Ring

Est.: $1,000-$1,500
Starting Bid: $500

56239
South Sea Cultured Pearl, Diamond, Gold Ring

Est.: $1,000-$1,500
Starting Bid: $650

56240
Diamond, Gold Ring

Est.: $2,000-$3,000
Starting Bid: $1,300

56241
South Sea Cultured Pearl, Diamond, Gold Ring

Est.: $1,000-$1,500
Starting Bid: $750

56242
South Sea Cultured Pearl, Diamond, Gold Ring

Est.: $1,000-$1,500
Starting Bid: $500

56243
South Sea Cultured Pearl, Diamond, Gold Ring

Est.: $2,000-$3,000
Starting Bid: $1,250

56244
Turquoise, Diamond, White Gold Ring

Est.: $3,000-$4,000
Starting Bid: $2,000

56245
White Onyx, Diamond, Enamel, White Gold Ring

Est.: $1,200-$1,600
Starting Bid: $900

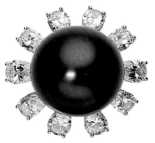

56246
South Sea Cultured Pearl, Diamond, Platinum Ring

Est.: $2,000-$3,000
Starting Bid: $1,000

56247
Coral, Diamond, Gold Ring

Est.: $2,000-$3,000
Starting Bid: $1,000

56248
Turquoise, Diamond, Ruby, Gold Ring

Est.: $3,000-$5,000
Starting Bid: $1,500

56249
Kunzite, Diamond, Gold Ring

Est.: $2,000-$3,000
Starting Bid: $1,000

56250
Tanzanite, Diamond, Gold Ring

Est.: $3,000-$4,000
Starting Bid: $1,500

56251
Fancy Sapphire, Diamond, Gold Ring

Est.: $3,000-$4,000
Starting Bid: $1,500

56252
Diamond, White Gold Ring

Est.: $2,000-$3,000
Starting Bid: $1,000

56253
Diamond, White Gold Ring

Est.: $3,000-$4,000
Starting Bid: $1,500

56254
Colored Diamond, Diamond, White Gold Ring

Est.: $2,000-$3,000
Starting Bid: $1,000

56255
Sapphire, Diamond, Gold Ring

Est.: $7,000-$9,000
Starting Bid: $5,000

56256
Diamond, Platinum, Gold Ring

Est.: $3,000-$5,000
Starting Bid: $1,500

56257
Diamond, Gold Ring

Est.: $4,000-$6,000
Starting Bid: $2,500

56258
Diamond, Enamel, Gold Ring, La Nouvelle Bague

Est.: $1,800-$2,400
Starting Bid: $1,150

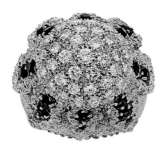

56259
Diamond, Sapphire, Gold Ring

Est.: $2,000-$3,000
Starting Bid: $1,500

56260
**Colored Diamond, Diamond,
Rose Gold Eternity Bands**

Est.: $3,000-$4,000
Starting Bid: $1,900

56261
**Diamond, Multi-Stone,
Platinum Eternity Bands**

Est.: $2,000-$3,000
Starting Bid: $1,000

56262
Diamond, Platinum Ring Set

Est.: $3,000-$4,000
Starting Bid: $2,300

56263
**Diamond, Platinum, White
Gold Jewelry Suite**

Est.: $1,500-$2,500
Starting Bid: $1,000

56264
Coral, Diamond, Gold Jewelry Suite

Est.: $1,500-$2,000
Starting Bid: $750

56265
Gold Jewelry

Est.: $2,500-$3,500
Starting Bid: $1,250

56266
**South Sea Cultured Pearl, Cultured
Pearl, Diamond, Gold Jewelry**

Est.: $4,000-$6,000
Starting Bid: $2,000

56267
**Opal, Black Onyx, Diamond,
White Gold Jewelry Suite**

Est.: $2,000-$3,000
Starting Bid: $1,500

56268
Ruby, Diamond, Gold Jewelry Suite

Est.: $2,000-$3,000
Starting Bid: $1,200

56269
Coral, Diamond, Gold Jewelry

Est.: $1,000-$1,500
Starting Bid: $500

56270
**Diamond, Black Onyx, White
Gold Jewelry Suite, Hertz**

Est.: $2,000-$3,000
Starting Bid: $1,500

56271
Chalcedony, Diamond, Rose Gold Jewelry Suite, Bucherer

Est.: $1,500-$2,000
Starting Bid: $1,100

56272
Turquoise, Gold Jewelry Suite

Est.: $1,000-$2,000
Starting Bid: $500

56273
Diamond, Gold Jewelry Suite

Est.: $1,000-$1,500
Starting Bid: $500

56274
Sapphire, Pearl, Gold Suite

Est.: $1,200-$1,600
Starting Bid: $600

56275
Tanzanite, Gold Jewelry

Est.: $2,500-$3,500
Starting Bid: $1,500

56276
Coral, Diamond, Gold Jewelry Suite

Est.: $3,000-$5,000
Starting Bid: $1,500

56277
Diamond, Gold Jewelry Suite

Est.: $2,500-$3,500
Starting Bid: $1,500

56278
Lapis Lazuli, Gold Jewelry Suite, Ippolita

Est.: $1,000-$2,000
Starting Bid: $500

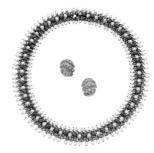

56279
Turquoise, Cultured Pearl, Gold Jewelry

Est.: $4,000-$6,000
Starting Bid: $3,000

56280
Micromosaic, Gold Jewelry

Est.: $3,000-$5,000
Starting Bid: $1,500

56281
Diamond, Gold Jewelry Suite

Est.: $1,000-$1,500
Starting Bid: $500

56282
Smokey Quartz, Citrine, Gold Jewelry Suite

Est.: $1,000-$2,000
Starting Bid: $500

56283
Diamond, White Gold Jewelry Suite

Est.: $3,000-$5,000
Starting Bid: $1,500

56287
**Diamond, Gold Jewelry
Suite, Kieselstein-Cord**

Est.: $2,500-$3,500
Starting Bid: $1,250

56291
**Gold, Sterling Silver Jewelry
Suite, David Yurman**

Est.: $3,000-$4,000
Starting Bid: $1,500

56284
**South Sea Cultured Pearl, Diamond,
White Gold Jewelry Suite**

Est.: $2,000-$3,000
Starting Bid: $1,000

56288
**Cultured Pearl, Diamond,
Platinum, White Gold Jewelry**

Est.: $4,000-$6,000
Starting Bid: $3,000

56292
**Diamond, Mother-of-Pearl,
Gold Jewelry Suite**

Est.: $1,000-$2,000
Starting Bid: $500

56285
Multi-Stone, Gold Jewelry

Est.: $2,000-$3,000
Starting Bid: $1,000

56289
Diamond, Gold Jewelry Suite

Est.: $1,500-$2,500
Starting Bid: $750

56293
Tourmaline, Emerald, Gold Jewelry Suite

Est.: $1,000-$2,000
Starting Bid: $500

56286
Gold Coin, Gold Jewelry

Est.: $1,000-$1,500
Starting Bid: $500

56290
Diamond, Gold Jewelry Suite

Est.: $4,000-$6,000
Starting Bid: $2,000

56294
Gold Coin, Gold Jewelry Suite

Est.: $2,000-$3,000
Starting Bid: $1,000

56295
Coral, Gold Jewelry Suite

Est.: $2,000-$3,000
Starting Bid: $1,000

56299
Unmounted Topaz

Est.: $1,000-$1,500
Starting Bid: $600

56303
**Baume & Mercier Lady's
Diamond, Gold Watch**

Est.: $1,000-$1,500
Starting Bid: $500

56296
Unmounted Diamond

Est.: $1,200-$1,600
Starting Bid: $800

56300
Unmounted Aquamarine

Est.: $1,500-$2,500
Starting Bid: $800

56304
**Omega Lady's Diamond, Gold
Covered Dial Watch**

Est.: $1,000-$1,500
Starting Bid: $500

56297
Unmounted Kunzite

Est.: $2,000-$3,000
Starting Bid: $1,000

56301
**Concord Lady's Diamond,
Gold Veneto Watch**

Est.: $1,500-$2,500
Starting Bid: $1,000

56305
**Baume & Mercier Gentleman's
Gold Watch**

Est.: $1,000-$1,500
Starting Bid: $500

56298
Unmounted Tourmaline

Est.: $1,000-$1,500
Starting Bid: $600

56302
Piaget Lady's Diamond, Gold Watch

Est.: $2,500-$3,500
Starting Bid: $1,500

56306
**Chopard Lady's, Diamond, Gold
Integral Bracelet Watch**

Est.: $3,000-$4,000
Starting Bid: $1,500

56307
Art Deco Hamilton Diamond, Platinum Watch

Est.: $1,000-$1,500
Starting Bid: $500

56308
Antique Enamel, Platinum, Gold Pendant Watch, Tiffany & Co., early 20th Century

Est.: $1,000-$1,500
Starting Bid: $500

56309
Baume & Mercier Lady's Diamond, Gold Watch

Est.: $2,000-$3,000
Starting Bid: $1,000

56310
Rado Lady's Diamond, Mother-of-Pearl, Ceramic, Stainless Steel, Titanium Sintra Jubilé Watch

Est.: $1,000-$1,500
Starting Bid: $500

56311
Baume & Mercier Lady's Diamond, Gold Watch

Est.: $1,200-$1,800
Starting Bid: $600

56312
Longines Lady's Diamond, White Gold Covered Dial Integral Bracelet Watch

Est.: $1,500-$2,000
Starting Bid: $800

56313
Breitling Lady's Mother-of-Pearl, Stainless Steel Starliner Watch

Est.: $1,000-$2,000
Starting Bid: $500

56314
Chopard Lady's Ruby, Sapphire, Stainless Steel Happy Sport, Leather Strap Watch

Est.: $2,000-$3,000
Starting Bid: $1,000

56315
Rolex Lady's Stainless Steel Oyster Perpetual Watch

Est.: $1,000-$1,500
Starting Bid: $800

56316
IWC Lady's Coral, Diamond, Gold Watch

Est.: $2,000-$3,000
Starting Bid: $1,500

56317
Charriol Lady's Diamond, Mother-of-Pearl, Stainless Steel Columbus Chronograph Watch

Est.: $1,000-$1,500
Starting Bid: $500

56318
Bvlgari Lady's Gold Watch

Est.: $800-$1,200
Starting Bid: $400

56319
**Piaget Lady's Gold Watch,
retailed by Tiffany & Co.**

Est.: $2,500-$3,500
Starting Bid: $1,250

56320
**Cartier Gentleman's Stainless Steel
Pasha Chronograph, Watch**

Est.: $2,000-$3,000
Starting Bid: $1,000

56321
**Franck Muller Lady's White Gold
Automatic Master Square Miroir Watch**

Est.: $3,000-$4,000
Starting Bid: $1,500

56322
**Cartier Lady's Stainless Steel
Automatic Pasha de Cartier Watch**

Est.: $2,000-$3,000
Starting Bid: $1,500

56323
**Hamilton Lady's Diamond,
Platinum Watch**

Est.: $3,000-$5,000
Starting Bid: $1,500

56324
**Swiss Lady's Diamond,
Gold Covered Dial Watch**

Est.: $3,000-$4,000
Starting Bid: $2,000

56325
**Longines Unisex Diamond,
White Gold Watch**

Est.: $1,000-$1,500
Starting Bid: $500

56326
**Swiss Lady's Diamond, Gold
Covered Dial Watch**

Est.: $1,000-$1,500
Starting Bid: $500

56327
**Rolex Lady's Gold, Stainless
Steel Datejust Watch**

Est.: $1,000-$2,000
Starting Bid: $500

56328
**Bueche Girod Lady's Gold
Integral Bracelet Watch**

Est.: $1,500-$2,000
Starting Bid: $800

End of Auction

Terms and Conditions of Auction

Auctioneer and Auction:

1. This Auction is presented by Heritage Auctions, a d/b/a/ of Heritage Auctioneers & Galleries, Inc., or Heritage Auctions, Inc., or Heritage Numismatic Auctions, Inc., or Heritage Vintage Sports Auctions, Inc., Currency Auctions of America, Inc., Heritage Auctions (HK) Limited, or Heritage Auctions – Europe Cooperatief U.A. as identified with the applicable licensing information on the title page of the catalog or on the HA.com Internet site (the "Auctioneer"). The Auction is conducted under these Terms and Conditions of Auction and applicable state and local law. Announcements and corrections from the podium and those made through the Terms and Conditions of Auctions appearing on the Internet at HA.com supersede those in the printed catalog.

Buyer's Premium:

2. All bids are subject to a Buyer's Premium which is in addition to the placed successful bid:
   - Fifteen percent (15%) on Domain Names & Intellectual Property Auction lots;
   - Nineteen and one-half percent (19.5%) on Comic and Movie Poster Auction lots;
   - Twenty percent (20%) on Currency, Sports Collectibles, US Coin, and World & Ancient Coin Auction lots;
   - Twenty-two percent (22%) on Wine Auction lots;
   - For lots in all other categories not listed above, the Buyer's Premium per lot is twenty-five percent (25%) on the first $250,000, plus twenty percent (20%) of any amount between $250,000 and $2,500,000, plus twelve percent (12%) of any amount over $2,500,000.
   - Minimum Buyer's Premium per lot is $19, except for Sports Collectibles lots wherein the Buyer's Premium is $14 per lot.

Auction Venues:

3. The following Auctions are conducted solely on the Internet: Heritage Weekly Internet Auctions (Coin, Currency, Comics, Rare Books, Jewelry & Watches, Guitars & Musical Instruments, and Vintage Movie Posters); Heritage Monthly Internet Auctions (Sports, World Coins and Rare Wine). Signature® Auctions and Grand Format Auctions accept bids from the Internet, telephone, fax, or mail first, followed by a floor bidding session; HeritageLive! and real- time telephone bidding are available to registered clients during these auctions.

Bidders:

4. Any person participating or registering for the Auction agrees to be bound by and accepts these Terms and Conditions of Auction ("Bidder(s)").

5. All Bidders must meet Auctioneer's qualifications to bid. Any Bidder who is not a client in good standing of the Auctioneer may be disqualified at Auctioneer's sole option and will not be awarded lots. Such determination may be made by Auctioneer in its sole and unlimited discretion, at any time prior to, during, or even after the close of the Auction. Auctioneer reserves the right to exclude any person from the auction.

6. If an entity places a bid, then the person executing the bid on behalf of the entity agrees to personally guarantee payment for any successful bid.

Credit:

7. In order to place bids, Bidders who have not established credit with the Auctioneer must either furnish satisfactory credit information (including two collectibles-related business references) or supply valid credit card information along with a social security number, well in advance of the Auction. Bids placed through our Interactive Internet program will only be accepted from pre-registered Bidders. Bidders who are not members of HA.com or affiliates should preregister at least 48 hours before the start of the first session (exclusive of holidays or weekends) to allow adequate time to contact references. Credit will be granted at the discretion of Auctioneer. Additionally Bidders who have not previously established credit or who wish to bid in excess of their established credit history may be required to provide their social security number or the last four digits thereof so a credit check may be performed prior to Auctioneer's acceptance of a bid. Check writing privileges and immediate delivery of merchandise may also be determined by pre-approval of credit based on a combination of criteria: HA.com history, related industry references, bank verification, a credit bureau report and/or a personal guarantee for a corporate or partnership entity in advance of the auction venue.

Bidding Options:

8. Bids in Signature Auctions or Grand Format Auctions may be placed as set forth in the printed catalog section entitled "Choose your bidding method." For auctions held solely on the Internet, see the alternatives on HA.com. Review at http://www.ha.com/c/ref/web-tips.zx#biddingTutorial.

9. Presentment of Bids: Non-Internet bids (including but not limited to podium, fax, phone and mail bids) are treated similar to floor bids in that they must be on-increment or at a half increment (called a cut bid). Any podium, fax, phone, or mail bids that do not conform to a full or half increment will be rounded up or down to the nearest full or half increment and this revised amount will be considered your high bid.

10. Auctioneer's Execution of Certain Bids. Auctioneer cannot be responsible for your errors in bidding, so carefully check that every bid is entered correctly. When identical mail or FAX bids are submitted, preference is given to the first received. To ensure the greatest accuracy, your written bids should be entered on the standard printed bid sheet and be received at Auctioneer's place of business at least two business days before the Auction start. Auctioneer is not responsible for executing mail bids or FAX bids received on or after the day the first lot is sold, nor Internet bids submitted after the published closing time; nor is Auctioneer responsible for proper execution of bids submitted by telephone, mail, FAX, e-mail, Internet, or in person once the Auction begins. Bids placed electronically via the internet may not be withdrawn until your written request is received and acknowledged by Auctioneer (FAX: 214-409-1425); such requests must state the reason, and may constitute grounds for withdrawal of bidding privileges. Lots won by mail Bidders will not be delivered at the Auction unless prearranged.

11. Caveat as to Bid Increments. Bid increments (over the current bid level) determine the lowest amount you may bid on a particular lot. Bids greater than one increment over the current bid can be any whole dollar amount. It is possible under several circumstances for winning bids to be between increments, sometimes only $1 above the previous increment. Please see: "How can I lose by less than an increment?" on our website. Bids will be accepted in whole dollar amounts only. No "buy" or "unlimited" bids will be accepted.

The following chart governs current bidding increments (see HA.com/c/ref/web-tips.zx#guidelines-increments).

Current Bid	Bid Increment	Current Bid	Bid Increment
< $10	$1	$10,000 - $19,999	$1,000
$10 - $49	$2	$20,000 - $49,999	$2,000
$50 - $99	$5	$50,000 - $99,999	$5,000
$100 - $199	$10	$100,000 - $199,999	$10,000
$200 - $499	$20	$200,000 - $499,999	$20,000
$500 - $999	$50	$500,000 - $999,999	$25,000
$1,000 - $1,999	$100	$1,000,000 - $1,999,999	$50,000
$2,000 - $4,999	$200	$2,000,000 - $9,999,999	$100,000
$5,000 - $9,999	$500	>= $10,000,000	$200,000

12. If Auctioneer calls for a full increment, a bidder may request Auctioneer to accept a bid at half of the increment ("Cut Bid") only once per lot. After offering a Cut Bid, bidders may continue to participate only at full increments. Off-increment bids may be accepted by the Auctioneer at Signature® Auctions and Grand Format Auctions. If the Auctioneer solicits bids other than the expected increment, these bids will not be considered Cut Bids.

Conducting the Auction:

13. Notice of the consignor's liberty to place bids on his lots in the Auction is hereby made in accordance with Article 2 of the Texas Business and Commercial Code. A "Minimum Bid" is an amount below which the lot will not sell. THE CONSIGNOR OF PROPERTY MAY PLACE WRITTEN "Minimum Bids" ON HIS LOTS IN ADVANCE OF THE AUCTION; ON SUCH LOTS, IF THE HAMMER PRICE DOES NOT MEET THE "Minimum Bid", THE CONSIGNOR MAY PAY A REDUCED COMMISSION ON THOSE LOTS. "Minimum Bids" are generally posted online several days prior to the Auction closing. For any successful bid placed by a consignor on his Property on the Auction floor, or by any means during the live session, or after the "Minimum Bid" for an Auction have been posted, we will require the consignor to pay full Buyer's

Premium and Seller's Commissions on such lot.

14. The highest qualified Bidder recognized by the Auctioneer shall be the Buyer. In the event of a tie bid, the earliest bid received or recognized wins. In the event of any dispute between any Bidders at an Auction, Auctioneer may at his sole discretion reoffer the lot. Auctioneer's decision and declaration of the winning Bidder shall be final and binding upon all Bidders. Bids properly offered, whether by floor Bidder or other means of bidding, may on occasion be missed or go unrecognized; in such cases, the Auctioneer may declare the recognized bid accepted as the winning bid, regardless of whether a competing bid may have been higher. Auctioneer reserves the right after the hammer fall to accept bids and reopen bidding for bids placed through the Internet or otherwise. Regardless that bids are made on a Property, Auctioneer reserves the right to withdraw the Properties, or any part of the Properties, from the Auction at any time prior to the opening of any lot containing such Properties for sale by the auctioneer (crier), or in the case of Internet-only auctions when the bid opens for either live bidding online or the beginning of the extended period, if any

15. Auctioneer reserves the right to refuse to honor any bid or to limit the amount of any bid, in its sole discretion. A bid is considered not made in "Good Faith" when made by an insolvent or irresponsible person, a person under the age of eighteen, or is not supported by satisfactory credit, collectibles references, or otherwise. Regardless of the disclosure of his identity, any bid by a consignor or his agent on a lot consigned by him is deemed to be made in "Good Faith." Any person apparently appearing on the OFAC list is not eligible to bid.

16. Nominal Bids. The Auctioneer in its sole discretion may reject nominal bids, small opening bids, or very nominal advances. If a lot bearing estimates fails to open for 40–60% of the low estimate, the Auctioneer may pass the item or may place a protective bid on behalf of the consignor.

17. Lots bearing bidding estimates shall open at Auctioneer's discretion (generally 40%-60% of the low estimate). In the event that no bid meets or exceeds that opening amount, the lot shall pass as unsold.

18. All items are to be purchased per lot as numerically indicated and no lots will be broken. Auctioneer reserves the right to withdraw, prior to the close, any lots from the Auction.

19. Auctioneer reserves the right to rescind the sale in the event of nonpayment, breach of a warranty, disputed ownership, auctioneer's clerical error or omission in exercising bids and reserves, or for any other reason and in Auctioneer's sole discretion. In cases of nonpayment, Auctioneer's election to void a sale does not relieve the Bidder from their obligation to pay Auctioneer its fees (seller's and buyer's premium) and any other damages or expenses pertaining to the lot.

20. Auctioneer occasionally experiences Internet and/or Server service outages, and Auctioneer periodically schedules system downtime for maintenance and other purposes, during which Bidders cannot participate or place bids. If such outages occur, we may at our discretion extend bidding for the Auction. Bidders unable to place their Bids through the Internet are directed to contact Client Services at 877-HERITAGE (437-4824).

21. The Auctioneer, its affiliates, or their employees consign items to be sold in the Auction, and may bid on those lots or any other lots. Auctioneer or affiliates expressly reserve the right to modify any such bids at any time prior to the hammer based upon data made known to the Auctioneer or its affiliates. The Auctioneer may extend advances, guarantees, or loans to certain consignors.

22. The Auctioneer has the right to sell certain unsold items after the close of the Auction. Such lots shall be considered sold during the Auction and all these Terms and Conditions shall apply to such sales including but not limited to the Buyer's Premium, return rights, and disclaimers.

Payment:

23. All sales are strictly for cash in United States dollars (including U.S. currency, bank wire, cashier checks, travelers checks, eChecks, and bank money orders, and are subject to all reporting requirements). All deliveries are subject to good funds; funds being received in Auctioneer's account before delivery of the Purchases; and all payments are subject to a clearing period. Auctioneer reserves the right to determine if a check constitutes "good funds": checks drawn on a U.S. bank are subject to a ten business day hold, and thirty days when drawn on an international bank. Clients with pre-arranged credit status may receive immediate credit for payments via eCheck, personal, or corporate checks. All others will be subject to a hold of 5 days, or more, for the funds to clear prior to releasing merchandise. (Ref. T&C item 7 Credit for additional information.) Payments can be made 24-48 hours post auction from the My Orders page of the HA.com website.

24. Payment is due upon closing of the Auction session, or upon presentment of an invoice. Auctioneer reserves the right to void an invoice if payment in full is not received within 7 days after the close of the Auction. In cases of nonpayment, Auctioneer's election to void a sale does not relieve the Bidder from their obligation to pay Auctioneer its fees (seller's and buyer's premium) on the lot and any other damages pertaining to the lot or Auctioneer. Alternatively, Auctioneer at its sole option, may charge a twenty (20%) fee based on the amount of the purchase. In either case the Auctioneer may offset amount of its claim against any monies owing to the Bidder or secure its claim against any of the Bidder's properties held by the Auctioneer..

25. Lots delivered to you, or your representative are subject to all applicable state and local taxes, unless appropriate permits are on file with Auctioneer. Bidder agrees to pay Auctioneer the actual amount of tax due in the event that sales tax is not properly collected due to: 1) an expired, inaccurate, or inappropriate tax certificate or declaration, 2) an incorrect interpretation of the applicable statute, 3) or any other reason. The appropriate form or certificate must be on file at and verified by Auctioneer five days prior to Auction, or tax must be paid; only if such form or certificate is received by Auctioneer within 4 days after the Auction can a refund of tax paid be made. Lots from different Auctions may not be aggregated for sales tax purposes.

26. In the event that a Bidder's payment is dishonored upon presentment(s), Bidder shall pay the maximum statutory processing fee set by applicable state law. If you attempt to pay via eCheck and your financial institution denies this transfer from your bank account, or the payment cannot be completed using the selected funding source, you agree to complete payment using your credit card on file.

27. If any Auction invoice submitted by Auctioneer is not paid in full when due, the unpaid balance will bear interest at the highest rate permitted by law from the date of invoice until paid. Any invoice not paid when due will bear a three percent (3%) late fee on the invoice amount. If the Auctioneer refers any invoice to an attorney for collection, the buyer agrees to pay attorney's fees, court costs, and other collection costs incurred by Auctioneer. If Auctioneer assigns collection to its in-house legal staff, such attorney's time expended on the matter shall be compensated at a rate comparable to the hourly rate of independent attorneys.

28. In the event a successful Bidder fails to pay any amounts due, Auctioneer reserves the right to sell the lot(s) securing the invoice to any underbidders in the Auction that the lot(s) appeared, or at subsequent private or public sale, or relist the lot(s) in a future auction conducted by Auctioneer. A defaulting Bidder agrees to pay for the reasonable costs of resale (including a 15% seller's commission, if consigned to an auction conducted by Auctioneer). The defaulting Bidder is liable to pay any difference between his total original invoice for the lot(s), plus any applicable interest, and the net proceeds for the lot(s) if sold at private sale or the subsequent hammer price of the lot(s) less the 15% seller's commissions, if sold at an Auctioneer's auction.

29. Auctioneer reserves the right to require payment in full in good funds before delivery of the merchandise.

30. Auctioneer shall have a lien against the merchandise purchased by the buyer to secure payment of the Auction invoice. Auctioneer is further granted a lien and the right to retain possession of any other property of the buyer then held by the Auctioneer or its affiliates to secure payment of any Auction invoice or any other amounts due the Auctioneer or affiliates from the buyer. With respect to these lien rights, Auctioneer shall have all the rights of a secured creditor under Article 9 of the Texas Uniform Commercial Code, including but not limited to the right of sale (including a 15% seller's commission, if consigned to an auction conducted by Auctioneer). In addition, with respect to payment of the Auction invoice(s), the buyer waives any and all rights of offset he might otherwise have against the Auctioneer and the consignor of the merchandise included on the invoice. If a Bidder owes Auctioneer or its affiliates on any account, Auctioneer and its affiliates shall have the right to offset such unpaid account by any credit balance due Bidder, and it may secure by possessory lien any unpaid amount by any of the Bidder's property in their possession.

Terms and Conditions of Auction

31. Title shall not pass to the successful Bidder until all invoices are paid in full. It is the responsibility of the buyer to provide adequate insurance coverage for the items once they have been delivered to a common carrier or third-party shipper.

Delivery; Shipping; and Handling Charges:

32. Buyer is liable for shipping, handling, registration, and renewal fees, if any. Please refer to Auctioneer's website HA.com/c/shipping.zx for the latest charges or call Auctioneer. Auctioneer is unable to combine purchases from other auctions or affiliates into one package for shipping purposes. Lots won will be shipped in a commercially reasonable time after payment in good funds for the merchandise and the shipping fees is received or credit extended, except when third-party shipment occurs. Buyer agrees that Service and Handling charges related to shipping items which are not pre-paid may be charged to the credit card on file with Auctioneer.
33. Successful international Bidders shall provide written shipping instructions, including specified customs declarations, to the Auctioneer for any lots to be delivered outside of the United States. NOTE: Declaration value shall be the item'(s) hammer price together with its buyer's premium and Auctioneer shall use the correct harmonized code for the lot. Domestic Buyers on lots designated for third-party shipment must designate the common carrier, accept risk of loss, and prepay shipping costs.
34. All shipping charges will be borne by the successful Bidder. On all shipments in which Heritage charges the Delivery, Handling, and Transit Fee *infra*, any risk of loss during shipment will be borne by Heritage until the shipping carrier's confirmation of delivery to the address of record in Auctioneer's file, this is the "Secure Location". A common carrier's confirmation is conclusive to prove delivery to Bidder; if the client has a Signature release on file with the carrier, the package is considered delivered without Signature. Auctioneer shall arrange, select, and engage common carriers and other transportation vendors on your behalf. Transit services are subject to the following terms and conditions:
    a. Scope of Transit Services: Your properties for transit will be insured under one or more insurance policies issued by an authorized broker to Auctioneer. The properties will be insured for the invoice price of the properties (hammer price plus Buyer's Premium) ("Insured Value"). For each shipment, you will provide a Secure Location to which the items will be delivered. NOTICE: **Auctioneer is neither an insurance company nor a common carrier of any type.**
    b. Auctioneer's Compensation for Transit Services: Auctioneer will provide transit services to Buyer for ¾ of 1% of the Insured Value, plus packaging and handling fees and fees for the common carrier (collectively, "Delivery, Handling, and Transit Fee"). You agree to pay Delivery, Handling, and Transit Fee and comply with all terms of payment as set forth in paragraphs 23 to 31 of this Agreement.
    c. Auctioneer's Limitation of Liability for Transit Services: You understand and agree that Auctioneer's liability for loss of or damage to the items, if any, ends when the items have been delivered to the Secure Location, and Auctioneer has received evidence of delivery. If you claim that any property has sustained loss or damage during transit, you must report any such loss or damage to Auctioneer within seventy-two (72) hours of the delivery date. Your recovery for loss of or damage to any property is limited to the lesser of actual cash value of the property or the Insured Value. **Under no circumstances is Auctioneer liable for consequential or punitive damages.**
35. Due to the nature of some items sold, it shall be the responsibility for the successful Bidder to arrange pick-up and shipping through third-parties; as to such items Auctioneer shall have no liability. Failure to pick-up or arrange shipping in a timely fashion (within ten days) shall subject Lots to storage and moving charges, including a $100 administration fee plus $10 daily storage for larger items and $5.00 daily for smaller items (storage fee per item) after 35 days. In the event the Lot is not removed within ninety days, the Lot may be offered for sale to recover any past due storage or moving fees, including a 10% Seller's Commission.

36A. The laws of various countries regulate the import or export of certain plant and animal properties, including (but not limited to) items made of (or including) Brazilian rosewood, ivory, whalebone, turtle shell, coral, crocodile, or other wildlife. Transport of such lots may require special licenses for export, import, or both. Bidder is responsible for: 1) obtaining all information on such restricted items for both export and import; 2) obtaining all such licenses and/or permits. Delay, failure, or incapacity to obtain any such license or permit does not relieve the buyer of timely payment, or afford them the capacity to void their purchase or payment. For further information, please contact Ron Brackemyre at 800-872-6467 ext. 1312.

36B. California State law prohibits the importation of any product containing Python skin into the State of California, thus no lot containing Python skin will be shipped to or invoiced to a person or company in California.

36C. Auctioneer shall not be liable for any loss caused by or resulting from:
    a. Seizure or destruction under quarantine or Customs regulation, or confiscation by order of any Government or public authority, or risks of contraband or illegal transportation of trade, or
    b. Breakage of statuary, marble, glassware, bric-a-brac, porcelains, jewelry, and similar fragile articles

37. Any request for shipping verification for undelivered packages must be made within 30 days of shipment by Auctioneer.

Cataloging, Warranties and Disclaimers:

38. NO WARRANTY, WHETHER EXPRESSED OR IMPLIED, IS MADE WITH RESPECT TO ANY DESCRIPTION CONTAINED IN THIS AUCTION OR ANY SECOND OPINE. Any description of the items or second opine contained in this Auction is for the sole purpose of identifying the items for those Bidders who do not have the opportunity to view the lots prior to bidding, and no description of items has been made part of the basis of the bargain or has created any express warranty that the goods would conform to any description made by Auctioneer. Color variations can be expected in any electronic or printed imaging, and are not grounds for the return of any lot. NOTE: Auctioneer, in specified auction venues, for example, Fine Art, may have express written warranties and you are referred to those specific terms and conditions. .
39. Auctioneer is selling only such right or title to the items being sold as Auctioneer may have by virtue of consignment agreements on the date of auction and disclaims any warranty of title to the Property. Auctioneer disclaims any warranty of merchantability or fitness for any particular purposes. All images, descriptions, sales data, and archival records are the exclusive property of Auctioneer, and may be used by Auctioneer for advertising, promotion, archival records, and any other uses deemed appropriate.
40. Translations of foreign language documents may be provided as a convenience to interested parties. Auctioneer makes no representation as to the accuracy of those translations and will not be held responsible for errors in bidding arising from inaccuracies in translation.
41. Auctioneer disclaims all liability for damages, consequential or otherwise, arising out of or in connection with the sale of any Property by Auctioneer to Bidder. No third party may rely on any benefit of these Terms and Conditions and any rights, if any, established hereunder are personal to the Bidder and may not be assigned. Any statement made by the Auctioneer is an opinion and does not constitute a warranty or representation. No employee of Auctioneer may alter these Terms and Conditions, and, unless signed by a principal of Auctioneer, any such alteration is null and void.
42. Auctioneer shall not be liable for breakage of glass or damage to frames (patent or latent); such defects, in any event, shall not be a basis for any claim for return or reduction in purchase price.

Release:

43. In consideration of participation in the Auction and the placing of a bid, Bidder expressly releases Auctioneer, its officers, directors and employees, its affiliates, and its outside experts that provide second opines, from any and all claims, cause of action, chose of action, whether at law or equity or any arbitration or mediation rights existing under the rules of any professional society or affiliation based upon the assigned description, or a derivative theory, breach of warranty express or implied, representation or other matter set forth within these Terms and Conditions of Auction or otherwise. In the event of a claim, Bidder agrees that such rights and privileges conferred therein are strictly construed as specifically declared herein; e.g., authenticity, typographical error, etc. and are the exclusive remedy. Bidder, by non-compliance to these express terms of a granted remedy, shall waive any claim against Auctioneer.
44. Notice: Some Property sold by Auctioneer are inherently dangerous e.g. firearms, cannons, and small items that may be swallowed or ingested or may have latent defects all of which may cause harm to a person. Purchaser accepts all risk of loss or damage from its purchase of these items and Auctioneer disclaims any liability whether under contract or tort for damages and losses, direct or inconsequential, and expressly disclaims any warranty as to safety or usage of any lot sold.

Dispute Resolution and Arbitration Provision:

45. By placing a bid or otherwise participating in the auction, Bidder accepts these Terms and Conditions of Auction, and specifically agrees to the dispute resolution provided herein. Consumer disputes shall be resolved through court litigation which has an exclusive Dallas, Texas venue clause and jury waiver. Non-consumer dispute shall be determined in binding arbitration which arbitration replaces the right to go to court, including the right to a jury trial.
46. Auctioneer in no event shall be responsible for consequential damages, incidental damages, compensatory damages, or any other damages arising or claimed to be arising from the auction of any lot. In the event that Auctioneer cannot deliver the lot or subsequently it is established that the lot lacks title, or other transfer or condition issue is claimed, in such cases the sole remedy shall be limited to rescission of sale and refund of the amount paid by Bidder; in no case shall Auctioneer's maximum liability exceed the high bid on that lot, which bid shall be deemed for all purposes the value of the lot. After one year has elapsed, Auctioneer's maximum liability shall be limited to any commissions and fees Auctioneer earned on that lot.
47. In the event of an attribution error, Auctioneer may at its sole discretion, correct the error on the Internet, or, if discovered at a later date, to refund the buyer's purchase price without further obligation.
48. Exclusive Dispute Resolution Process: All claims, disputes, or controversies in connection with, relating to and /or arising out of your Participation in the Auction or purchase of any lot, any interpretation of the Terms and Conditions of Sale or any amendments thereto, any description of any lot or condition report, any damage to any lot, any alleged verbal modification of any term of sale or condition report or description and/or any purported settlement whether asserted in contract, tort, under Federal or State statute or regulation or any claim made by you of a lot or your Participation in the auction involving the auction or a specific lot involving a warranty or representation of a consignor or other person or entity including Auctioneer { which claim you consent to be made a party} (collectively, "Claim") shall be exclusively heard by, and the claimant (or respondent as the case may be) and Heritage each consent to the Claim being presented in a confidential binding arbitration before a single arbitrator administrated by and conducted under the rules of, the American Arbitration Association. The locale for all such arbitrations shall be Dallas, Texas. The arbitrator's award may be enforced in any court of competent jurisdiction. If a Claim involves a consumer, exclusive subject matter jurisdiction for the Claim is in the State District Courts of Dallas County, Texas and the consumer consents to subject matter and in personam jurisdiction; further CONSUMER EXPRESSLY WAIVES ANY RIGHT TO TRIAL BY JURY. A consumer may elect arbitration as specified above. Any claim involving the purchase or sale of numismatic or related items may be submitted through binding PNG arbitration. Any Claim must be brought within two (2) years of the alleged breach, default or misrepresentation or the Claim is waived. Exemplary or punitive damages are not permitted and are waived. A Claim is not subject to class certification. Nothing herein shall be construed to extend the time of return or conditions and restrictions for return. This Agreement and any Claim shall be determined and construed under Texas law. The prevailing party (a party that is awarded substantial and material relief on its damage claim based on damages sought vs. awarded or the successful defense of a Claim based on damages sought vs. awarded) may be awarded its reasonable attorneys' fees and costs.
49. No claims of any kind can be considered after the settlements have been made with the consignors. Any dispute after the settlement date is strictly between the Bidder and consignor without involvement or responsibility of the Auctioneer.
50. In consideration of their participation in or application for the Auction, a person or entity (whether the successful Bidder, a Bidder, a purchaser and/or other Auction participant or registrant) agrees that all disputes in any way relating to, arising under, connected with, or incidental to these Terms and Conditions and purchases, or default in payment thereof, shall be arbitrated pursuant to the arbitration provision. In the event that any matter including actions to compel arbitration, construe the agreement, actions in aid of arbitration or otherwise needs to be litigated, such litigation shall be exclusively in the Courts of the State of Texas, in Dallas County, Texas, and if necessary the corresponding appellate courts. For such actions, the successful Bidder, purchaser, or Auction participant also expressly submits himself to the personal jurisdiction of the State of Texas.
51. These Terms & Conditions provide specific remedies for occurrences in the auction and delivery process. Where such remedies are afforded, they shall be interpreted strictly. Bidder agrees that any claim shall utilize such remedies; Bidder making a claim in excess of those remedies provided in these Terms and Conditions agrees that in no case whatsoever shall Auctioneer's maximum liability exceed the high bid on that lot, which bid shall be deemed for all purposes the value of the lot.

Miscellaneous:

52. Agreements between Bidders and consignors to effectuate a non-sale of an item at Auction, inhibit bidding on a consigned item to enter into a private sale agreement for said item, or to utilize the Auctioneer's Auction to obtain sales for non-selling consigned items subsequent to the Auction, are strictly prohibited. If a subsequent sale of a previously consigned item occurs in violation of this provision, Auctioneer reserves the right to charge Bidder the applicable Buyer's Premium and consignor a Seller's Commission as determined for each auction venue and by the terms of the seller's agreement.
53. Acceptance of these Terms and Conditions qualifies Bidder as a client who has consented to be contacted by Heritage in the future. In conformity with "do-not-call" regulations promulgated by the Federal or State regulatory agencies, participation by the Bidder is affirmative consent to being contacted at the phone number shown in his application and this consent shall remain in effect until it is revoked in writing. Heritage may from time to time contact Bidder concerning sale, purchase, and auction opportunities available through Heritage and its affiliates and subsidiaries.
54. Rules of Construction: Auctioneer presents properties in a number of collectible fields, and as such, specific venues have promulgated supplemental Terms and Conditions. Nothing herein shall be construed to waive the general Terms and Conditions of Auction by these additional rules and shall be construed to give force and effect to the rules in their entirety.

State Notices:

Notice as to an Auction in California: Auctioneer has in compliance with Title 2.95 of the California Civil Code as amended October 11, 1993 Sec. 1812.600, posted with the California Secretary of State its bonds for it and its employees, and the auction is being conducted in compliance with Sec. 2338 of the Commercial Code and Sec. 535 of the Penal Code.

Notice as to an Auction in New York City: This Auction is conducted in accord with the applicable sections of the New York City Department of Consumer Affairs Rules and Regulations as Amended. This a Public Auction Sale conducted by Auctioneer. The New York City Auctioneers conducting the sale of behalf of Heritage Auctions No. 41513036 ("Auctioneer") are licensed Auctioneers including Dawes, Nicholas 1304724, Guzman, Kathleen 762165, Luray, Elyse 2015375, or as listed at HA.com/Licenses and as posted at the venue site. All lots are subject to: the consignor's right to bid thereon and consignor's option to receive advances on their consignments. Auction may offer, in its sole discretion, advances on consignments and extended financing to registered bidders, in accord with Auctioneer's internal credit standards. Auctioneer will disclose to bidders, upon request, a list of lots subject to an advance, reserve, guarantee, or Auctioneer's financial interests of any kind. All Terms and Conditions of Sale are available at HA.com and in the printed catalog, including term #21 which states: Consignor, auctioneer's affiliates and, its employees may bid on their lots or other lots for their own account in accordance with the laws of New York and they may have information as to the lots not available to the public. On lots bearing an estimate, the term refers to a value range placed on an item by the Auctioneer in its sole opinion but the final price is determined by the bidders.

Notice as to an Auction in Texas: In compliance with TDLR rule 67.100(c)(1), notice is hereby provided that this auction is covered by a Recovery Fund administered by the Texas Department of Licensing and Regulation, P.O. Box 12157, Austin, Texas 78711 (512) 463-6599. Any complaints may be directed to the same address.

Rev. 8-12-2014

Terms and Conditions of Auction

Additional Terms & Conditions:
JEWELRY, WATCH & LUXURY ACCESSORY AUCTIONS

JEWELRY, WATCH & LUXURY ACCESSORY TERM A: JEWELRY: As most jewelry sold at auction has been worn, and may have been previously repaired, altered, or embellished, ALL LOTS are sold AS IS. Such wear, repairs or changes may display varying levels of evidence, so it is the responsibility of each prospective bidder to fully inspect each lot before bidding and rely upon their own judgment prior to placing a bid. Bidder acknowledges that the absence of any reference to their condition does not imply the absence of wear, repairs, or defects.

JEWELRY, WATCH & LUXURY ACCESSORY TERM B: WATCHES: As most watches sold at auction have been worn, and may have been previously repaired, altered, or embellished, ALL LOTS are sold AS IS. Such wear, repairs or changes may display varying levels of evidence, so it is the responsibility of each prospective bidder to fully inspect each lot before bidding and rely upon their own judgment prior to placing a bid. Bidder acknowledges that the absence of any reference to their condition does not imply the absence of wear, repairs, or defects. No item shall be considered eligible for return unless its original Heritage security tag remains attached and intact.

JEWELRY, WATCH & LUXURY ACCESSORY TERM C: All descriptions and statements in this catalog and subsequent invoices regarding measurement, authorship, source or origin, or other aspects are qualified opines and do not constitute a warranty or representation, and are provided for identification purposes only. Auctioneer warrants only such authorship, period or culture of each lot as is set out in the BOLD faced type heading in the catalog description of the lot, with the following exclusions: this warranty does not apply to any catalog description where it was specifically mentioned that there is a conflict of specialist opinion on the authorship of a lot; or authorship which on the date of Auction was in accordance with the then generally accepted opinion of scholars and specialists, despite the subsequent discovery of new information, whether historical or physical, concerning the artist or craftsman, his students, school, workshop or followers; or opines which may be proven inaccurate by means of scientific processes not generally accepted for use or which were unreasonably expensive or impractical to use at the time of publication of the catalog. Such limited warranty as to authorship is provided for a period of one (1) year from the date of the auction and is only for the benefit of the original purchaser of record and is not transferable, and any claim regarding a bold-faced provision must be accompanied by two written letters by independent and authorized appraisers in support of the claim. It is specifically understood that any refund agreed to by the Auctioneer would be limited to the purchase price.

JEWELRY, WATCH & LUXURY ACCESSORY TERM D: The Auction is not on approval. Under extremely limited circumstances not including authenticity (e.g. gross cataloging error), a purchaser who did not bid from the floor may request Auctioneer to evaluate voiding a sale; such request must be made in writing detailing the alleged gross error, and submission of the lot to Auctioneer must be pre-approved by Auctioneer. A bidder must notify the appropriate department head (check the inside front cover of the catalog or our website for a listing of department heads) in writing of the purchaser's request within three (3) days of the non-floor bidder's receipt of the lot. Any lot that is to be evaluated for return must be received in our offices within 30 days after Auction. AFTER THAT 30 DAY PERIOD, NO LOT MAY BE RETURNED FOR ANY REASONS. Lots returned must be in the same condition as when sold and must include any Certificate of Authenticity. No lots purchased by floor bidders may be returned (including those bidders acting as agents for others). Late remittance for purchases may be considered just cause to revoke all return privileges.

JEWELRY, WATCH & LUXURY ACCESSORY TERM E: Pre-auction estimates of value or "bidding estimates" are opines provided solely as a convenience to clients, and should only be used as approximations of current market value. Estimates do not include Buyer's Premiums or sales tax.

JEWELRY, WATCH & LUXURY ACCESSORY TERM F: In the event Auctioneer cannot deliver the lot or subsequently it is established that the lot lacks title or the bold faced section of description is incorrect, or other transfer or condition issue is claimed, Auctioneer's liability shall be limited to rescission of sale and refund of purchase price; in no case shall Auctioneer's maximum liability exceed the high bid on that lot, which bid shall be deemed for all purposes the value of the lot. After one year has elapsed, Auctioneer's maximum liability shall be limited to any commissions and fees Auctioneer earned on that lot.

JEWELRY, WATCH & LUXURY ACCESSORY TERM G: Provenance and authenticity are not guaranteed by the consignor or the Auctioneer. While every effort is made to determine provenance and authenticity, it is the responsibility of the Bidder to arrive at their own conclusion prior to bidding. Provenance or other information regarding history of ownership may be provided if known, or may be excluded at the request of the consignor.

JEWELRY, WATCH & LUXURY ACCESSORY TERM H: On the fall of Auctioneer's hammer, Buyers assume full risk and responsibility for lot, including shipment by common carrier or third-party shipper, and must provide their own insurance coverage for shipments.

JEWELRY, WATCH & LUXURY ACCESSORY TERM I: Watches in waterproof and water-resistant cases have been opened to identify type and condition. Auctioneer cannot guarantee that the watches are waterproof or water-resistant at the time of purchase. Buyers are advised to have the watches checked by a competent watchmaker with respect to such attributes.

JEWELRY, WATCH & LUXURY ACCESSORY TERM J: All dimensions in catalog descriptions are approximate.

JEWELRY, WATCH & LUXURY ACCESSORY TERM K: Condition reports are provided as a service to clients. Buyers should note that descriptions of property are not warranties and that watches may need general service, change of battery or further repair work for which the buyer is solely responsible.

JEWELRY, WATCH & LUXURY ACCESSORY TERM L: Watch bands made from protected species (i.e. alligator, crocodile) and items made of ivory and tortoise may be subject to restrictions in certain countries.

JEWELRY, WATCH & LUXURY ACCESSORY TERM M: Any property made of or incorporating endangered or protected species or wildlife may have import and export restrictions established by the Convention on International Trade in Endangered Species of Wild Fauna and Flora (CITES). These items are not available to ship Internationally or in some cases, domestically. By placing a bid the bidder acknowledges that he is aware of the restriction and takes responsibility in obtaining and paying for any license or permits relevant to delivery of the product. Lots containing potentially regulated wildlife material are noted in the description as a convenience to our clients. Heritage Auctions does not accept liability for errors or for failure to mark lots containing protected or regulated species.

JEWELRY, WATCH & LUXURY ACCESSORY TERM N: Descriptions of Handbags, Purses, and Wallets may denote that the hardware is "gold" or "silver". Such terms refer to the metal color of the hardware, rather than that the hardware is made of a precious metal. Unless there is specific mention as to carat weight or precious metal weight of the hardware, all descriptions using the terms "gold" or "silver" are descriptive of color of the hardware, not a reference to the hardware being made or platted with a precious metal.

JEWELRY, WATCH & LUXURY ACCESSORY TERM O: California State law prohibits the importation of any product containing Python skin into the State of California, thus no lot containing Python skin will be shipped to or invoiced to a person or company in California.

For wiring instructions call the Credit department at 877-HERITAGE (437-4824) or e-mail: CreditDept@HA.com

---

Notice as to an Auction in New York City

This Auction is conducted in accord with the applicable sections of the New York City Department of Consumer Affairs Rules and Regulations as Amended. This a Public Auction Sale conducted by Auctioneer. The New York City Auctioneers conducting the sale of behalf of Heritage Auctions No. 41513036 ("Auctioneer") are licensed Auctioneers including Dawes, Nicholas 1304724, Guzman, Kathleen 762165, Luray, Elyse 2015375, or as listed at HA.com/Licenses and as posted at the venue site.

All lots are subject to: the consignor's right to bid thereon and consignor's option to receive advances on their consignments. Auction may offer, in its sole discretion, advances on consignments and extended financing to registered bidders, in accord with Auctioneer's internal credit standards. Auctioneer will disclose to bidders, upon request, a list of lots subject to an advance, reserve, guarantee, or Auctioneer's financial interests of any kind. All Terms and Conditions of Sale are available at HA.com and in the printed catalog, including term #21 which states: Consignor, auctioneer's affiliates and, its employees may bid on their lots or other lots for their own account in accordance with the laws of New York and they may have information as to the lots not available to the public. On lots bearing an estimate, the term refers to a value range placed on an item by the Auctioneer in its sole opinion but the final price is determined by the bidders. Rev 6-8-2016

How to Ship Your Purchases

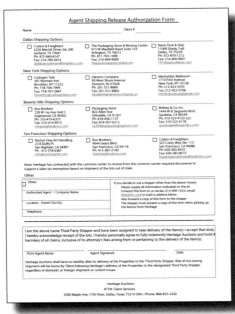

Agent Shipping Release
Authorization form

Heritage Auctions requires "Third Party Shipping" for certain items in this auction not picked up in person by the buyer. It shall be the responsibility of the successful bidder to arrange pick up and shipping through a third party; as to such items auctioneer shall have no liability.

Steps to follow:

1. Select a shipping company from the list below or a company of your choosing which will remain on file and in effect until you advise otherwise in writing.

2. Complete, sign, and return an Agent Shipping Release Authorization form to Heritage (this form will automatically be emailed to you along with your winning bid(s) notice or may be obtained by calling Client Services at 866-835-3243). The completed form may be faxed to 214-409-1425.

3. Heritage Auctions' shipping department will coordinate with the shipping company you have selected to pick up your purchases.

Shippers that Heritage has used are listed below. However, you are not obligated to choose from the following and may provide Heritage with information of your preferred shipper.

Navis Pack & Ship
11009 Shady Trail
Dallas, TX 75229
Ph: 972-870-1212
Fax: 214-409-9001
TX1062@GoNavis.com

The Packing & Moving Center
915 W Mayfield Road Suite 103
Arlington, TX 76014
Ph: 817-795-1999
Fax: 214-409-9000
thepackman@sbcglobal.net

Craters & Freighters
2220 Merritt Drive, Suite 200
Garland, TX 75041
Ph: 972-840-8147
Fax: 214-780-5674
dallas@cratersandfreighters.com

- It is the Third Party Shipper's responsibility to pack (or crate) and ship (or freight) your purchase to you. Please make all payment arrangements for shipping with your Shipper of choice.

- Any questions concerning Third Party Shipping can be addressed through our Client Services Department at 1-866-835-3243.

- Successful bidders are advised that pick-up or shipping arrangements should be made within ten (10) days of the auction or they may be subject to storage fees as stated in Heritage's Terms & Conditions of Auction, item 35.

NOTICE of CITES COMPLIANCE; When purchasing items made from protected species.
Any property made of or incorporating endangered or protected species or wildlife may have import and export restrictions established by the Convention on International Trade in Endangered Species of Wild Fauna and Flora (CITES). These items are not available to ship Internationally or in some cases, domestically. By placing a bid the bidder acknowledges that he is aware of the restriction and takes responsibility in obtaining and paying for any license or permits relevant to delivery of the product. Lots containing potentially regulated wildlife material are noted in the description as a convenience to our clients. Heritage Auctions does not accept liability for errors or for failure to mark lots containing protected or regulated species.

rev 5_2017

TIMEPIECES SIGNATURE® AUCTION
October 24 | New York | Live & Online

Featuring a Collection from an Influential Tech Entrepreneur

Patek Philippe Very Rare And
Important Ref. 3974J Yellow Gold
Automatic Perpetual Calendar
Minute Repeating Wristwatch With
Moon Phases, circa 1991
Estimate: $250,000+

Inquiries:

Jim Wolf
JWolf@HA.com | 214.409.1659

Jonathon Burford
JonathonB@HA.com | 310.492.8664

NATURE & SCIENCE
November 4, 2017 | Dallas | Live & Online

Featuring Over $1 Million
in Gold Nuggets and
Crystalline Specimens

GOLD NUGGET
Bendigo Goldfields,
City of Greater Bendigo
Victoria, Australia
7.28 x 6.22 x 1.57 inches (18.50 x 15.80 x 4.00 cm)
3,623 grams (116.48 oz t)
Estimate: $200,000-$300,000

Inquiries: 877-HERITAGE (437-4824)

Craig Kissick | ext. 1995 | CraigK@HA.com

Department Specialists

For the extensions below, please dial
877-HERITAGE (437-4824)

Comics & Comic Art
HA.com/Comics
Ed Jaster, Ext. 1288 • EdJ@HA.com
Lon Allen, Ext. 1261 • LonA@HA.com
Barry Sandoval, Ext. 1377 • BarryS@HA.com

Animation Art
HA.com/Animation
Jim Lentz, Ext. 1991 • JimL@HA.com

Entertainment & Music Memorabilia
HA.com/Entertainment
Margaret Barrett, Ext. 1912 • MargaretB@HA.com **
Garry Shrum, Ext. 1585 • GarryS@HA.com
Giles Moon, Ext. 1725 • GilesM@HA.com

Vintage Guitars & Musical Instruments
HA.com/Guitar
Mike Gutierrez, Ext. 1183 • MikeG@HA.com

Fine Art

American Indian Art
HA.com/AmericanIndian
Delia E. Sullivan, Ext. 1343 • DeliaS@HA.com

American & European Art
HA.com/FineArt
Ed Jaster, Ext. 1288 • EdJ@HA.com
Aviva Lehmann, Ext. 1519 • AvivaL@HA.com *
Ariana Hartsock, Ext. 1283 • ArianaH@HA.com
Alissa Ford, Ext. 1926 • AlissaF@HA.com ***
Marianne Berardi, Ph.D., Ext. 1506 • MarianneB@HA.com
Janell Snape, Ext. 1245 • JanellS@HA.com ***

Asian Art
HA.com/FineArt
Richard Cervantes, Ext. 1927 • RichardC@HA.com *
Moyun Niu, Ext. 1864 • MoyunN@HA.com **

Decorative Arts
HA.com/Decorative
Karen Rigdon, Ext. 1723 • KarenR@HA.com
Carolyn Mani, Ext. 1677 • CarolynM@HA.com **
Rachel Weathers, Ext. 1536 • RachelW@HA.com

Design
HA.com/Design
Brent Lewis, Ext. 1577 • BrentL@HA.com **
Karen Rigdon, Ext. 1723 • KarenR@HA.com

Illustration Art
HA.com/Illustration
Ed Jaster, Ext. 1288 • EdJ@HA.com

Tiffany, Lalique & Art Glass
HA.com/Design
Nicholas Dawes, Ext. 1605 • NickD@HA.com *

Modern & Contemporary Art
HA.com/Modern
Frank Hettig, Ext. 1157 • FrankH@HA.com
Holly Sherratt, Ext. 1505 • HollyS@HA.com ***
Leon Benrimon, Ext. 1799 • LeonB@HA.com *
Taylor Curry, Ext. 1304 • TaylorC@HA.com *
Naomi Thune, Ext. 1816 • NaomiT@HA.com

Photographs
HA.com/Photographs
Nigel Russell, Ext. 1231 • NigelR@HA.com *
Ed Jaster, Ext. 1288 • EdJ@HA.com

Fine Silver & Objects of Vertu
HA.com/Silver
Karen Rigdon, Ext. 1723 • KarenR@HA.com

Texas Art
HA.com/TexasArt
Atlee Phillips, Ext. 1786 • AtleeP@HA.com

Handbags & Luxury Accessories
HA.com/Luxury
Diane D'Amato, Ext. 1901 • DianeD@HA.com *
Max Brownawell, Ext. 1693 • MaxB@HA.com *
Barbara Stone, Ext. 1336 • BarbaraS@HA.com

Historical

Americana & Political
HA.com/Historical
Tom Slater, Ext. 1441 • TomS@HA.com
Don Ackerman, Ext. 1736 • DonA@HA.com
Michael Riley, Ext. 1467 • MichaelR@HA.com

Arms & Armor, Civil War & Militaria
HA.com/Arms
HA.com/CivilWar
David Carde, Ext. 1881 • DavidC@HA.com
Jason Watson, Ext. 1630 • JasonW@HA.com

Automobilia
HA.com/Automobilia
Nicholas Dawes, Ext. 1605 • NickD@HA.com *

Historical Manuscripts
HA.com/Manuscripts
Sandra Palomino, Ext. 1107 • SandraP@HA.com *

Judaica
HA.com/Judaica
David Michaels, Ext. 1606 • DMichaels@HA.com **

Rare Books
HA.com/Books
James Gannon, Ext. 1609 • JamesG@HA.com

Space Exploration
HA.com/Space
Michael Riley, Ext. 1467 • MichaelR@HA.com

Texana
HA.com/Texana
Sandra Palomino, Ext. 1107 • SandraP@HA.com *

Domain Names & Intellectual Property
HA.com/IP
Aron Meystedt, Ext. 1362 • AronM@HA.com

Jewelry
HA.com/Jewelry
Jill Burgum, Ext. 1697 • JillB@HA.com
Jessica DuBroc, Ext. 1978 • JessicaD@HA.com
Eva Violante, Ext. 1872 • EvaV@HA.com *
Peter Shemonsky, Ext. 1125 • PeterS@HA.com ***
Gina D'Onofrio, Ext. 1153 • GinaD@HA.com **
Ana Wroblaski, Ext. 1154 • AnaW@HA.com **
Tracy Sherman, Ext. 1146 • TracyS@HA.com *****
Ruth Thuston, Ext. 1929 • RuthT@HA.com ******

Luxury Real Estate
HA.com/LuxuryRealEstate

Nate Schar, Ext. 1457 • NateS@HA.com
Thania Kanewske, Ext. 1320 • ThaniaK@HA.com
Rochelle Mortenson, Ext. 1384 • RochelleM@HA.com

Vintage Movie Posters
HA.com/MoviePosters

Grey Smith, Ext. 1367 • GreySm@HA.com
Bruce Carteron, Ext. 1551 • BruceC@HA.com

Nature & Science
HA.com/NatureAndScience

Craig Kissick, Ext. 1995 • CraigK@HA.com

Numismatics

Coins – United States
HA.com/Coins

David Mayfield, Ext. 1277 • David@HA.com
Win Callender, Ext. 1415 • WinC@HA.com
Mark Feld, Ext. 1321 • MFeld@HA.com
Jason Friedman, Ext. 1582 • JasonF@HA.com
Sam Foose, Ext. 1227 • Sam@HA.com
Bob Marino, Ext. 1374 • BobMarino@HA.com
Harry Metrano, Ext. 1809 • HarryM@HA.com **
Sarah Miller, Ext. 1597 • SarahM@HA.com *
Al Pinkall, Ext. 1835 • AlP@HA.com
Kyle Kavanagh, Ext. 1156 • KyleK@ha.com

Rare Currency
HA.com/Currency

Allen Mincho, Ext. 1327 • Allen@HA.com
Len Glazer, Ext. 1390 • Len@HA.com
Dustin Johnston, Ext. 1302 • Dustin@HA.com
Michael Moczalla, Ext. 1481 • MichaelM@HA.com
Luke Mitchell, Ext. 1859 • LukeM@HA.com
Kenneth Yung • KennethY@HA.com ****

World & Ancient Coins
HA.com/WorldCoins

Cristiano Bierrenbach, Ext. 1661 • CrisB@HA.com
Warren Tucker, Ext. 1287 • WTucker@HA.com
David Michaels, Ext. 1606 • DMichaels@HA.com **
Matt Orsini, Ext. 1523 • MattO@HA.com
Michael Peplinski, Ext. 1959 • MPeplinski@HA.com
Sam Spiegel, Ext. 1524 • SamS@HA.com
Zach Beasley, Ext. 1741 • ZachB@HA.com
Kenneth Yung • KennethY@HA.com ****

Sports Collectibles
HA.com/Sports

Chris Ivy, Ext. 1319 • CIvy@HA.com
Calvin Arnold, Ext. 1341 • CalvinA@HA.com **
Peter Calderon, Ext. 1789 • PeterC@HA.com
Tony Giese, Ext. 1997 • TonyG@HA.com
Derek Grady, Ext. 1975 • DerekG@HA.com
Mike Gutierrez, Ext. 1183 • MikeG@HA.com
Lee Iskowitz, Ext. 1601 • LeeI@HA.com *
Mark Jordan, Ext. 1187 • MarkJ@HA.com
Chris Nerat, Ext. 1615 • ChrisN@HA.com
Rob Rosen, Ext. 1767 • RRosen@HA.com
Jonathan Scheier, Ext. 1314 • JonathanS@HA.com
Nick Cepero, Ext. 1878 • NickC@HA.com

Timepieces
HA.com/Timepieces

Jim Wolf, Ext. 1659 • JWolf@HA.com
Jonathon Burford, Ext. 1132 • JonathonB@HA.com **

Wine
HA.com/Wine

Frank Martell, Ext. 1753 • FrankM@HA.com **
Amanda Crawford, Ext 1821 • AmandaC@HA.com **
Ian Dorin, Ext. 1805 • Idorin@ha.com *

Services

Appraisal Services
HA.com/Appraisals

Meredith Meuwly, Ext. 1631 • MeredithM@HA.com
Courtney Christy, Ext. 1109 • CourtneyC@HA.com

Careers
HA.com/Careers

Corporate Collection and Museum Services
Meredith Meuwly, Ext. 1631 • MeredithM@HA.com

Credit Department
Marti Korver, Ext. 1248 • Marti@HA.com

Media & Public Relations
Elon Werner, Ext. 1599 • ElonW@HA.com
Eric Bradley, Ext. 1871 • EricB@HA.com
Steve Lansdale, Ext. 1699 • SteveL@HA.com

Special Collections
Nicholas Dawes, Ext. 1605 • NickD@HA.com *

Trusts & Estates
HA.com/Estates

Mark Prendergast, Ext. 1632 • MPrendergast@HA.com
Michelle Castro, Ext. 1824 • MichelleC@HA.com
Elyse Luray, Ext. 1369 • ElyseL@HA.com *
Carolyn Mani, Ext. 1677 • CarolynM@HA.com **

Locations

Dallas (World Headquarters)
214.528.3500 • 877-HERITAGE (437-4824)
3500 Maple Ave.
Dallas, TX 75219

Dallas (Fine & Decorative Arts – Design District Showroom)
214.528.3500 • 877-HERITAGE (437-4824)
1518 Slocum St.
Dallas, TX 75207

Beverly Hills
310.492.8600
9478 W. Olympic Blvd
Beverly Hills, CA 90212

Chicago
312-260-7200
215 West Ohio
Chicago, Illinois 60654

New York
212.486.3500
445 Park Avenue
New York, NY 10022

Palm Beach
561-693-1963
250 Royal Palm Way, Suite 307
Palm Beach, Florida 33480

San Francisco
877-HERITAGE (437-4824)
478 Jackson Street
San Francisco, CA 94111

Europe
+31-(0)30-6063944
Energieweg 7, 3401 MD
IJsselstein, Nederland

Hong Kong
+852-2155 1698
Unit 1105, 11/F Tower ONE,
Lippo Centre, 89 Queensway Road,
Admiralty, Hong Kong

Houston: 713.899.8364

Corporate Officers

R. Steven Ivy, CEO & Co-Chairman
James L. Halperin, Co-Chairman
Gregory J. Rohan, President *
Paul Minshull, Chief Operating Officer
Todd Imhof, Executive Vice President
Kathleen Guzman, Managing Director, New York

* Primary office location: New York
** Primary office location: Beverly Hills
*** Primary office location: San Francisco
**** Primary office location: Hong Kong
***** Primary office location: Palm Beach
****** Primary office location: Chicago

8-16-2017

Numismatic Auctions	Location	Auction Dates	Consignment Deadline
US Coins & Currency and World Coins and Currency	Long Beach	September 6-12, 2017	Closed
US Coins - The Eric P. Newman Collection Part IX	Dallas	November 1-3, 2017	Closed
US Currency - The Eric P. Newman Collection Part VIII	Dallas	November 1-3, 2017	Closed
US Coins	Dallas	November 1-3, 2017	September 18, 2017
World Coins & Currency	Hong Kong	December 6-8, 2017	October 9, 2017
US Coins, US & World Currency	Tampa	January 3-9, 2018	November 13, 2017

Fine & Decorative Arts Auctions	Location	Auction Dates	Consignment Deadline
Asian Art	New York	September 12, 2017	Closed
Fine & Decorative Arts featuring the Gentleman Collector	Dallas	September 22-25, 2017	Closed
Photographs	New York	October 11, 2017	Closed
Illustration Art	Dallas	October 13, 2017	Closed
Fine Silver & Objects of Vertu	Dallas	October 17, 2017	August 22, 2017
Modern & Contemporary Art - Prints & Multiples	Dallas	October 21, 2017	August 28, 2017
20th & 21st Century Design	Dallas	October 24, 2017	August 29, 2017
Texas Art	Dallas	October 28, 2017	September 1, 2017
American Art	Dallas	November 3, 2017	September 8, 2017
Nature & Science	Dallas	November 4, 2017	September 8, 2017
Ethnographic Art: American Indian, Pre-Columbian & Tribal	Dallas	November 13, 2017	September 18, 2017
Pre-War Design including Tiffany & Lalique Art Glass	Dallas	November 14, 2017	September 19, 2017
Modern & Contemporary Art	Beverly Hills	November 30, 2017	October 5 ,2017
European Art	Dallas	December 1, 2017	October 6 ,2017
Fine & Decorative Arts, Including Estates	Dallas	December 9 – 10, 2017	October 13, 2017

Memorabilia & Collectibles Auctions	Location	Auction Dates	Consignment Deadline
Sports: 1933 Goudey PSA Registry Set	Dallas	September 21, 2017	Closed
Entertainment and Music – The Connie Francis Collection	Beverly Hills	October 1, 2017	Closed
Guitars & Musical Instruments	Dallas	October 27, 2017	September 5, 2017
"Heroes of Sports" Platinum Night Auction	New York	October 28, 2017	Closed
Entertainment & Music	Dallas	November 11, 2017	September 20, 2017
Comics & Original Comic Art	Beverly Hills	November 16-17, 2017	October 3, 2017
Sports Collectibles	Dallas	November 16-18, 2017	September 25, 2017
Movie Posters	Dallas	November 17, 2017	September 25, 2017
Animation Art	Beverly Hills	December 9, 2017	October 26, 2017

Historical Collectibles Auctions	Location	Auction Dates	Consignment Deadline
Rare Books	Dallas	September 14, 2017	Closed
Historical Manuscripts	Dallas	October 19, 2017	August 28, 2017
Americana and Political - The David and Janice Frent Collection	Dallas	October 21, 2017	Closed
Space Exploration	Dallas	November 10, 2017	September 19, 2017
Americana & Political	Dallas	December 2, 2017	October 11, 2017
Arms & Armor and Civil War & Militaria	Dallas	December 10, 2017	October 19, 2017
Texana	Dallas	February 10, 2018	December 1, 2017
Rare Books	New York	March 7, 2018	January 15, 2018

Luxury Lifestyle Auctions	Location	Auction Dates	Consignment Deadline
Fine & Rare Wine	Beverly Hills	September 8, 2017	Closed
Fine Jewelry and Luxury Accessories	Beverly Hills	September 25-26, 2017	Closed
Fine & Rare Wine	Beverly Hills	October 13-14, 2017	August 31, 2017
Fine & Rare Timepieces	New York	October 24, 2017	Closed
Luxury Real Estate	TBD	Fall 2017	September 1, 2017
Fine & Rare Wine	Beverly Hills	December 1, 2017	October 16, 2017
Fine Jewelry and Luxury Accessories	New York	December 4-5, 2017	September 12, 2017
Fine and Rare Timepieces	New York	June 5, 2018	March 28, 2018

Domain Names	Location	Auction Dates	Consignment Deadline
Domain Names	Dallas	Fall 2017	September 1, 2017

HA.com/Consign | Consignment Hotline 877-HERITAGE (437-4824) | All dates and auctions subject to change after press time. Visit HA.com/Auctions for a current schedule.

HERITAGE INTERNET-ONLY AUCTIONS with Live Sessions

Comics: 6PM CT Sundays
Movie Posters: 6PM CT Sundays
Sports: 10PM CT Sundays (Extended Bidding)
U.S. Coins: 7PM CT Sundays & Tuesdays
Currency: 7PM CT Tuesdays

Nature & Science: 10PM CT Thursdays
World Coins: 8PM CT Thursdays
Wine: 10PM CT 1st Thursdays
Monthly World Coins: 8PM CT final Sundays
Fine Jewelry: 9PM CT Tuesdays

8/14/2017